Merchant Marine
Survivors of World War II

# Merchant Marine Survivors of World War II

*Oral Histories of Cargo Carrying Under Fire*

MICHAEL GILLEN

McFarland & Company, Inc., Publishers
*Jefferson, North Carolina*

**A Note to the Reader:** This is an oral history of the U.S. Merchant Marine in World War II and, as such, most of what you will read here will be taken directly from transcripts of the voices of the seamen themselves on tape. To retain authenticity little has been changed, except where, to reduce confusion, a word or two has been added [in brackets]. Also, to reduce repetition, words have been cut in certain instances. But the "color" of the language has been retained, whether that be a certain regional inflection, or usage of an occasional indelicate expression at which some merchant seamen are known to be particularly skilled.

*Frontispiece:* The author as he appeared on a U.S. Merchant Mariner's Document, 1980 (collection of Michael Gillen).

LIBRARY OF CONGRESS CATALOGUING-IN-PUBLICATION DATA

Gillen, Michael, 1948–
    Merchant marine survivors of World War II : oral histories of cargo carrying under fire / Michael Gillen.
        p.    cm.
    Includes bibliographical references and index.

    **ISBN 978-0-7864-9467-5** (softcover : acid free paper) ∞
    **ISBN 978-1-4766-1887-6** (ebook)

    1. World War, 1939–1945—Naval operations, American.
    2. Merchant marine—United States—Interviews.  3. Sailors—United States—Interviews.  4. Merchant marine—United States—History—20th century.  5. Armed merchant ships—United States—History—20th century.  6. Shipwrecks—United States—History—20th century.  7. Shipwreck survival—Anecdotes.
    8. World War, 1939–1945—Personal narratives.  I. Title.
    D773.G56 2015
    940.4'59730922—dc23                                    2014043151

BRITISH LIBRARY CATALOGUING DATA ARE AVAILABLE

© 2015 Michael Gillen. All rights reserved

*No part of this book may be reproduced or transmitted in any form or by any means, electronic or mechanical, including photocopying or recording, or by any information storage and retrieval system, without permission in writing from the publisher.*

Front cover: SS *Mary Luckenbach*, loaded with ammunition, explodes with loss of all hands after being struck by aircraft torpedo in Convoy PQ-18 to North Russia, September 1942. See Chapter 16 for an eyewitness account (War Shipping Administration).

Printed in the United States of America

*McFarland & Company, Inc., Publishers*
    *Box 611, Jefferson, North Carolina 28640*
        *www.mcfarlandpub.com*

To the Merchant Marine veterans of World War II
who participated in this project,
and to all others who served
in the U.S. Merchant Marine during that war

# Table of Contents

*Acknowledgments*   ix
*Preface: The Ship*   1

| | | |
|---|---|---|
| 1 | William J. "Bill" Bailey: "I just couldn't take it any longer" | 7 |
| 2 | Howard Bethell: "No longer bums, they were heroes" | 11 |
| 3 | Daniel J. Bradley: "I've been on borrowed time" | 25 |
| 4 | Rexford Dickey: "He died from a broken heart" | 32 |
| 5 | Stanley E. Gorski: The Minefields of Manila Bay | 36 |
| 6 | Jack A. Holt: "We all piled out on deck" | 43 |
| 7 | Paul J. Jarvis: "Okinawa was absolute hell" | 50 |
| 8 | Eric H. Johanson: "We were scared to death" | 60 |
| 9 | Ruel N. Lawrence: "The ship pulled me down" | 62 |
| 10 | John M. Le Cato: "*Norluna*, you're supposed to be sunk!" | 70 |
| 11 | Edward A. MacMichael: One Step Ahead of the Japs | 84 |
| 12 | Edward C. March: Torpedoes and Molasses Don't Mix | 91 |
| 13 | John S. "Jack" McCusker: "Did you ever hear a ship die?" | 102 |
| 14 | Harry E. Morgan: Walnuts and Bauxite for the War | 114 |
| 15 | Dennis A. Roland: A Prisoner of the Japanese | 120 |
| 16 | William J. Shearer: "She was there, and all of a sudden it wasn't" | 135 |
| 17 | Henrik E. "Hank" Sievers: Cargo for Pearl and Nawiliwili | 139 |

| | | |
|---|---|---|
| **18** | Robert B. Smolen: "Captain, they're gonna machine-gun us!" | 142 |
| **19** | John H. Tiencken: "I hated to see her lost" | 147 |
| **20** | Donald E. Zubrod: 42 Days in a Lifeboat | 161 |

*Appendix A: Glossary*     171

*Appendix B: The Crew of a Typical Liberty (Dry Cargo) Ship During World War II*     175

*Chapter Notes*     177

*Bibliography*     195

*Index*     197

# Acknowledgments

It takes a crew, and though the writing of a book is very much a solitary experience, moving it ahead after a long voyage to safe harbor usually involves many people. For their participation and input in any form to bringing this book to fruition, I am especially grateful to the following:

Howard Bethell, a Merchant Marine veteran of World War II who figures prominently here (Chapter 2), and probably got me going on this project in the first place simply by telling his story—in a way that only he could. He was a friend, had a keen sense of history, and was an early supporter of Project Liberty ship.

W. D. "Bill" Ehrhart, poet, memoirist, teacher, and essayist of the Vietnam War—and then some—a longtime friend, and once a merchant seaman himself, for offering to take a preliminary version of this project to McFarland, the publisher of his first Vietnam War–related memoir, *Vietnam-Perkasie*.

Captain Arthur C. Moore, another Merchant Marine veteran of World War II, for compiling his invaluable history of U.S. Merchant Marine ship and personnel losses during the war, *A Careless Word—A Needless Sinking* (1983), for his friendship, words of encouragement, and guiding me to Stanley Gorski, subsequently interviewed for this project (Chapter 5).

John Gorley Bunker, maritime historian (*The Liberty Ships, Heroes in Dungarees*), Merchant Marine "black gang" veteran of World War II, friend and colleague at the Seafarers Union, and a mentor if ever there was one, for his encouragement in the early goings.

Dayl Koffler-Wise, my friend, best man at my wedding, and founder of Post Traumatic Press, which published an earlier chapbook version of parts of this oral history.

Eliz Anderson, National Liberty ship Memorial, San Francisco, for putting me in touch with Joanie Morgan.

Joanie Morgan, for providing photographs and documents relating to the life and long maritime career of her husband, Harry Morgan (Chapter 14), for her knowledge and sharp eye as proofreader of chapters relating to Harry, and Capt. Ed MacMichael (Chapter 11), with whom she worked on SS *Jeremiah O'Brien*, National Liberty Ship Memorial, San Francisco, and for backing this project with a will. Joanie is a kindred spirit, devoted to the cause of ship preservation, currently involved with Steam Tug *Hercules*, to which her husband had also dedicated himself for a period of time, bringing the tug back to life.

Captain John L. MacMichael, Jr., USN, grandson of Capt. Ed MacMichael, for his interest, and for putting me in touch with his father.

Capt. John L. MacMichael, Sr., USN, retired, for his interest, invaluable assistance providing photographs and documents, and answering questions that relate to the life and service of his father.

Joanie Wittenburg, who, with the support of her brother, Henry Holt, responded enthusiastically to my initial request for assistance relating to their father, Jack Holt (Chapter 6), and provided photographs and documentation that proved to be very helpful.

Daniel J. Bradley, Jr., for his interest, and for providing photographs and information relating to the life and career of his father, Daniel J. Bradley (Chapter 3).

Audrey Ivey, for her and her sister's interest, and for providing photographs of their father, Capt. Edward March (Chapter 12).

John W. Zubrod, for his interest, and for providing the photograph of his father, Donald Zubrod (Chapter 20), which appears here.

Claudia Jew, Mariners' Museum, for her great patience and help searching the vast photographic archives of the museum and providing many of the ship images that appear here.

Alissa Cafferky, Steam Ship Historical Society of America, for searching the photographic archives of the society and providing some of the ship images that appear here.

Professors Daniel J. Walkowitz and Paul Mattingly, New York University, for inviting me to participate with the initial class of their new Program in Public History at NYU—which provided me with so much support as I pursued my doctoral degree—and who appreciated the importance of oral history methods and the work of many of us in that area.

Roger S. Durham, my longtime friend and the author of books about the American Civil War, for words of wisdom relating to writing and the publication process.

Edward William Blythe, my son-in-law, for his interest in this book, and for reading and commenting on several chapters of a late manuscript draft.

And to Fern Zeigler, my wife and soulmate, for her encouragement, keen eye, providing an environment that is a writer's dream—and safe harbor otherwise—and for her love.

They have brought us our lifeblood and they have paid for it with some of their own. When their ships were not blown out from under them by bombs and torpedoes, they have delivered their cargoes to us who needed them so badly.

—General Douglas MacArthur

# Preface: The Ship

The ship loomed ahead at a Hudson River pier as I made my way slowly southward in the morning mist along New York City's West Side Highway. With its flush-deck profile, characteristically capped stack, and wartime gun tubs still in place, the ship was unmistakably a Liberty, a merchant cargo ship type built in unprecedented numbers in the United States during World War II.[1]

This was early 1978—more than 32 years after the end of the war—and by then a Liberty ship was already a rare sight to behold, as most had been scrapped, relegated to a few "boneyard" reserve fleets, or converted by ignominious fate into such things as stationary fish processing plants. A few others were still tramping around the world, no doubt, under foreign flag, but they were few and far between, their days certainly also numbered.

She was, I soon found out, the SS *John W. Brown*, a veteran of many wartime voyages. She was then being used, as she had since soon after the war ended, as a stationary school ship for teaching the maritime trades. Her days were numbered too for such use, and I learned she had already become the focus of a preservation effort spearheaded by the fledgling Project Liberty Ship under the aegis of the National Maritime Historical Society.[2]

My involvement in that project, as editor of its first newsletter, assistant director, and then director, proved ultimately successful, but not until a dedicated group had taken the helm and initiative in Baltimore to return the ship to that city, where she had been launched in 1942.[3]

As so often happens, one thing led to another, and it was through my involvement with Project Liberty Ship, and other work in New York that actually paid a salary, that seeds were sown for this oral history of the U.S. Merchant Marine in World War II.

1

The Liberty ship *John W. Brown* as she appeared at her Hudson River pier, New York City, circa 1978 (photograph by Michael Gillen).

Having just moved back from Georgia, where I had been a landlocked historic site curator for the state, I was now at the right place and time for finding and interviewing Merchant Marine veterans of World War II. I did not know it at first, of course, but my initial conversations with one Howard Bethell, an early member of Project Liberty ship and a still-working mariner who had had two ships shot out from under him during the war, was probably what got this whole thing underway.

These were the ships then—Libertys along with a number of other types—that were either fresh off the ways, as Libertys were, or had seen service stretching back to World War I, and even earlier. Sailed by thousands of civilian merchant seamen, they—crews and ships—are often considered as having made the difference between victory and defeat against the forces of fascism during World War II. It was, after all, a *world* war, and that required these fleets of dry cargo and tanker ships to provide the logistical support that supplied the "lifeblood" to all the beachheads where the fight had been taken. And, for a time, principally because of the U-boat menace and aerial attack, it was not clear that construction of these ships would keep pace with their losses.[4]

## Preface: The Ship

The 20 Merchant Marine veterans whose recollections of wartime service appear here came to the ships for the first time for different reasons and at different points in time, starting seafaring careers in the 1930s, some in the 1920s, and a few during or soon before the war officially began for the United States in late 1941.

For some, it was a family tradition to finally ship out as a grandfather, father, or uncle had done before them. For others who had grown up in port cities, or up river or down river from one, it was a dream come true to finally go where ships and seamen they had watched outbound had gone before them. And for still others, shipping out was simply something to do—perhaps what seemed the only thing available to do—during the economic hard times of the Great Depression of the 1930s. And then there was the war: for some others here, the thought of shipping out did not occur, and the opportunity did not present itself, until war itself came.

These twenty, while not entirely representative, perhaps, came from as many places across the United States as they might have had reasons for going to sea in the first place. From Maine to Florida on the East Coast, they shipped out from the major ports of Boston, New York, Philadelphia and Baltimore. On the West Coast, from San Pedro to Portland, Seattle, San Francisco and Sacramento, they found their way to the ships as well. To the Gulf Coast, from such places as Mobile, Alabama, and north to Racine, Wisconsin, to first get a taste of seafaring on the Great Lakes, they also found their way to the ships.

When I went to sea, briefly, in the late 1960s—and it was another war, in Vietnam, that made that happen—it was something I had long wanted to do, perhaps due to mucking around in boats on a Connecticut lake or to a certain Viking gene I would later come to learn was part of my DNA. When I finally did ship out in 1967, from Morrisville, Pennsylvania, on a World War II–vintage T-2 tanker that had been converted to carry steel bars and sheeting for U.S. Steel Corp., most of my watch-partners, men like Joe Gotz, Mel Woods, and Eddie Means—able seamen all—were Merchant Marine veterans of World War II.

As a 19-year-old, greenhorn ordinary seaman, I had few of my own stories to tell. But during long voyages to the West Coast, Southeast Asia, and, later, Europe, my shipmates had plenty of time for telling sea stories, often about their experiences during World War II. As always, I was all ears. Thus was planted even earlier seeds for what would become a project on which I would work, off and on, for too many years: this oral history of the U.S. Merchant Marine in World War II.

As originally conceived, and because of Howard Bethell's particular experience, this project was intended to focus on the experiences of seamen who had survived the torpedoing and loss of one or more ships. When they were finally rescued and landed back ashore again after having been plucked from oil-slicked waters or retrieved from a box-shaped raft that kept them afloat but offered little protection from the elements, they had become "survivors" of the experience while so many thousands of other mariners were lost forever.[5] That seemed compelling, but did not, I came to realize, address a broader fact: that all who served, whether torpedoed or not, contributed vitally and "paid with some of their own" in multiple ways, we've come to understand, that could, from the trauma of it, endure for years.

As we consider that the U.S. Merchant Marine suffered, in proportion to its total numbers, a casualty rate a close second to only the U.S. Marine Corps during World War II, the appellation of "survivor" seems all the more fitting.[6] Many of those who survived their war service continued to ship out in the Merchant Marine, because, simply put, and as they had done before, that's what they were, that's what they did, and that's what they intended, as always, to continue to do. They would do that, many of them, going where the jobs took them—and to other battlefronts in Korea and Vietnam—well into the 1970s and 1980s.

There were others, however, who, and despite their service during the war and intentions to pursue their trade after the war, were screened off the ships in the 1950s—"blacklisted," as it were, for their political beliefs and affiliations—and unable to secure Coast Guard clearance documentation to ship out again. In the face of political hysteria and political opportunism that would become known as McCarthyism—so named for the U.S. senator who had actually fabricated his own war record for political expediency—these seamen, some of whom had actually fought fascism as volunteers during the Spanish Civil War—years before World War II began—would come ashore to look for and pursue other trades. Some of them are represented here as well, as they deserve to be.

It was my privilege, and to my benefit and enrichment, to work with and get to know many of these Merchant Marine veterans, both at sea and ashore. I am proud to say, too, that some of them also became good friends. But sadly, most of those who participated in this project—as so many other veterans of World War II—have not survived to this point in time.

I began this project decades ago, but the twists and turns of my life since then, it seems, have prevented it from coming to fruition in this form before now. Fortunately, it has kept calling me back.

This book will at least serve in some small measure, it is hoped, to honor those who participated in this project, as well as all those who served in the U.S. Merchant Marine during World War II, and to begin the process of making these stories more widely available to others.

# CHAPTER 1

# William J. "Bill" Bailey: "I just couldn't take it any longer"

*William J. "Bill" Bailey was born in Jersey City, New Jersey, in 1910 and shipped out from New York for the first time at the age of fifteen as ordinary seaman in the SS Lake Gaither. He continued to ship out through the 1930s, was active in the maritime labor movement, and went to Spain in 1937 as a volunteer with the Abraham Lincoln Brigade. He fought against fascist forces at Belchite and other areas and returned to the United States after 18 months. Bailey shipped out again soon after that and continued to do so, usually in unlicensed Engine Department ratings, and at the time of the attack on Pearl Harbor had just been elected port agent of the New York branch, Pacific Coast Marine Firemen, Oilers, Watertenders and Wipers Association.*[1]

I decided I just couldn't take it any longer, you know, watching these kids coming in. I said to myself, "How the fuck can I go through this war—when people ask me 'What did you do during the war?'—all I'll be able to say will be 'I helped win it by pushing kids out, by manning ships.'"

To me, that would have been a cop-out. I just couldn't do it.

I was in the Paramount Theater when I learned about the attack on Pearl Harbor. They blacked the screen out, and the lights came on, and the loud speakers came on saying, "All men in the armed forces, emergency has been declared. Get back to whatever unit you've come from."

Then Roosevelt's speech came on, and they kept repeating it, that it was a "day of infamy" and all that. The movie went on, but you could hear wailing and moaning and people rushing out. And some were elated, others were sad, confused and didn't know what the hell was happening.

My feeling was that it had to come, but I was hoping it would have

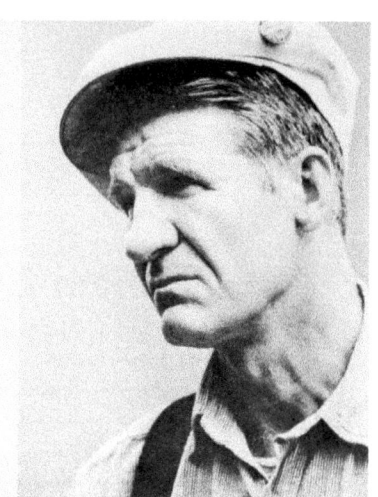

Bill Bailey as he appeared on an early postwar labor union election card, date and photographer unknown (collection of Michael Gillen).

come another way: by way of Germany. Japan was an enemy too, but the bastard enemy was the goddamned Hitler Germany. But that's the way it was.

Then I caught all the pressure, of supplying ships, with all the Liberty ships coming out—and assigned to us, and getting the crews for these. It was a vital thing to do, servicing those ships, and I thought I did my part up to that point. But still, I used to go home at night and figure, Jesus Christ, I just had to get in on the action.

I talked with some guys who had just come back from the Murmansk Run [to North Russia], you know, no fingers left, no toes. And here they are fighting to go back again. You know, what greatness![2]

And here I was sitting at a goddamned desk pushing these kids out, you know, telling them they have to go out there and do their patriotic duty and all that stuff. And am I *uncomfortable*. I could never ... there was no way I was gonna go through that war without seeing if I could take the same bullshit.

So one day I just said, "That's it, I've had it, I'm going to the West Coast to attend school." I had already made application to go to the maritime school for the 30 or 60 days, whatever it took, and get my license and sail.

There were some four other guys, and we got two of them "drive a car to the West Coast" deals. You know, they'll supply the gas coupons or something. So we drove two cars all the way to San Francisco. And I wasn't there one day before I went into the maritime officers school.

I'll be a son of a bitch if they didn't throw me out of school the next day, on some basis when it says, "Have you ever been arrested?" I put "no," see, and the guy said, "Well, we've got to have honest people here."

I said, "Hey, man, what the hell's that got to do with it?"

He said, "Well, you lied, so we have to kick you out."[3]

So I went to what they call the "Doby School" where you pay $50 and they help supply the answers and help you with arithmetic and all that type of stuff. And it was a tough 30 days. I never knew anything about arithmetic, long division, square roots and all that stuff. I had to learn all that within 30 days.

But I sat for my ticket and I got it like on a Tuesday. And I'm out on a ship that was sailing on Friday, for the war zone, as a third assistant engineer. And then from then on I got another ticket after that, and always sailed as Third or First, up to the Aleutians and all them other places.[4]

The Liberty ship *John Paul Jones*, on which Bailey served as third assistant engineer to New Guinea and South America during World War II (Mariners' Museum, Newport News, Virginia).

Like I say, I was happy when I was out there. I felt good that I was doing my part. You know, I thought, I can take that shit. But before, I would've been extremely unhappy. Man, I would've been a son of a bitch to live with.

*Bailey served throughout the war on a series of Liberty ships—SS John Paul Jones, SS Samuel Gompers, and SS George Powell—and finally a Victory ship, SS Laredo Victory, to Naha, Okinawa. The ship was at anchor there when atomic bombs were dropped on Hiroshima and Nagasaki, Japan. Finally, and after dealing with the typhoon that hit Okinawa in October, the* Laredo Victory *was ordered to leave Okinawa for the United States in early November 1945. Bailey continued to ship out after the war, until 1950 when his political beliefs and affiliations caused him to be "blacklisted" and he was unable to obtain the required Coast Guard clearance documentation to ship out. Screened out of the Merchant Marine despite his service during the war, he had to find work ashore. Bailey found work as a longshoreman, and retired from that in 1973 to write, lecture, and appear in such films as* The Good Fight. *He served as President of the Marine Workers Historical Association (MWHA), published an autobiography,* The Kid from Hoboken *(1993), and passed away in San Francisco at 84 in 1995.*

CHAPTER 2

# Howard Bethell: "No longer bums, they were heroes"

*Howard Bethell was born into a seafaring family in Liverpool, England, in 1914. Some of his ancestors were in the slave trade, and his father was a seaman in the* Carpathia *when that ship "ran through the ice fields at full speed" to rescue survivors of the* Titanic. *After the outbreak of World War I Bethell was brought to Boston by his mother, and years later he would say he had been going to sea in wartime, off and on, since 1914. He first shipped out in 1932 in the passenger ship* Morro Castle, *two years before it was destroyed by fire off Asbury Park, New Jersey. He shipped out regularly in the 1930s, and was an Ordinary Seaman on the SS* Idaho *at the time of the attack on Pearl Harbor.*[1]

## "Your country is at war"

On Pearl Harbor Day, December 7, 1941, I was in a C-1 making her maiden voyage.[2] *Idaho* was her name. She had come around from the West Coast and I joined her in New York.

We went to Cape Town, Durban, and from Durban up to Lourenço Marques in Portuguese East Africa.[3] Of course, there was a difference in the time. I think it was a Monday when we heard the news. Somebody told us that the United States was at war, but we didn't believe him.

So we were walking around in Lourenço Marques and we met this Englishman and asked him, "Listen, have you heard anything about the United States being at war?"

He said, "Yes, your country is at war. The Japanese have attacked your fleet in Pearl Harbor and smashed it." So then we knew it was true.

Howard Bethell, left, leaning on cargo hatch of SS *Mansfield*, with unidentified seaman. Undated, early postwar, photographer unknown (Howard Bethell).

The next morning the American consul came down to the ship and gave the captain his orders: we would take the ship home. Naturally they had standard orders for merchant ships at a time like that.

So we sailed back the way we came. We stood double watches. Ordinarily you'd go from wheel to lookout to standby. [On standby] you'd make coffee, call the watch, and stuff like that.

But in this situation we didn't: standby was on the bridge, you were a lookout. We had two lookouts, day and night. And the [life] boats were all swung out and ready.

We went to Durban, Port Elizabeth, and Cape Town. We were in Cape Town when the *Prince of Wales* and the *Repulse* were there on their way up. They were on their way to reinforce the American fleet in the Indian Ocean. This would be about two weeks before they were both sunk.[4]

We did some drinking in the bars with the crews off the ships. I remember we had an electrician who was a loudmouthed character. We were sitting at a table with a couple of English sailors, and one of the Englishmen picked up his mug and said, "The Queen, God bless her."

And Francis, the loudmouthed jerk, sounds off and says, "Ah, fuck the Queen!"

So the Englishman put down his beer and hit Francis right in the mouth and broke all his teeth. They had to take him to the hospital and pick them out with forceps. And all the way home Francis ate soup and mumbled. So I used to imitate the way he sounded. I'd say, "Hey, Francis, tell me what you said to the English sailor!"

A couple of our guys were in a whorehouse there. There was a waiting line with a couple of big, limey Royal Marines in it. So one of our guys says, "What do you have to do, wait?" So one of the marines says, "Yeah, everyone has to wait."

So our guy said, "Fuck it, I wouldn't wait for the Queen of England!"

And this Royal Marine got up and said, "Don't you mention Her Majesty's name in a place like this!"

So we proceeded from Cape Town to Boston: no guns, no escorts, no nothing. We crossed the South Atlantic and then the North Atlantic. On the way we put all the paint we could find into big ash cans. GI cans. We had white, buff, gray, blue, green—any color—and we mixed it all together. It came out sort of a pinkish gray. We painted the ship out to camouflage her on the way home.

We had a "guarantee engineer" on board at this time. Since this was the ship's first voyage they had what they call a "guarantee engineer." He's sent along by the builder of the engines. He sort of rides along and helps out and is supposed to be the expert if anything happens. Well, this guy we had on board hadn't been to sea in years, I don't suppose. He was as nervous as a cat. If you dropped a spoon on deck he'd come running out of his cabin with his life jacket on.

So we proceeded to Boston. In the meantime, the Coast Guard had turned out all the navigation lights. They had taken in the lighthouses and there were no navigation landmarks along the coast. So we overshot Boston by about 40 miles—well, nearly 40 miles. We ended up in Newburyport. The Coast Guard came out in a 40-foot picket boat and asked us what we wanted. We said, "We're looking for Boston." He said, "That way."

So we finally got into Boston. When we got there a couple of the crew got cold feet. There were sinkings all up and down the coast at that time and they didn't want to take the ship back to New York. So the shipping commissioner read the articles to them. He looked at the articles and told them, "You signed on for a voyage. The voyage is not over until the last sling comes out of the holds. Then you must be paid off within 24 hours. You will take the ship to New York."

Well, coming up from Boston a couple of ships had been in a collision. The seamen weren't used to this blackout stuff. So there was this collision, and the captain took his sweet time bringing our ship up to this one that was on fire. So later on a couple of those guys who'd wanted to get paid off in Boston and didn't went up to the Coast Guard and made charges against the Old Man. They claimed he hadn't performed his duty. I was told that I had to go up and testify.

So I went up there to the commissioner and he asked me about it. I said, "I'm an ordinary seaman. Who am I to tell the captain of a ship how he should handle the ship? If he didn't think it was safe to come up too close to that burning ship, that's his duty."

So that was all I heard from the commissioner. And that was the end of that voyage.

## *Abandoning Ship: "We did it in style"*

*After returning from his first wartime voyage, Howard Bethell shipped out again in February 1942 in the* SS Lihue, *a 410' freighter built in 1919, as*

*Ordinary Seaman for a voyage with war cargo from New York to the Red Sea.*[5]

We took her out after the loading was completed and anchored in the North River, just above the Battery. I remember it was a bitter cold day. We had to store the gear away and finish getting the ship secured for sea. One of the runners fouled in the block, so I went aloft in a bosun's chair to haul down the runner. It was so cold that when I got down I couldn't get out of the chair. They took the chair off me.

Then we sailed. And of course this was all new to us. You know, guns, blackouts, security and all this stuff. Well, we proceeded towards Trinidad. We were going to bunker [take on fuel] in Trinidad and then go around the Cape of Good Hope to the Red Sea. We weren't in a convoy; the Navy hadn't organized the [preparations for] war yet, so we proceeded alone.

We had guns fore and aft, guns on the bridge, and a gun crew and gunnery officer. He was a real character from some freshwater college in Minnesota or Wisconsin. And I believe this was the first time he'd seen the ocean.[6]

I had had the last wheel and got relieved by the 12 to 4 watch. I went aft along the catwalk over the deck cargo, and down to the stern where the fo'c'sle was. I was sitting in the rec room—I had just lit a cigarette, bent forward to light it—and the torpedo hit and knocked me out of the chair. So I ran up on deck and went forward. The spray was still coming down from where the torpedo had hit. It felt like rain.

I went to my station, which was in the gun tub aft. I was to pass the shell from the ammo locker and give it to the Navy man to put in the gun. We were standing up there and this gunnery officer made me take off this radium dial wristwatch. He said that the enemy could see it.

The sub came up—I think it surfaced on our lee side—and started firing. Then it put up a star shell, but the wind blew it back again. It was bright as day [and] it illuminated the whole area. So we started firing, and the gunnery officer claimed we hit it. She was going full speed ahead and away from us, so I don't know if we hit it or not.[7] You don't hear and see very much with the concussion of the gun and the flash when you're right up close to it.

The gunnery officer had gone up to the bridge when the torpedo hit. He assumed that because he was a naval officer—in the naval reserve— that he was in command of the ship, that the captain, the master of the ship, was just a technician who ran the ship day to day. Well, the captain

Prewar photograph of SS *Lihue* (pronounced as lih-WHO-ee), the first of two ships that would be shot out from under Bethell during the war (Mariners' Museum, Newport News, Virginia).

sure changed his mind. He told him, "You get your ass back there with that gun, and you get your little boys and start firing. *I'm* running this ship!" So he went back and took charge [of the deck gun]. That's what the man at the wheel told me.

She was going down by the head all the time, taking on water and spewing out cargo as she went along. She went down by the head, but we stood by the guns all night long until dawn. They started getting the boats ready to abandon ship. The word was passed that at noon we're going to abandon ship. They had both boats swung out, full of provisions and ready to go.

We had an injured seaman whose name, I think, was Johnson. He was an old man who must have been at least 70. He had been on lookout when the torpedo hit. The concussion knocked him down, and he had a broken leg. We put him in one of the lifeboats and made him safe and secure. And then we got ready to lower the boats, to abandon ship.

The word was passed: "We're going to abandon ship at eight bells." The man at the wheel secured the wheel. At 11:20 he struck seven bells that called the watch. At, I believe, 10 minutes of the hour he struck another bell for the mate to come to the bridge. At noon he struck eight bells. And when the officer of the watch gave the order "secure the wheel" he put the wheel amidships. We did it in style. Everything was done in first-class style.

Then we lowered the boats and started rowing away. A friend of mine, one of the oilers in the boat ahead of me, said, "There's one good thing about this. I won't have to listen to any more goddamned wisecracking from you!" So we were rowing away and trying to tow the rafts. Some of the crew were on the rafts, and those rafts were jerry-built. They were breaking up. But we were picked up by a British tanker that brought us into Trinidad.

We stayed on that ship I think overnight, and then they brought us into Trinidad. The Caribbean was infested with submarines at that time. In fact, the night before we got into Trinidad a submarine came in and sank two ships, including one that was alongside the dock discharging cargo. When we landed, she was resting on the bottom but was still discharging cargo.

## "No longer bums, they were heroes"

*After his experience with the sinking of* SS Lihue *in the Caribbean, 28-year-old Howard Bethell shipped out again in the spring of 1942, this time for North Russia in the* SS Kentucky.

I shipped out on a ship called the *Kentucky*, States Lines, Captain Richard Childs.[8] That was around Easter 1942. On May 2 we sailed out of New York as a two-ship convoy. We went up through the Cape Cod Canal. I'll never forget it. It was a bright, sunny day, and all the automobiles were honking as we went past. Merchant seamen were no longer bums, they were heroes.

Then we went up to Halifax where the main convoy formed. From there [departing May 22] we went across to Scotland, to Glasgow and Loch Ewe. From Loch Ewe we went around the east coast of Scotland. It was beautiful weather—I've never seen a better day. We went down to Edinburgh, waited there, and then went back to Glasgow or Loch Ewe. From there we went to Iceland to a fjord near Reykjavik. We finally rendezvoused and sailed for Russia.

We sailed for Murmansk in early September 1942. That was Convoy PQ-18. PQ-17 was the one that was wiped out.[9] We were the next one. We heard about PQ-17, of course. Word gets around amongst seamen. In fact, one of the [Navy] Armed Guards shot himself through the hand so he wouldn't have to go. But we sailed.

There were two famous ships in our convoy: the *Virginia Dare* and the *Patrick Henry*. They acted as column leaders. We followed them because they used gyro-compasses. The old type magnetic compasses were useless up there. They were erratic or they'd freeze and wouldn't move. Those Liberty ships were considered big, fast ships in those days: they made 10 knots. Our ship only made eight.

We left the rendezvous point in Iceland and headed north [and] went north of Bear Island. You could just see the sun shining on the ice in Spitzbergen Island. We proceeded onwards and got attacked up there. Waves of bombers came over—fifty or sixty of them. In the haze and overcast we'd have high-altitude bombers dropping bombs on us. And there were submarines underneath.

I remember once when the bosun yelled, "Hey, look, there's hundreds of planes!" But it wasn't hundreds of planes; it was a big flock of sea gulls. At that moment they looked like planes coming in to attack.

I was one of the youngest men on deck in the *Kentucky*, and I was 28 at the time. People tend to think of the Merchant Marine as a bunch of kids. One of the AB's on my watch had sailed around the world in Teddy Roosevelt's Great White Fleet. He didn't have to go. And my [watch] partner and I were both 4-F. We'd both been rejected by the draft. We didn't have to go. But that's what kept the Merchant Marine going: old-timers who wouldn't quit, and young guys who didn't have to worry about the draft.

A lot of the younger guys were drafted out of the Merchant Marine. And some joined the Navy. They decided that if they were gonna fight a war, they'd rather fight it in the Navy. Some were drafted and had no choice. But of those that were drafted, some were discharged later on because there was such a shortage of merchant seamen. A bosun I sailed

**Wartime photograph of SS *Kentucky*, not dated but probably early 1942 (Mariners' Museum, Newport News, Virginia).**

with after the war told me that he sailed in a ship out of New York during the war and he was the only man on deck who could steer. There was a desperate shortage of merchant seamen.

Anyway, back to PQ-18. When the [aerial] torpedo was coming at the ship, the bosun tried to hit it with a gun, to deflect it, but he missed. The concussion of the torpedo was so—great that it knocked my glasses off. I had my sea boots on, but there was no time to get anything. I went out on deck and then up to the [wheel] house.

I met the old man and asked him, "What are your orders, Captain?"

He gave me the ship's papers, and said, "Put these in the [life] boat."

My battle station was on the bridge. My watch did all the steering; we'd either be on the wheel or on standby. And my job when we went to battle stations was to report to the bridge, check the old man's gun, and give it to him. And check the papers.

I got the papers and dropped them into the lifeboat—the port lifeboat. The papers were in a metal box with holes in it so it would sink if we had to get rid of them in a hurry. Then I went up to my boat station, abandon ship station. My job was to lower the boat. And while I was doing that one of the oilers came along, put one foot on my shoulder, one foot on my head, and dived right into the boat.

When the boat was away, me and the chief engineer went through the engine room to make sure that everybody was out. Then we went and climbed onto one of the save-all nets, the scramble net over the side. The third mate, Mr. Kelly, a big Black Irishman from Chicago, brought a boat back and took me off the net hanging over the side. The captain and another man—Chips [carpenter]—went over the stern in a raft. They were the last ones off the ship.

The *Kentucky* was going down as we left.

We were picked up by a small British minelayer or minesweeper. Those seamen on the minesweepers were miserable bastards. There was no place to sleep—two guys to a bunk. You slept on the deck and ate whatever you could get. They were miserable ships. The British said you had to have "granite guts" to sail in them.

Then we came up that river that flows into the White Sea. We went up to Archangel. We went alongside a Russian ship, but they wouldn't let us cross over to go ashore. So the skipper of the minesweeper said, "To hell with 'em." And then he put us alongside an American ship, which we went on and stayed on that night. There was no place to sleep so I slept under the mess room table. We got bombed that night but I was so goddamned tired I never moved.

The next day we went ashore in Russia.

## Ashore in Russia, 1942

*Howard Bethell and the surviving merchant seamen and members of the armed guard from SS* Kentucky *were put ashore in Archangel, Russia, after having been rescued by a British minesweeper. They were under almost constant attack by submarine and enemy aircraft in convoy PQ-18. The air attacks continued during their time ashore in Archangel.*

Well, they got us organized and put us ashore in the hotel there. It was run by Intourist, the Russian tourist organization. They put us—about 18 of us guys—in one room. It was a big room [and] they just put all the cots in there. They did what they could for us, but they didn't have very much.

I remember there was a rat in that room. So we told the maid, "Hey, get a cat!"

She said, "No good: cat *this* big, rat *that* big!"

So we got our knives. We all carried knives because seamen were getting jumped and robbed ashore. So we all carried sheath knives. Well, we closed the door and chased that rat around and around and around until we got him in the corner and bayoneted him.

We couldn't get used to the Russian system. We'd be in the head [bathroom] and the woman would be in there with us, scrubbing the deck. We couldn't get used to that: it wasn't the American style.

And I remember one of the little girls was crying. I asked her what she was crying for, and she said she was being sent to the front to be a nurse. All the good jobs in Archangel were run by girls from Moscow. The desk clerks and people like that. They spoke English and they said, "Ah, Moscow is lovely. You should see Moscow. This Archangel is nothing." And they had a nice soft job. The poor natives, they were exploited. The women were doing the police duty, doing most of the labor, and they'd given them longshore work. Most of the men, I imagine, were at the front. But then that's the Russian style.

Well, we got bombed out about every other night they got raided. The Germans were flying out of Finland. We had a Finnish-American in the ship, and he was quite a drinker. But he was scared to drink because when he drank he'd start singing Finnish songs, and he was afraid they'd pick him up as a Finn and he'd never be seen again.

I would say that the city was bombed every other night, they'd come over. The city was built mostly of logs, it seemed. Two layers of logs. In other words, a house within a house [and] they'd put sawdust in between for insulation. Well, the Germans used firebombs. They'd come whistling down like nothing. We used to go out and watch them, but when the worst came we'd go down in the cellar.

We were down in the cellar one night with all kinds of seamen. It was an air raid shelter. There were British, American, Canadian and what have you. All kinds of seamen: Chinese, Laskars, Hindus and God knows what. The Orientals always brought everything they owned with them down there.

Well, we were down there one night and a Russian woman came down. She said, "The city's on fire! Women and children are being burned to death! We need volunteers to come up and help save them!" So all the English and Irish and Scots and Swedes and Americans and Canadians and Australians all went to help save the women and children. All the Asiatics just sat there, guarding their possessions.

So we went out there. The city was on fire, and they wanted us to save a lathe. The lathe was fastened to the bed of the shop it was in. Well, our bosun was about six foot five, and 250 pounds. He and five of us got together and we rocked it back and forth and we tore it off the deck. We dragged it and took it out into the street, but we needed some help so we grabbed some Russians and said, "Lift!" So we went down the street with the lathe, away from the fire. The fire was advancing.

Well, the lathe got awfully heavy. We looked around and the Russians were gone. The bosun grabbed a couple more Russians and said, "Lift!" and gave them a kick in the ass. We lifted it up, but it got heavy again: *they'd* gone! So we said the hell with it. If they didn't worry about it, why should we. And we left it in the street.

Me and one of the officers were walking along, and some woman came up to us. She was hysterical. Her house was on fire and she was pointing up to it. Well, we got the idea that her baby was up there. So we got a ladder and he and I climbed up and we went in the room. It was full of smoke. He went to one side, and I went to the other on our hands and knees crawling around. We couldn't find any baby. So we looked again, and still no baby. So we went down the ladder and told her, "No baby." But it wasn't a baby she was after, it was her most prized possession: it was a sewing machine.

We used to have sort of a thieves' market in Archangel. You could peddle anything, like a jackknife with a broken blade. It was valuable. If you needed a jackknife it was better than nothing. So the guys were selling anything they could. And I remember talking to some Estonian or Latvian sailor there. So I said to him, "How do you like this country?"

He looks around and he says, "I've been to England and I've been to Boston, so you know what I think of this country." He spoke good English. Those Estonian and Latvian—the Baltic people—they don't like Russians. A lot of them were seafaring types.

We used to eat at the hotel and at other places. There was a social club where we went and ate reindeer meat and cabbage soup and black bread. We used to dip it in salt. It's delicious.

Well, I used to sneak a couple pieces of bread to this kid. He was maybe 12 years old. He didn't look like any of the Russian kids, he looked like an Irish kid: red hair and freckles. I used to give him bread. He had picked up English—you know how a 12-year-old kid is. There was one

Left to right, Howard Bethell's Merchant Marine uniform service emblem and his honorable service pin (photograph by Michael Gillen).

streetcar that used to run right past the Intourist Hotel. We used to sit there and make bets: women trying to get aboard with their bundles, how many cars would pass before they'd make it. People would just shove them out of the way. The kid used to ride on the back of the car like all kids, yelling, "Jigge, jigge Yankee bastards!" as he went past us. Or "Limey bastards," according to which ones he passed.

A couple of days before we were going to sail, he slipped me a coin about a little bigger than a silver dollar. A silvery metal. So I kept it, but I gave it to some girl who admired it in England. I found out later that it was platinum, pure platinum. For a while they used platinum in coins. It was an old coin, and I wish I still had it.

Well, the kid told me, "Tomorrow you go," He was a streetwise kid, a smart kid. And he was right. The next day we sailed.

## "Lady, how the hell do you think I got here?"

*After returning from Russia, Bethell took time off to attend radio operator's school. When that did not work out, he shipped out again as Able Seaman, in the Liberty ship* Isaac Coles. *After having had two ships torpedoed out from under him—first in the Caribbean, and then in a convoy to Russia— his ship departed from New York in convoy, and eventually arrived in July 1943, in support of the invasion of Sicily.*[10]

We went into the Mediterranean on the *Isaac Coles* [and] were sailing in the invasion of Sicily. Once there, we came under attack once. And then we were in the port of Palermo. I think we were the second ship into that port, came alongside, secured and made fast. And on the dock there were cases of Italian hand grenades called "Red Devils." We discharged cargo there, all kinds of military supplies. The longshoremen were local longshoremen, and they were guarded by colored troops in, I believe, the transport corps.

There would be an air raid, oh, maybe every other night or every day for a while.

During the time I wasn't working I roamed all around the city. I was in the fascist headquarters, where they were still paying dues up until the invasion. The dues cards were laying all around. I picked up a pennant: black velvet with fascist [logo] in silver thread, which I still have.

The city had been badly bombed. The water was unsafe. The Army had—what do you call those things?—like big bladders of water hanging on a tripod. You were supposed to drink that because the water was contaminated.

So I was thirsty one day, and I walked into the Red Cross. I was in dungarees—clean dungarees; I wasn't in uniform. And the hostess bustled up to me and wanted to know what I was doing there. She said, "Who are you, what are you doing here?"

I told her, "I'm a seaman off a merchant ship."

She said, "You can't come in here, this is for our boys fighting this war!"

And I said, "Well, lady, how the hell do you think I got here?"

And I walked out.[11]

*After discharging in Palermo, the* Isaac Coles *carried German and Italian prisoners of war to North Africa, discharged them into barges, and then returned to the United States without mishap, arriving in Norfolk, Virginia, some weeks later. Bethell left the ship there, returned to New York and continued to ship out from there for the duration of the war. He continued to ship out for many years after the war, as AB and Quartermaster, often in liners running between Hawaii and the West Coast. In 1981 while serving as AB in the* President Jackson *he was involved in the rescue of Vietnamese "boat people" in the South China Sea. He passed away in 1982, at 67, while serving as AB in the* President Wilson *in the Pacific. He was buried at sea, as he would have wished.*

# CHAPTER 3

# Daniel J. Bradley: "I've been on borrowed time"

*Daniel J. Bradley was born into a seafaring family in Boston, Massachusetts, in November 1921.*[1] *A self-professed "tanker stiff" who shipped out only in tankers, he first went to sea in December 1940 as ordinary seaman (OS) in the tanker* Beacon *(Esso), and then as able seaman (AB) in the H.H. Rogers.*[2] *He was AB in the tanker* Typhoon *in the Caribbean when Pearl Harbor was attacked on 7 December 1941.*[3]

I heard it on my radio, and I went up and told the Old Man that Pearl Harbor was attacked. And he as much as chased me off the bridge and told me I was full of it [and] "get the hell out of here with them goddamned stories!"

And then a while later the radio operator, he come up and told him. So then we started taking precautions. We started running blackout. We were at sea when it happened. In fact, we were on our way to Guantanamo Bay [and] were coming down from Havana—had discharged part in Havana—and were coming down to discharge the rest of it.

We were in Aruba the night they threw the shells out and blew up a bunch of ships outside the reef. [This was] in around February because I know the American soldiers had just come into Aruba and relieved Scotchmen within about a three-day span of the American soldiers getting in there.[4]

We were at the dock at the time. I was sound asleep and they called me and I got up on deck, and there was nothing but flames from one end of the island to the other outside. But it was all to the leeward of us, so that's what saved the island.

They hit, I think, three tankers, and they hit one of the high-octane tanks up in the [tank] farm and put a shell into the BOQ and blew that up.

*Bradley returned to New York, signed off the* Typhoon *in March 1942, and continued to ship out from there on tankers to the Caribbean. He eventually joined the Esso* Manhattan—*a brand new T-3 type tanker—and as an AB on the 12 to 4 watch took her out of the shipyard in Chester, Pennsylvania, where she was built.*

We made a couple of trips coast-wise [and] had a Navy gun crew and a specialty crew [for] a paravane up forward, for mine sweeping. We ran alone down in the Gulf and back up to New York. We made a couple of trips on the *Manhattan*, and we got into New York and discharged.

I went up to Boston for the weekend, and damn near missed the ship coming home. But they were held up on account of some repairs, so I got back on it. And we left the dock at about seven o'clock in the morning. It was a nice day in March—overcast, but it was clear. And we'd been going down the channel, and we dropped the pilot, and it was just shortly after we dropped the pilot—about an hour or so—we had actually passed Ambrose [Light] and we were down around Asbury Park and were around point "Zed"—the last buoys of the swept channel—close by [and] I had just sat down to have some soup. It was about six minutes after twelve and she just went—boom!—like that and the sea come up over the stern. So everybody started running out the after door. I grabbed 'em and said, "Go up forward, go up forward!" And I went forward.

We had six lifeboats, and we were putting lifeboats over—aft—and we got the lifeboats away. All

**Daniel and Marie Bradley, possible wedding portrait, November 1945. Marie Bradley is shown in the uniform of U.S. Navy WAVES, in which she served during the war (Daniel J. Bradley, Jr.).**

the lifeboats and the life rafts were away. And there were six of us left on the ship.

So the blimp came down and she was—kept on homing in on us, and swerving off to see if there was anything [submarine] down there.[5]

She stayed together, and what held her together were all these degaussing wires along the side and the cables running up. And as she kept working up and down in the seaway, why, then she parted. That was the "longest ship in the world," they said. See, they brought the stern in first, and they put the stern in the dock. And then they put the bow in and the bow was up against the stern. So she was known as the longest ship in the world.[6]

I got off on a Coast Guard cutter.[7] The Coast Guard cutter came out and they came up under the stern, and we—one by one—we jumped from the quarterdeck stern onto the boat. And we were carried back into New York. They processed us at Pier Six on Staten Island, and then they put us in different hotels in the city.

I got on the *Norfolk* after I left the *Manhattan*, and made the North Atlantic trip and came back. And then I got on the *Harrisburg* in New York in July of '43. She was a brand new ship, too.[8]

We loaded and ran up to Argentia, Newfoundland. And it was [with] the *Cherry Valley*, the *Oriente*, the *Cristobal*, and one other big troopship. There was three troopships [and] just five of us: two tankers and three troopships, plus the escort. And we left Argentia and went across the Atlantic to Greenock, Scotland.

We had to slow down for the *Cherry Valley* to keep up. She was a T-2 but she's only a 15-knotter.[9] And the *Harrisburg*, she was reported to do 17 and a half, 18 knots. She was a T-3, so she's a little faster. And she was a good sea boat. And we came back from there, and came back into New York.

We loaded bunker fuel in Aruba, and we headed for the Canal. And on the west coast of the Canal we picked up part of Squadron Seven—PT Boats, three of them [as deck cargo].

There was us—the *Harrisburg*—and the [Esso] *Pittsburgh*. *Pittsburgh* was a Sun-built job [with a] Sundoxford Diesel.[10] She was supposed to run with us out to the South Pacific. We were supposed to go to Australia with the PT boats, and we ended up in Milne Bay in New Guinea. We put the PT boats off [there] and discharged into these different fuelers that the Navy had. In fact, we discharged into the *George Henry*, and also the *Typhoon* came alongside. I took one look and I said, "I know that thing!" They didn't even have a name on it; they just gave it a number—the X145.

They wouldn't give it a name. But the old *George Henry*, she was known [by the Navy] as the USS *Victoria*.

So we discharged there, and then we left there and came back through the Canal, picked up another load and went into Espiritu Santos. Then another, came back and took another load to [a port] in the Friendly Islands, and then we came back.

Oh, we also towed a Liberty ship at Christmas of '43. We towed [it] at about 14 knots and then we lost all the [towing] gear in bad weather. And we had to lay-to and stick around until the seagoing tug came and brought her into New Zealand. We were in New Zealand [on] Christmas Day of '43, and then we came back through the Canal again. And we stopped in Cartagena, in July.

I think we started loading the 4th of July in Cartagena, Colombia, and we were going from there to New York. We were loaded with Colombian bottoms—real heavy—and we left there and were on our way to New York when we got torpedoed.

**Wartime photograph of tanker SS *Esso Harrisburg*, with deck cargo. Dated 31 May 1943 (Mariners' Museum, Newport News, Virginia).**

It was a fantastic night, the lovers' night: the full moon was just rising. It was beautiful. We had this one Navy gunner named Davey O'Brien. The kid had eagle eyes and he spotted the sub on the surface and called the alarm. We were running on one boiler and we had about 36 inches of grass on the bottom. So the skipper pulled the ship away, giving the stern to the sub, but they threw one of the so-called acoustic fish and that's where they got us—right in the stern.[11]

I was up on the gun deck. I was hot-shell man on the 4"/50. I would take the empty shells out and carry them away from the action. I was right on the stern and I had my big asbestos gloves on for when you catch the hot shell coming out, to carry it away. But we never did fire a shot there. The forward gun got a couple of shots off but they couldn't do anything because the gun was jammed in one position after the initial shock. But the 20-mm gunners were still firing as the ship went down.

We had another Navy gunner, the trainer on the 4"/50. He was unlucky. They have a handle there that you lift up to swing the gun in an arc or raise it or lower it. And that handle came down and hit him right on the knee and broke his kneecap. So they carried him over to a lifeboat and they put him in the forward end of the lifeboat. And as they were releasing the lifeboat in the water one of the release blocks came over and almost took his head off. Later, when they were picking him up, one of the Navy rescue vessel's sailors threw a heaving line, and the monkey fist struck him on the other side of the head. The poor son of a gun.

I was black and blue from my ankle all the way up, because when the first one hit it just knocked everybody flat, and I went down. But that's all it was. I was black and blue from, let's say, the calves of my legs all the way up my side. And I didn't know what the hell it was until I realized later that's what caused it.

All I had on was a pair of shorts, khaki shorts. No hat, no nothing. And I lost all my papers. One guy was crying about the fact that he had ruined his watch, and I said, "Hey, you gotta be thankful that you're still alive." So then he started to talk a little bit different.

I'll tell you how foolhardy I was. I went down to the inside to see if there was anybody left in the rooms. I helped lower one lifeboat and then I went down and around and checked. I went down forward and through the quarters and up the after ladder back up onto the boat deck. Then I swung out with the manrope and went down. The stern had already started to settle, and of course we were loaded. So I didn't have too far to go. I went down maybe 15 or 20 feet.

The ship didn't burn. I think you'd need a blowtorch to light that stuff off that we had.

The first torpedo hit right in the stern, right underneath us. The next one hit right in the bunker tank just forward of the after house. Then the third one hit number five [cargo tank], starboard, and that's when oil went all over everything on the lee side. We had four boats on her. The boats forward, they had gotten away clean. The boat I was in, everybody was covered in oil. We were away after the second one hit, but we got covered with bunker oil. What we were carrying was also similar to bunker oil, and that also got laid on us. So we were kind of crummy out there. The other three boats, the guys were clean.

The ship didn't go down right away, she stayed up all night. Her bow—just her bow—was sticking up out of the water. And then, at about four or five o'clock in the morning, you could see her starting to go down. The buoyancy was being worked out of the bow. We were quite a ways—a couple of miles by then—but you could see her go down. And let me tell you, that's a heartbreaking sight. I was on her almost a year, and she was a good ship.

We lost eight men: four in the merchant crew—all in the deck department, and we lost four in the Navy crew. We lost the skipper, the bosun, and two ABs. The skipper was last seen on the foc'sle'head. He handed somebody his wallet, and they said they saw him go forward. I don't think he was injured.[12]

We had heard so many of these stories about machine-gunning, so we all sort of scattered so that none of them would be near us. The sub went up to one boat but they didn't come near our boat.

We put up the sail in the morning and started sailing. It was crowded. We had about 17 men in the boat. There was one guy who had to go, so the second mate, Hayden, said to him, "Use a bucket." That was a mistake. He used the bucket and just about everybody wanted to go over the side!

Hayden, the second mate, was really good, a good seaman.[13] He started right off the bat passing out the provisions the way they're supposed to be passed out. We had water and food. And the guy who didn't smoke had four packs of cigarettes with him. He had a little survival kit that he carried, and he had all this stuff. And of course he passed it out to the guys who were really on the nicotine kick. I was a smoker but I didn't smoke them because I didn't need it that bad.

Three days later we were picked up—the boat I was in—by the *Queen Wilhemina*, a Dutch destroyer. One of the boats made Santa Marta

[Colombia] five days later, and some of the fellas were picked up by an American minesweeper about 36 hours later.[14] We were brought back to Aruba [and] were in Aruba for six or seven days at the USS [United Seamen's Service] Club. Then they sent us on a minesweeper over to Curacao. We were there a day or so, and then they flew us on a Pan Am Clipper to Miami. We were a day in Miami, and then we took the train up to New York.

They gave us survivor's leave and vacation time, and that's when I went home, went and started going to that Boxell's School of Navigation in Boston. I decided to try for a third mate's license. And I got a third mate's license.

I'll tell you—this is my own feeling—I feel that I've been on borrowed time since 1944. To me this is all bonus. Why, with other ABs getting killed there—was it the fact that I wasn't at that spot at that moment, or was it because I was over there at that moment?

I've always wondered about that.

*Bradley continued to ship out for the duration of the war and saw service in the Pacific as well as Atlantic. He settled with his family in Staten Island, New York, soon after the war and continued to ship out—ultimately as chief mate—on Esso tankers. He retired initially in 1972, worked ashore in security for a while, then shipped out again with Cove Shipping until retiring again in 1982. Bradley was involved with the Shriners, and was a 32nd degree Mason. He passed away in Staten Island, New York, in 2004.*

# CHAPTER 4

# Rexford Dickey: "He died from a broken heart"

*Rexford "Rex" Dickey was born in Sangerville, Maine, in 1902. He was raised in Bangor and first went to sea in the early 1920s on 6-masted lumber schooners along the Maine coast. He then made his way to New York and shipped as a mess boy in a tanker around 1922. He sailed regularly out of New York through the 1920s and early 1930s, was involved in the maritime strike of 1934, and then made his way to Baltimore. He was in Baltimore, working as a patrolman for the Seafarers International Union, when Pearl Harbor was attacked. He decided to go back to sea at that point. He shipped out as AB in the SS* Joseph Hewes, *and paid off that ship in New York in January 1943. He then shipped out as AB in the Liberty ship* Wade Hampton.[1]

I picked the ship up in Baltimore, and then we went to New York and loaded, foodstuffs mostly. We were in New York about a week. The captain came around and asked if we wanted to make the trip, said that we were going to Russia. He couldn't tell us which port. He asked if we wanted to stay on, and, if not, said we could get off now before we signed any [shipping] articles when it would be too late. Some got off, but most stayed on.

When we left, we were in a big convoy and proceeded straight out across the Atlantic.[2]

We were in ice fields, and then after we got out of the ice fields it was blowing like the devil. And that night when I went on watch, why, we all figured there was no danger of getting torpedoed tonight: it was blowing too hard.

At 8 o'clock that night we got torpedoed.[3] I was at the wheel when we got hit. The torpedo hit around the after mast, between number four and number five hatch. I think it was on the port side, but I'm not sure.

It blew the tail right off, from the after end of number four hatch back. We lost—I don't know how many of the gun crew, because they lived back aft there.[4]

We were ordered to abandon ship, and the bosun and I lowered the lifeboats. After we got the lifeboats lowered on the two sides we grabbed the life raft; it was one of those box type [wooden] rafts. When the raft came up after hitting the water, I jumped for it. I only got a little wet. But when the bosun jumped for it, he missed. He went into the water, and then I pulled him out.

Visibility wasn't very good. We were on the life raft maybe an hour or so. At that time there was a destroyer picking up the gang from the lifeboats. We weren't

Rex Dickey, Baltimore, 1982 (photograph by Michael Gillen).

very far from them; we could hear them talking, and all that. So I turned on the flashlight to make sure they'd know where we were. And they hollered out, "Turn that light out or we'll shoot it out!" Well that was enough for me. I turned it out. By the time daylight came, there was nothing around. They'd all gone off and left us. The next day a ship passed us, but it was quite a ways off. They didn't spot us.

Our raft was about six feet by eight feet. We did have a little bit of food, but the water, in cans, had already frozen. We had no water at all except what we could get when it snowed. We had a mast that we put up and had flags flying from. And we had canvas about a foot high that we put up around the raft to cut down on the spray.

We passed the whole day and another night, and the next day a ship passed by us real close. If we'd seen anybody walking on deck we could've recognized him—that's how close they came to us. We jumped up and hollered and hooted and all that, but it didn't do any good.

I think the bosun gave up when that last one passed us by. He went over into his corner, and I went over to another and sat down, out of the spray as much as we could. He didn't talk, and he didn't move from that time on. I can see myself now, lying there on my back with my legs up in the air paddling like on a bicycle, trying to keep warm. Anything to keep warm, and pass the time away.

**The Liberty ship SS *Wade Hampton* (Mariners' Museum, Newport News, Virginia).**

At one point I dozed off, and I was dreaming that a convoy was coming. I woke up quick and started to holler, and all of a sudden it came to me that I was dreaming—I was seeing things. Everything goes through your mind. I thought that I'd make it somehow or the other. Even when that last ship went by us and didn't pick us up, I thought, "Well, there'll be another one coming along." I never considered for a moment that I wouldn't make it.

Well, anyway, I was beginning to see things again, or thinking I was. I'd doze off, and then I saw this convoy and I thought, "Hell, this is just a dream." All of a sudden, I said, "I'd better look again." I looked again, and sure enough it was a convoy. I got up and started hollering to beat the band. I could see the convoy going off in the distance, way off there. I could see that convoy leaving there, and gave one more yell.

All of a sudden, somebody right behind me says, "We see you, we see you. We'll pick you up." Well, I looked behind me, and there's this destroyer about 50 or a 100 feet from us. It was one of those old four-stack destroyers.⁵ The destroyer drew right alongside us, and they threw a ladder over and I went up it.

After I got aboard, I said, "How about the bosun?"

He said, "Well, he's gone."

I don't know if he died from exposure or if he died from a broken heart. I think he died mostly from a broken heart. I think he gave up the will to live after that last ship passed us by.⁶

So from the destroyer they transferred me over to this hospital ship they had. We were heading for Newfoundland, I think. So this doctor they had was an Australian [and] I think he would've had me walking in no time. They cut the toe off—what was frozen—and then put me ashore in Halifax.

*From Halifax Dickey eventually made his way back to New York and then to Baltimore. He did not ship out again during the war but worked as a patrolman for the Seafarers International Union (SIU). Dickey continued to work for the SIU into the early post-war period, then shipped out again from 1948 until 1953. He continued to work with the SIU as patrolman and port agent in Baltimore before retiring in 1970. He passed away at 84 in 1986.*

CHAPTER 5

# Stanley E. Gorski: The Minefields of Manila Bay

*Stanley E. Gorski was born in Connecticut in 1914 and raised in Racine, Wisconsin. He joined the U.S. Coast Guard in 1933 and received training and initial experience on the Great Lakes. He transferred to the East Coast after a year, served in the cutter* Mojave, *and was honorably discharged in 1937. He then joined the Merchant Marine, shipping out initially from New York through the Eastern and Gulf Sailors (later National Maritime Union)—as AB, quartermaster, and bosun. He shipped out later from the West Coast with Oceanic-Oriental Line to Australia and the Far East. In late 1941 Gorski shipped out in the MS* American Leader *from San Pedro, California.*[1]

In early September of 1941 I shipped on a brand new ship called the *American Leader* in San Pedro, California. *American Leader* was a C-1 type ship with all the latest gear aboard.[2] I actually signed on as an ordinary seaman, but by the time we left the United States bound for the Far East I was bosun in this thing.

My government maintained [before the attack on Pearl Harbor] that a convoy of five ships never existed.[3] Well I was *in* the bloody thing and so were five other ships I can name and the cruiser *Boise*.[4] We left the Hawaiian Islands for Manila [Philippines] on November 27, a convoy of five ships escorted by *Boise*, when this country was still neutral.

The last six months prior to [the U.S. entry in] the war we all had ideas that something was going to happen sooner or later. Because, don't forget, the war had been on since 1939 in Europe. We had talked of the possibility should it occur and all that, and naturally Manila would be one of the first places that would be hit. [But] nobody had any idea that it would be the Hawaiian Islands.

On December the 8th—which is the 7th here—our radioman got a message to the effect that Pearl Harbor had been attacked, but the news did not go out to the crew immediately. I knew of it, chief officers knew of it, the captain, etcetera, but it was kind of kept from the crew because you never know what the reaction is gonna be.

We arrived in Manila the day after Pearl Harbor was attacked; we were at sea a day, day and a half out of Manila [when word was received of the attack].[5] We arrived in Manila and, of course, began discharging cargo, because we had aboard various materiel for the military out there. And general cargo, of course.

This [the blackout procedures] was ordered by the USS *Boise*, and the five ships—four of the five ships—blacked out per the orders finally under duress. They logged it as "under duress" because we were not at war, and the *Boise* ordering us to run blacked out was contrary to international law.

So at any rate, under duress, we ran blacked out, that is, the four freight ships. The *President Grant*, which was sort of designated as convoy command, carried passengers, so the result was that the captain of the *President Grant*, an American President Line ship, he was used to dark ship because under international law in those days—and I remember that so distinctly—because, hell, we ran with our lights all night displayed on American flags painted on both sides of our ship. And by international law the message had already been given out that if anyone—if any ship were to carry women and children and passengers they were to display that blue light in the truck of the foremast, and if that was not displayed the Germans would presume that the ship was an enemy, and they would attack. And I was bosun in the ship [so] it was my job to take care of all of that.

We discharged our cargo, and the first attack on Manila took place on December 10th. I counted the first—for those of us aboard the ship—there were many of us—but a bunch of Japanese bombers—72 by my count—were flying at an extremely high altitude, and, of course, they were bound for Cavite across the bay from us about four miles distant. And about, oh, maybe three planes peeled off and dropped bombs around us in the harbor there. We knew that the war was on, and we knew that it was a question of a short time before Manila itself would be attacked.

We arrived there on the day after, which was actually the 9th of December—Manila time—and the first attack of those 72 bombers over our immediate area, although other parts of the island had already been attacked, and the bombers went over to Cavite. And in 25 minutes, approximately, Cavite was for all intents useless.

You could see the bombers going, certainly could hear the bombs dropping and all that. You could see the smoke. And, of course, with the sirens going and—our shore gangs—the stevedores—as soon as they heard a siren go off, why, they would all leave the ship. And I had to make certain that my gangs were situated on the fore and afterdecks in case these guys departed without even shutting off the machinery part of the time to keep from wrecking our rigging and stuff. We had to watch very, very closely, and as a matter of fact we took care of that pretty well. And in the end it pretty much amounted to our own crews discharging of the cargo, because you couldn't get the people to stay aboard the ship—they were afraid that they were going to be bombed.

We didn't get it all unloaded—we had orders to leave there on December 12th. On December 12th I had a conference with the skipper, the chief mate, and some naval officer had come aboard. And they told us if there was any chance of getting out, we would have to leave by evening twilight on the 12th of December.[6]

MS *American Leader*, **unarmed and showing typical United States (then noncombatant) identification of immediate pre–Pearl Harbor period (Mariners' Museum, Newport News, Virginia).**

We were supposed to be guided through the minefields of Manila Bay by a United States submarine. But if the submarine didn't show, then we were to proceed out of Manila by ourselves. In other words, Captain [Haakon A.] Pederson was to con that ship through the minefields using some charts that were given to him by the naval officer. Of course, this was a very hairy thing, you know, and that's the way it was—the sub didn't show up.[7]

And, of course, we didn't batten down our hatches thoroughly because we had to get out that night, because they figured there was going to be a big attack on the harbor the following day. That's what the rumors were, and that was the news that was conveyed to us by the military.

So we left hurriedly, of course, and in going through the minefields I had all hands—by order of the skipper and the chief mate—anybody who wasn't on watch had to wear their life preserver at all times, and of course to stay within the confines of the ship. In other words, don't be on deck if you didn't have to be [while] going through those minefields. It was the most extensive minefield under our jurisdiction in those days.

And it was an extremely tense and hairy time for all hands, because if we were to hit one of those mines, of course, if you were on deck chances were you would've been injured worse than if you'd been inside the deck house. We did crank out the lifeboats to make certain they were ready for launching as quickly as possible. And of course I had plenty of training in the Coast Guard in that kind of stuff, and later on it would come into good use for it.

But anyway, we left Manila on the 12th at evening's twilight, and we arrived off the northeast coast of Australia on Christmas Day, December the 25th. To our knowledge we were the last of about five ships, of about five ships that escaped from Manila, and only two of us arrived in Australia safely. [Another] ship that we didn't know—came in with a bad list. She'd been attacked by aircraft, and came in to anchor. She had a big list, to her port, as I recall.

On the way we ran into some trouble. This was a brand new C-1 type ship—and a diesel-powered job—and one of our pistons became hot and we had to shut down. And of all places. We had to pull that piston in an area where Japanese submarines were supposed to be operating quite heavily. But it had to be done; we were either going to be crippled or we had to pull that piston. We just had to drift. And here was the point: the piston had to be pulled as quickly as possible, but how were you going to do it? You had to have enough men to help out in this procedure to get out of there as quickly as possible [and] with a certain amount of vibration.[8]

So my deck crew had to get in on the act too, and we had left a few men in Manila who never got back to the ship [before] we sailed. So we were short-handed in the first place. But at any rate we did discuss the whole thing, and there were no arguments in any way.[9] And what we did—all the men that we could spare, and any volunteers, went down with the "black gang" and pulled the piston—disconnected the piston—and we proceeded on there. You could feel the vibration—it was quite heavy—and it dropped our speed from a top speed of 15 knots to 13.

And we were very fortunate that nothing happened as far as any—no attack on us. We drifted for about three and a half hours, and got out of it very nicely. So we then proceeded down to Thursday Island and had orders to anchor off Thursday Island. And when we identified ourself, apparently there had been reports that we had been sunk, 'cause we had a terrible time in there. We were at anchor quite a long time.

We had to stay there, oh, about nine to 12 hours before we finally got permission to proceed on down the coast, to Brisbane, and we discharged a small amount of cargo in Brisbane, and had orders to proceed to Sydney. We were in Sydney approximately 10 days, discharging our cargo and taking on other types of cargo.

And there were negotiations going on as to whether we might [have deck guns installed]. But [without plating reinforcement] we were unable to carry anything like that.

And the day came finally when we had orders to head back to the United States. Now, again, this was a trying thing, because the war was on and we had a tremendous long voyage to make to the Panama Canal. And on the way we were to stop at New Caledonia to load ore, which was an absolute necessity for the steel industry. And when we pulled in there, again we couldn't understand why we had been reported as being sunk so often. And everybody was hoping we'd get the heck out of there as fast as we could. And we took on a load of ore.[10]

We came in through the west coast entrance of the Panama Canal, and as far as we could see it didn't look much different. But there was the military guard: military personnel stationed in all different parts of the ship, as guards, with side arms and rifles, and they were stationed on the bridge. It was unusual but everything went off smoothly, and we felt we were safe. But when we got on the Atlantic side we sure had something to learn. In 1942 we took a terrible pounding there. But we were a fast ship and did proceed on our own—all the time—and we were bound for Boston.

And en route a lot of things happened. We were fired upon by somebody—don't even know who it was—off Cape Hatteras—in a storm. This was in the early part of February and the [unspecified ship] was sunk about 27 miles on our starboard bow [but] we couldn't change course to try to pick up survivors or anything like that.

And it was a very hairy trip ahead, going up there. We had a tanker blown up on our starboard quarter off of Florida that knocked some of our deck crew [who were] on their last smoke before evening blackout—knocked them onto the deck. It was about three-quarters of a mile from us. Because you're all pretty close together and trying to take advantage of the Gulf Stream. So you get into the fastest portion in order to make the best time. We felt it [the explosion], saw it, and a couple of the crew members were bruised from being thrown to the deck. But there was no such thing as stopping or turning around or anything like that. What happened to it we don't know.

We arrived in Boston as I recall it on February 12th: fifty-one or two days from the time we left Australia. I took my discharge with me [to a Coast Guard recruiter]. And I said, "Well, I've got an honorable discharge [from the Coast Guard], and I've been trained on the five-inch gun, and I figured that I'd be of more use in the military, in the Coast Guard." And I was told, "Well, you can't do it. You either have to stay with the ship you are in or report to your local draft board." Now, my local draft board was in Racine, *Wisconsin*!

I went over to Scully Square to the Navy recruiter, pulled out my discharge, showed it to the recruiter, and he did the same thing: pulled out a directive or letter and he read it to me, and it said, "No merchant seaman is permitted to enlist in the Navy but must stay in the [merchant] ship. He is needed more in the merchant ship."

We had no idea how *bad* this sinking thing was that was taking place in those early days on the East Coast.

So, the result was, what am I to do? We discharged the crew—they were paid off. And I was the only guy—plus the "black gang"—to turn over the machinery while we were in port. We of course went ahead and discharged our cargo—this was all done by shore people. But at any rate, there I was. So the chief officer who was assigned to *American Leader* when she was in port asked me if I had any people in my family, and "why don't you take a trip home?"

So I took a bus trip, stayed on the darn bus all the way to Chicago, Illinois, and then on to Milwaukee, Wisconsin. They kept me on the [ship's] books. In other words, I had been aboard her already for one trip, and then the captain wanted me aboard that ship, you know, when we were refitted in the Navy yard with guns and all the rest of it. Anyway. So I came for a short visit to Racine, and [then] I went back. *American Leader* went into a yard in New Jersey, where she was fitted with guns and armor plating and all the rest of the stuff. And there were a bunch of publicity photographs that were shot. And one of the Cisco Brothers came aboard *America Leader* one morning. The marine superintendent told the shore mate to get the bosun and have him work with this photographer. And it was one of the Cisco boys—a news photographer—and I recognized him. But anyway, there was a bunch of photographs shot for the United States Merchant Marine—that is, PR stuff—and a series of photographs by Ernie Cisco for the magazine section of the *New York Times* which was to be published in May. Many years later I got copies of that magazine.

So we staged a number of photographs, and word is, supposedly one of the most famous photographs that was used in the Merchant Marine publicity and as a stock shot was a group of guys heaving on a heaving line [and] showing *muscle*.

*Stanley Gorski was aboard* American Leader *as bosun when the ship set sail again, probably in March 1942, for another long, wartime voyage. But as luck would have it, and after having been turned down for reenlistment in the Coast Guard and enlistment in the Navy, the* American Leader *was attacked by the German commerce raider* Michel *on that voyage and was sunk. Gorski spent the rest of the war as a POW, first aboard* Michel *itself, and then in a Japanese POW camp in Sumatra where he was forced to work on the Sumatra Railway. Of the original 49 merchant seaman on* American Leader *when she set sail on that second voyage, 10 were killed in the initial attack by* Michel, *two died in a Japanese POW camp in Sumatra, and an additional 12 were lost when Japanese ships on which they were being transferred to Japan were torpedoed.*[11] *This included the SS* Junyo Maru, *sunk by the British submarine HMS* Tradewind *on 18 September 1944 while en route to Sumatra. Gorski survived that sinking—the second time a ship would be shot out from under him during the war, while three of his former shipmates in* American Leader *were lost. He shipped out into the early post-war period, and for many years was an executive with Rae Motors Corp. Gorski passed away in Racine, Wisconsin, in 2003.*

CHAPTER 6

# Jack A. Holt:
# "We all piled out on deck"

*Jack A. Holt was born in Cincinnati, Ohio, in March 1921.[1] The son of a career Army officer, he was raised in Washington, D.C., and Tidewater, Virginia, and first went to sea at the age of 16 in the three-masted schooner* Daniel Getson. *After finishing high school in 1939 he joined the Merchant Marine and began shipping out regularly. He was an ordinary seaman in SS* Dakotan *in the Pacific at the time of the Japanese attack on Pearl Harbor.[2]*

We were right off Acapulco, Mexico, hugging the coast, when the war began. I was on watch or had just come off watch when somebody came back in the fo'c'sle and said, "Hey, the Japs have just attacked Pearl Harbor!"

Everybody said, "Aw, get out of here," you know. This was one of those ship's clowns anyway and nobody paid any [attention] but he said, "No, it's the truth. I was there on the wheel when the Old Man got the message from Sparks." And he said, "He and Sparks are up there in the radio room right now."

It wasn't long until the Old Man hit the general alarm, and we all piled out on deck. Some of the fellows had their own little radios and had picked it up. And we were just aghast; nobody could believe it. But some of the more sober ones said, "Hey, wait a minute, this has been brewing for a long time." Especially the old Pacific hands that had been running out to China and Japan. They said, "Shit, [General Douglas] MacArthur tried to tell us; everybody tried to tell us."

Some guys were saying things like, "Those little sneaky so and sos, why, we'll whip them in a week!" But I wasn't too sure about that. I was just stunned, 'cause I had a real good buddy—a high school chum—who was stationed at Kaneohe Bay there and it got pretty well wiped out.[3] As it turned out, it almost destroyed him: he lost most of his hands. I had just visited him on my last ship, and I was just sick over that, worried about him and some other friends I had out there, plus the fact that it was such a dirty, nasty thing.

So the Old Man announced it formally. He said, "We are at war. It's official now. I know you boys have heard it, but it is official that Pearl Harbor was attacked this morning, apparently with a heavy loss of life and a terrific loss to the U.S. fleet. It looks now like the entire fleet in the harbor has been destroyed. Well, they did save a few of them, but the [battleship] *Oklahoma* and them all went to the bottom."[4] And he said, "We will institute wartime security measures." And he said, "Mister mate, I want you to blacken the ship: we're gonna paint all the portholes, dog all doors at night regardless of the heat, and paint over all white work."

And here we'd been working our butts off getting everything sougeyed and cleaned up so that she'd look nice, you know, coming into the Panama Canal.

So we turned to with the black paint—any kind of paint we could find—and we started. We had black paint, and green and blue and— We made our own usually, just carbon black and oil and whatnot. And we just slapped paint on like mad. I mean, those ships have, I forget what their color scheme was. Seems to me they had some yellow on the stack. We went right to work on the stack and on the booms and on the mast. And even painted out the name with man-helpers. And that night was my first experience with a blackout.

Well, naturally, there's some guy out on deck with a flashlight trying to get up on lookout. After enough broken shins and whatnot, we learned to paint little marks on deck to guide us up. And we learned to take flashlights and cover them with tissue paper or something, and hold them way down on deck, 'cause it was just hazardous: you were just stumbling and clattering all over.

The foc'sles were not air-conditioned, and it was absolutely stifling down below deck there. And some of the fellows was careless about it so the Old Man just simply went down and took out all the lights, except the emergency lights. And we put little shields over them.

So we got to the [Panama] Canal, and I must say the Canal was in a top-notch state of readiness. Boy, they picked us up just as soon as we got

**Third mate Jack A. Holt at sea circa 1943 (courtesy Joanie Wittenberg).**

close: there were planes all *over* us. And then I believe an escort met us outside of the Canal. If I remember right, some Navy people come aboard and they had guys right on there. And from then on, in the Canal, when you took a ship through there was a soldier or sailor right there beside you with a—sometimes a 45 in his *hand*. You didn't make any bobbles when you were steering in the Canal.

And the same went for the engine room, because they did have some known spies. Later on I was on a ship that went through where they jerked a Dutchman off of there. Come to find out he was sailing for 20 years and didn't even have his [licensing] papers; he just had first papers. So what they'd do with him, they'd take him off the ship, they blindfold him, and take him across the Isthmus [of Panama] on a passenger train and they'd bring him back on the other side.

The Canal was in tip-top security. I don't think they would've ever taken the Canal the way they did Pearl Harbor.

I did get home—the 24th of December I was in Norfolk [Virginia]— I did get Christmas Eve. And then the next day we went up to Baltimore, and I paid off.

*After completing the voyage on SS* Dakotan, *Holt had second thoughts about shipping out again in the Merchant Marine and decided to "tell it to the Marines" in early 1942.*

## SS Honolulan

By that time the war was going full blast. So I went down and tried to get in the Marines or something. But I had a little eye problem. I wanted to go for officer's training but I couldn't make it on account of this eye problem. Then I found out that they wouldn't hardly take a merchant seaman anyway, because by that time the ships were going down like nine pins out there. So I gave up trying to go into the service, and about a week later I was on another ship, the *Honolulan*. I joined her in Baltimore.[5]

We went around to New York, and I saw my first ship sunk up there. It had been sunk the night before and hadn't gone all the way down; it was just the bow sticking up off of Cape May [New Jersey]. I said to myself, "This looks rough." Because we were right in sight of land almost.

Well, we went to New York and loaded—general military cargo for the British Eighth Army, which at that time was fighting in the Middle East. We left New York and it took 35 straight days to get to Cape Town. We never saw a ship. We ran all alone, darkened and everything. The only thing I saw, one night at sundown, I just saw the top hamper of a big battleship, and I'm sure it was one of those German pocket raiders. There was a raider operating in the South Atlantic at about that time.

The convoys were pretty ragged at that time. We didn't have the expertise and all that the Limeys had. They were trying to teach the Americans. Everybody was running by themselves and they were going down.... At one time they were losing 27 ships a week between New York and the

**Prewar photograph of SS *Honolulan* (Mariners' Museum, Newport News, Virginia).**

Caribbean.⁶ But we got through the Caribbean all right, and out across the ocean and then went into Cape Town: 35 days, a long, long haul.

But it was a good old ship, the *Honolulan*. She was a leftover from World War I. She was what they call one of them "west" boats. They were kind of like the Luckenbach ships. They were a regular forest of booms. They had six hatches, and I think they had two Sampson posts. They had about 22 booms on there. They were fine old ships, riveted ships. They were tough and had been fairly well taken care of. She was traded around like an old horse, you know. But she was a fine old ship, and they could lift a lot of cargo with them. It kept the deck department hopping because we just had the standard bosun and three watches. In those days you did all your cargo work—the hatches and battens and strong backs. And we always—there was always seamanship. You were always splicing or doing something *all* the time on the ship. Especially after the Arabs [stevedores] got through and then the Indians gave her a good working over.

We stayed in Cape Town about six or eight hours for bunkers and fuel and some groceries, and then went around the Cape and up to Basra,

Iraq. We got up there without any incident. We had a bunch of airplanes on deck, which we unloaded for the Limey air force. And the rest of the stuff was ammunition and Lord knows what all was in there. It was just crates, but I'm sure it was mostly ammunition and food and whatnot.

We had a bunch of them Hudson Bombers—A-20As. They were all the way through. This was a flush-deck ship, and we had quite a bunch of them. But we didn't lose any of them. I thought sure, you know, the Roaring Forties and all, we'd get it. But we delivered every one of them in good shape.

It seemed like we were going to be in Basra, Iraq, forever, because of the way the Arabs worked [and] a lot of them were German sympathizers. We stayed there, I guess we were there a month. And then we went on down to Bombay, and we laid out at anchor there for about two or three weeks. And then another couple, three weeks in His Royal Highness's dockyards, whatever they called it there. We stayed in Bombay, I guess a month and a half between anchoring and unloading.

Then we started out for Cape Town again. And we stayed in Cape Town—we got a few more hours in Cape Town—overnight, I guess. We got to go ashore again. It was strictly wartime. The British couldn't get through the Med so they had to go around. There were big troopships there, and the town was simply swarming with—mostly British. There were very few Americans although we did see a sister ship, one of the American-Hawaiians. I think it was the *Columbian*. We left Cape Town—it must've been the first or second week in July. It was beautiful weather. We had a load of manganese ore and we finished it out with jute, bales of jute.

Well, we were minding our own business and tooting along there—we hadn't seen a soul—and just at suppertime, we were all eating, and I had the second wheel—that's right, I had got my supper and I just—got up first. I took a shortcut through the galley, and to this day I don't know what saved my life, because I had just stepped out of the galley on the starboard side when the first torpedo hit right aft of where I was at. Right amidships. It hit right in number four [hatch], I guess that was, on that ship.[7]

And it blew me up. I remember hitting the overhead. It just raised me right off the [deck and] I hit the overhead and it must've knocked me out because when I came to one of the ABs was lifting me up.

*Soon after the SS* Honolulan *was torpedoed and sunk, the German submarine that had done the deed—U-582—surfaced and ordered one of the lifeboats to come alongside. The crew were questioned about the ship's cargo and destination and were then given directions to the Cape Verde Islands, along with two cartons of cigarettes. Some six days later, at 1830 GCT on 28 October 1942, all members of the SS* Honolulan's *crew were picked up by the British MS* Winchester Castle. *They were landed at New York on 7 August 1942.*[8] *Holt took time off soon after to sit for his third mate's license. He continued to ship out for the duration of the war as an officer, and then into the postwar period until 1950. He came ashore, worked as a horse wrangler, and then had a long career as a dispatcher with the Texas Department of Public Safety. He retired in 1976 and went back to sea, upgrading eventually to Master. He came ashore for good in 1986, lived in Edna, Texas, where he passed away, at 89, in 2011.*

CHAPTER 7

# Paul J. Jarvis:
# "Okinawa was absolute hell"

*Paul J. Jarvis was born in Tennessee in 1917 and raised in a "white" Benedictine orphanage in Arkansas. He went to sea in the 1930s, and participated in major maritime labor strikes of the period. He was ashore living in Richmond, Virginia, and employed as an ironworker "driving rivets" at the time of the attack on Pearl Harbor. He soon made his way to Baltimore, where he rejoined the Merchant Marine, shipping out as able seaman in SS* William Few *for a voyage, with ammunition, tanks and other war materiel, to South Africa, the Middle East, and Brazil. He then shipped out as bosun in SS* Richard Henderson *on 27 July 1943 for a voyage to the Mediterranean.*[1]

## Barrage Balloons in the Med

The ship had been in drydock and we went straight to Philadelphia and loaded everything in Philadelphia. She was a heavy ammo ship. The only ship hold we didn't have ammo in was number five—and number five got hit with the torpedo.

As far as I can remember it was uneventful loading in Philadelphia. I remember that was the first time I ever heard the Ink Spots singing "I want to buy a paper doll." I can remember that was a very popular song at that time. I remember hearing it in Philadelphia. Not that I'm a songster or anything about the popular music going on, but I heard it so damn much I got sick of it.

We had a tremendous deck cargo. Big boxes. Broken down airplanes and things like that. I really don't know where in the hell we were destined for. I'll tell you the truth, I don't recall.[2] I know when we sailed from here we went straight across the Atlantic. We went straight across in convoy. I don't think we came to New York to make up convoy. But we went on to the Mediterranean by way of Gibraltar and met a big convoy there. I remember we joined a convoy coming down from England then; I remember making that up.[3]

Getting across on that ship I know I did an awful lot of work on the ship—like slushing the stays—she was in horrible shape. The crew before, the mate told me, got absolutely nothing done on the damn ship. And I had the crew—that was the ship that had the gunnery officer on there that was a lawyer, and he was a no-good son of a bitch. But in spite of that, the crew did participate in [support of] the [gun crew].

Paul Jarvis as he appeared on seaman's identification for Port of Baltimore, circa 1942 (Paul J. Jarvis).

This balloon, this barrage balloon, I don't know if crew members were ever instructed in handling that barrage balloon or not, but I was never offered a chance to go to a school or read the instructions or anything. But I know we got to sea and the [chief] mate said, "Hey, Boats, do you know anything about these things?"

I said, "Hell, no, but maybe we can read the instructions on the thing."

And actually, we put that thing together. I think one of the engineers—first assistant—helped us. He was riggin' on it some too. It came in crates, and we had these great big gas bottles, a tremendous number of them. How many, I don't know but [they were] just like oxygen [or] acetylene tanks, and so forth. They were stored all on the afterdeck. And it came in three or four crates, parts of it, different parts of it and so forth, all rolled up—and of course the balloon itself. And it was a helluva big thing; it looked like a damn "Goodyear" thing when you got it blown up!

But we struggled—we had actually started working on it at sea. As I recall, we had it up on the boat deck, spread out. And the skipper was down, and other people and everybody putting their ideas together, how you work it and so forth. Finally, we got it assembled, the parts assembled and we carried it back on #5 hatch, and I remember that's where we put in a charge—a partial charge—in the thing and weighted it all down because it was actually flat when we put it all out. It was flat. And we had a nose assembly, because that's where you load it [gas] through.

And we put a partial charge in it, and we had a helluva time figuring out how to get the partial charge out of it because the damn thing was doing like this [gestures] up and down on the hatch. Well, I had spread a lot of canvas and old tarps and things across it so that the hatch battens wouldn't puncture it. We were being very careful about it. The damn thing's made of rubber, or semi-plastic or something like that. [It was a] great big silver thing.

Now they also had wire that you attach on either side of the thing, where if a plane—the object being if a plane went underneath it—of course you'd have the one wire [tether]. But, hell, give him 40 or 50—you might as well fuck him up good while he's at it, see. I don't remember, there might have been 25 to 40 wires.

And they were bastard things to put on. And the way they were made up, as I recall, they were made up and sort of coiled [and] as the balloon went up they would unroll automatically. And then when you got that damn balloon back down again, you had all them damn wires to make 'em back up in this thing. And they didn't roll up well. It was a misfit thing altogether. She was a *mess*. The whole damn thing was a mess.

I recall the first time we put it up. We said, hell, we won't put the wires on it. It was a good thing we didn't or we would've fouled the whole damn ship up. Because as the balloon went up, I know the mate and I were both up aloft on the after mast. He and I were up aloft because we had to rig the wire through fair leads and then a shive up on top. And we had a helluva time [because] the damn shive was jammed. We had a helluva time getting the shive where it was freed to go from side to side.

Naturally, the ship's forward motion would offer wind resistance to the thing, and here we got this damn balloon. We had to go up on top and bring the wires down through that to the nose of the balloon, and then feed this thing up by hand lines. It took the crew—to let it go up to keep it clear of the mast until it got free to take up on the line itself.

And the damn thing began flopping from side to side. It actually touched the water on the starboard side, it touched the water on the port side, and I thought sure as hell we had just lost the balloon. If I had my option I would've cut the damn line and gone off without and let it float on the ocean. But we got it back aboard again, and so forth.

And of course the line was going up [on deck] and we had to heave it aboard, and we had the goddamnedest mess 'cause the line had gotten outside of the pulley, gotten outside between the pulley and the cheeks of the block, and we had a helluva time getting it out.

Working with [chief mate] Bill Montgomery I developed a tremendous admiration of the guy's seamanship. He had come up on a school ship; he was not a "jack come up through the hawespipe"—but it was a mutual respect for each other on the thing.

But anyway, we got it all rigged up and we figured out that we had to put some more gas in it. We were guessing at the gas pressure, and I think the chief engineer or one of the assistant engineers figured out that it took more. But we got the idea that we had to blow her up tighter.

I know I had been reading a book when the [chief] mate came down and said, "We'd better get that [barrage] balloon up." See, the bosun's a day man. I was finished work at five o'clock, had dinner, and then you usually sat around—the guys sat around on the hatch and bullshit and things like that. But I had gone to get my book, and I was sitting on the hatch and was reading my book, and the book's name was *Only Yesterday*—a guy by the name of Bellamy wrote the book, and he was talking about the early [nineteen] twenties and turn of the century and so forth.[4] By the way, I haven't finished that book *yet*. But the mate came. I had gone to my room, and the mate came and knocked on the door, and he said, "I think we'd better get the balloon up." And while we were actually working on the balloon [earlier] the GQ [intelligence officer] had gotten something, I expect, about this idea—expecting air raids that night, [so he said] to get the damn balloon up.[5]

The night we got orders to put it up—they were expecting an air raid—we were going along the North African coast at that time. She went up like a kite. We were probably the first ones to get ours up, because we were congratulating each other about the fact that we had gotten her up so well. But he and I went aloft to check because you had to put it on a winch head to bring it down, and we knew damn well that that wire had gotten out of the sheaf again. And sure enough that's where the damn thing was: she had gotten out, jumped out. It was a very poor rig up there, is what it was, and I knew—I liked to cut my hands, and he was using an implement to get it back in. But the balloon was up already, you see, and everybody was on alert—we were on torpedo alert already, or, you know, air raid alert really is what we were on, and all the ships were getting their balloons up. But we felt good that ours was the first one—one of the first ones, if it wasn't the first. We were looking around the whole convoy laughing like hell about the fact we'd been such experts and we'd been such retards before. And he and I had been aloft, and actually the way that he and I got that thing back on—'cause I sat up in the truck and put my feet up against the damn stanchion, took the wire—even with gloves on it—took everything I could. But the balloon would get slack every once in a while [with] the wind and we got the damn thing—just timed it—and got the thing in. Of course we'd of never got the balloon down had we—but we never had to take it down *anyway*.

But the two of us got down—we were down on the deck cargo, and he said, "Hell, I'm gonna go take a bath." It was during general alert anyway, and he said, "I don't give a damn."

It was about 8:30—just at dusk—[and] hot as hell that night. I was actually standing on top of the deck cargo back by the after mast, between number four and five hatch, when the *John Bell* got hit. And when she got hit there was a tremendous ball of fire—a tremendous roar and a ball of fire. She was over on our starboard side, abreast of us. I was looking straight at the damn ship when she got hit.[6]

Then I ran midships—I had my life jacket on—and I wound up with potatoes and coal sacks around me. I'll always believe I was in midair when that ship got hit, jumping from the catwalk to the boat deck.[7] All I know is that the coal and goddamned potatoes was all over the after part of the boat deck.

The next thing I know, when I got up, I see we were sinking fast. The day man I had on there was a Swede—his name was Carlson—he was the first guy I saw after we were torpedoed. He said, "Boats, I think she's gonna go down pretty quick."

I stood up, and I saw these guys from the gun crew carrying this kid named Murdock. They were sort of carrying him, as I recall, by his hands and by his feet, belly up. So I got this kid and put him over my right shoulder, and carried him—he was bleeding from his face—down the catwalk, got on the boat deck and carried him to the forward end of the boat deck on the port side. The next day when I got to see my clothes, I was bloody from the butt down. I put him down and that's where the gun crew took over and carried him into the gun crew lifeboat. I learned later that the kid wasn't dead; he lived.

But what happened was that our boat—we went off the port side. I was in the boat with the chief mate. He and I were the last two to get off of that ship, of that I'm sure because I saw the boats were gone on the starboard side. I went across over there. He went up and actually brought the sextants. He brought that down, and I'll say I always thought Bill

Montgomery was one of the coolest guys I ever saw in my life: cool as a cucumber.

We had lowered the boat already—I'd say that the crew was well drilled, but it went off like clockwork. And that's when fire and boat drills pay off at sea, really pay off. I used to take 'em seriously. I think—all the thing went off without a flaw, without a flaw. I know I helped a guy in the gun crew's boat. I'd gotten down on the main deck, and I was watching both ends on the thing, the boat that Murdock was in. And lo and behold our third mate winds up in that goddamned boat and he belonged in command of one astern of us. But the son of a bitch ended up in the other one. He was a nut anyhow. But—who in the hell took the after boat on the port side I don't know. Possibly one of the ABs.

Lo and behold, we went off on the port side, and he and I went down on the monkey ropes—man rope with knots in 'em and so forth. We lowered the sextant down to, I think, the—chief steward [who] was in our boat—a long, tall, thin guy—and Bill Montgomery had a pair of binoculars around his neck, I remember that—and the two of us swung off.

But anyway we lowered ourselves down to the boat, and we pulled away. Of course the big thing that's in your mind—is that if the *John Bell* hadn't gone off with such a horrible fire—and she stayed afire, by the way—it was dark by then and she was lighting the seas up.

One of the oilers, a nice young man, actually put the main stop on the engine. He was on watch at the time, [and] he was the one who closed the steam stops down.

And as I say, having a good skipper, and having a good set of officers really paid off because that ship was well drilled. I venture to say that was one of the best abandoned ships—I don't know, it was the only one I ever had all during that time—but it went off like clockwork. But the oiler coming up out of the engine room closed the main stops, otherwise the ship would've kept headway on it.

Now the fact that the *John Bell* was on fire—the biggest problem is that in a helluva big convoy the other ships are ducking—but couldn't see *you*, you knew *that*—and you're pulling on the oars as hard as you could to get out of the way of this ship, and of course they break convoy—they break formation—and your biggest concern because they can't see you is that you're gonna get run down by a damn ship, and you come pretty close to 'em. And the guys that go by they holler to you, you know, and ask if you're all right, but there wasn't a damn thing *they* could do. They had to keep goin' because the escorts are assigned to come in and pick up survivors.

And this British trawler—I call it a trawler, whatever it was, frigate or corvette—I have a picture of that ship, called the *Southern Maid*—and they picked us up.[8] I don't know, we were in the water three or four, five hours—they picked us up during the night—so they came alongside[9] And of course they were sub-chasing and sounding all the time we were aboard, looking and so forth. There were depth charges going off all night around us.

Our ship went down not too long after we were picked up. We were circling around, and I asked one of the British officers—she went down by the stern—the whole stern got awash, and then she stopped. She just sat there.

I watched our ship actually go down. Naturally the crew all gave us their bunks on the British ship, but I couldn't sleep. So we were around. And, you know, you'd lose sight of it as they'd sweep—they'd make these big sweeps all around and everything. But the *John Bell* burned all the way into the next day, and she was giving light. She wasn't far astern of us—and other ships were burning—and you could get a glimpse of your [ship]—the silhouette against—the fire, where you were and so forth. But we actually saw her go down, sort of about a 60-degree angle. Her bow came up before it was over, and she went down vertically by that time. She sank stern first.

The hope was, you know, that maybe she'd be afloat in the morning. But I know the British skipper told us, "No, she'll never make it; the bulkheads have collapsed." And of course—they ask you right away what she had—it was ammo—so they obviously stayed away from it because you never know if fire was smoldering. All it had to do was get to #4 hold and the whole thing would've blown the Mediterranean apart! With what we had in there.

[Of] course, that goes through your mind, I want to tell you. There was no extra bravery on my part or anybody else's part, but I always in retrospect, I always said the *training*, the fact that you had good training. And I always felt so highly of Bill Montgomery—a fine gentleman, one of the finest I ever met [while] going to sea—and Captain Lawrence [J.] Silk, because they were strict men for, really, training: they went ahead right away as soon as the crew got formed. And I think they had respect for me because I went along with that and pushed the crew along with them too. But it really paid off. If I had to write the script for it I couldn't've written it better.

Anyway, I never saw Captain Silk until I got back to New York after that. I didn't see the biggest part of the crew after that because we scattered. Some of us got picked up and taken to Bizerte. Other guys went to Algiers, and other guys went to different places. In fact, the Swede—the day man—I didn't see him again until I got back to New York, and he had been the first man I saw after we got torpedoed. And I didn't see him again until I got all the way back to New York.

And I ended up in Bizerte—a goddamned Army camp over in Bizerte. And there, I've got to say, the WSA [War Shipping Administration] was miserable; they were not organized to take care of torpedoed seamen.[10] They had no makeshift—they had to go beg the Army. The Army had good facilities. The Army had it fine. But the WSA—we had to report to the WSA, and that's where I met the skipper off the *Henry Middleton*. He was screaming his ears off, blowing his stack at this WSA representative down there in Bizerte.

We lived in Bizerte on different ships, you know. Then we wound up in some tents on the Army base. We wouldn't get up for anything, and the goddamned food was horrible. It seems we were in Bizerte a hell of a long time. We came back on the *John Sergeant*.[11] They were equipped for troops, you know, and prisoners, and they brought all kinds of survivors back. But we had the MP's quarters down in #3 hold. And coming back on the *John Sergeant* was worse: beets and beans, and Spam. Till this day I won't eat Spam, and I still won't eat canned beets and I won't eat canned string beans, or dehydrated potatoes. That's all we had on that ship.

The *John Sergeant*, she came into Norfolk, Virginia. And you go through a hell of a reentry clearance. You go back to the FBI, the immigration, you go through the same bullshit and everything else, see. And each guy has got to ask his questions, he's got a set form. To me, I never had trouble acclimating to that stuff because I knew he had a certain thing; he wasn't the guy who made the rules. Somebody'd wound him up, so let him unwind on ya. What the hell's the difference? Give him the information he wanted: where you were born, where did it happen, this and the other.

And we rode the train up to New York. I know I got put up in a hotel on Central Park South for a day or two. Yeah, the treatment ran from cruel to—majestic! [We] got a $100 [survivor's allowance] for our clothes, for your [lost] belongings. I was probably one of the few guys that ever lost more than that. I don't know why, but I had three suits of clothes I went to sea with that trip. I always had clothes. But I'll never forget, I had this very fine suit. Now what the hell I took it for, I don't know. It was stupid even to take it to sea with me—I damn sure wasn't going anywhere I needed it. But, you know, you used it in port before you sailed, and so forth. I had three suits and I [had] wrapped them up in a sheet of canvas [for protection].

*After surviving the torpedoing and loss of the Liberty ship SS* Richard Henderson *in the Mediterranean in 1943, Paul Jarvis upgraded in Baltimore to third mate and continued to ship out as licensed deck officer on various merchant ships until, In March 1945 he shipped out as chief mate in the Liberty ship* Augustine Heard. *He would spend the rest of the war on that ship, including support of the campaign to invade and take Okinawa from the Japanese.*[12]

Until I die I'll swear [ours] was the first ship that ever touched Okinawa. The Liberty ship went in there first, with all the troops. They *beached* these Liberty ships: took 'em up on the tide—took 'em up on the mid-tide—and then we were supposed to back out on high tide. We had dropped our anchor. There's a maneuver you do: you swing starboard, drop an anchor, then swing port, go out and get another anchor, and then go forward on your anchors. So you can use the anchors [later] to pull you astern on the thing. Except that didn't work with some of them [that] got the hell shot out of them.

But actually what happened in Okinawa was the invasion of Naha there. It backfired a lot. A lot of guys were lost in that whole area there. It looked too damn hot to me, you know, after we got in there. The Liberty ships came under tremendous fire; many of them were shot to pieces and never got off the damn beach, and blew up by mines and everything else.[13]

And that was the damnedest thing, bodies floatin' all over the place.

The only thing I consider of any danger while I was in there—of course, the ship sinking was a danger which I didn't have to face. The ammo didn't go off. But I didn't think I was gonna come out of Okinawa. I never thought I'd come out of Okinawa. Okinawa was absolute hell.

I think I worked awfully hard [and] I think that was good for me. Nobody could sleep during those six days, because everything came in. Later on when the Kamikazes started and things like that, you saw the kamikazes hit the *Pennsylvania*. I saw a kamikaze fly right over us and hit the stern of the *Pennsylvania*.[14] You're damn right, I saw it. We were anchored, oh, maybe three-quarters of a mile from her at the time. It happened at Buckner Bay in Okinawa.

Your biggest thought was that one of these things [would] explode

Wartime photograph of the Liberty ship *Augustine Heard*, fully armed, date unknown (Mariners' Museum, Newport News, Virginia).

and wipe out the harbor, which you knew could happen. But you don't think about it, and after a while you can sleep.

Oh, yes, I saw the kamikazes. And until you witness it you really don't realize that it's a human being sitting behind the thing, highly trained— I don't know what they did to him—but up 'til the last fraction of a second he had the option of pulling out—and some did, by the way. Some did not go through with it. I saw some hit the water, miss the ship that they were aiming at—sail straight into the water—and seen others shot right down. Buckner Bay was a helluva place. The Japanese came in, [the] Japanese were tough.[15]

There was absolutely the most boring goddamned thing a person could be put through [after] all that action, and then it totally—subsides. Then you started worrying about the typhoon. The October 9th typhoon came up, crossed Okinawa. And that was all hell. If I *ever* thought I was gonna die, that's the only time that it ever really crossed my mind.[16]

*Paul Jarvis continued to ship out into the early postwar period, ultimately earning his master's license. Though "blacklisted" for his political beliefs and affiliations in the early 1950s and unable to obtain the required Coast Guard clearance documentation to follow his chosen career at sea, Jarvis continued to renew his master's license for many years. But the opportunity to use it again never came. He founded the Turner Trade School in New York, and served as its president. Also active with the Marine Workers Historical Association (MWHA), Jarvis passed away in New York in 2002.*

CHAPTER 8

# Eric H. Johanson: "We were scared to death"

*Eric H. Johanson was born in New York, New York, in 1910 and raised in Valley Stream on Long Island.[1] He first went to sea in 1931 as a wiper in the Cherokee, a coastal passenger ship out of New York. As he explained it, "it was the depression, I didn't have a job, so I went out to get a job." During a labor strike he hopped boxcars to the West Coast, then continued to ship out in unlicensed ratings with American Export Line. By the time of the attack on Pearl Harbor he had upgraded and had shipped out as first assistant engineer in the SS* West Notus, *McCormick Steamship Company, then in Buenos Aires, Argentina.[2] He shipped out again for a second voyage on that ship, and was en route from Argentina to New York with a load of flax seed when the ship encountered a German submarine running on the surface.*

I was on watch in the engine room. They sounded the alarm and then I could hear we were being shelled. I noticed that when the bullets went through the metal it was so hot that the paint caught on fire.[3]

The captain got killed on the bridge—he was the first man killed—and the chief mate took over. We stopped the engine and abandoned ship.[4] I ran to my room and got my ring and my wristwatch and cut the lights out.

I could see the submarine laying off the stern quarter, starboard side. Somehow they lowered the lifeboat and I got in. We were scared to death because we had read several accounts where the submarine would come up and machine-gun the men in the lifeboats. We saw the submarine coming after us, and we thought "this is it," you know.

But they didn't machine-gun us. They come up, and their captain talked good English. He talked to the mate and he talked to all of us in

The SS *West Notus*, outbound, on 27 February 1942, three months before her encounter with the German submarine *U-404* in the Caribbean (courtesy the Steamship Historical Society of America, Inc.).

general. He gave us directions to Cape Hatteras, and we asked him how things were going and did he think this thing would last.[5]

He said, "I've had enough. I wish this thing was over now."

They gave us some additional water and some pea soup. We headed for Cape Hatteras, and a couple of days later we were picked up by a Swiss ship that brought us into Hamilton Avenue, Brooklyn.[6]

That was it.

*After returning to New York, Johanson took time off to upgrade to chief engineer. He went aboard a ship in Mobile, Alabama, soon after, again as first assistant engineer, for that ship's initial trial run after construction.*

I'll never forget the first ship I took out of Mobile on the trial run and going down the Mobile River and seeing sea buoys. It made me sick: it looked like submarines. I don't know why, I just had that feeling. Then I went down in the engine room, and I wouldn't look out anymore. I was better off there. And I wouldn't go on deck any more. But of course that wore off after a while.

A lot of times we'd go through areas with fuel [oil] on the surface—miles and miles at a time—where a ship had sunk. And you don't know if you're next or not.

*After upgrading to chief engineer, Johanson continued to ship out in that capacity for the duration of the war. During that time he served in the Liberty ships* James Longstreet *and* James R. Randall. *Though retiring from active seafaring in 1962, he renewed his Chief Engineer's license in the 1980s. A chief surveyor for several years with International Cargo Gear Bureau, he passed away in Old Tappan, New Jersey, at 90, in 2000.*

## CHAPTER 9

# Ruel N. Lawrence: "The ship pulled me down ... and I thought that was it"

*Ruel Nathan Lawrence was born in Mobile, Alabama, in 1924 and, as his brothers George and Harold had before him, decided to join the Merchant Marine. He did so at the age of 16 in 1940, shipping out of Mobile initially as crew messman in the SS* Alcoa Cutter.[1]

### Not a Good Time (to Be a Whale)

I'd say she was about 6,000 tons, a freighter with hatches, and we carried bauxite in the hatches. It was a flush-deck, in a way, but you had your ladders going up to your midship house and everything, you know. I was a crew messman, and I had about three other, four other guys in the room with me.

Well, we were in Port o' Spain, Trinidad, on the bauxite run, and were at the dock there and, as you know, the British were already at war. When we were there they'd bring wounded in from sea. And we'd see all that. We got acquainted with a lot of British sailors and merchant seamen.

And while we was in Port o' Spain the Japanese attacked Pearl Harbor, December the seventh. It was on the radio. And as soon as we got word of the attack we immediately started painting the ship gray—everything was gray. And we had to start fixing things for blacking out—fixing curtains so at night the light wouldn't shine out, 'cause we knew we were at war and we had to take precautions.

We hit other ports too. We went to Dutch Guiana—we went up

there—and we hit the Triangle, all different islands around through there, also British Guiana and Port o' Spain, Trinidad. And we hit the Virgin Islands, around through there, picking up bauxite and things like that. If I'm not mistaken I think we went back to Mobile. We had a regular run out of Mobile; it was strictly an Alcoa port.[2] We brought the bauxite back to Mobile, and then I got off. I stayed home about a month, and then I got aboard the *Arizpa*, a Waterman ship.[3]

And we went down to Tocopilla, Chile, to pick up nitrates, or whatever it is we loaded down there.[4] But on the way down there they spotted a whale and they thought it was a submarine. We had general quarters, you know, went to general quarters, and they fired the 4"/.50 at it. The first shot—they hit the whale. They found it was a whale and—the first shot, you know, it was remarkable that they did it.[5]

I caught the SS *Pan Atlantic* in Mobile in April of 1942. We loaded—we knew we was going to Murmansk, Russia. They told us.[6]

*After first shipping out in SS* Alcoa Cutter *in 1940 in Mobile, Alabama, and then on the SS* Arizpa—*in both cases to the Caribbean—Ruel Lawrence shipped out again, in April 1942, as ordinary seaman in the SS* Pan Atlantic, *again from Mobile, but this time for the North Russia run. The ship loaded in Mobile, Philadelphia and New York before joining one of the east-bound HX-designated convoys in Halifax, Nova Scotia. Lawrence picks up the story here after the Atlantic crossing and final departure in Convoy PQ-17 from Iceland for North Russia.*

## "The ship pulled me down ... and I thought that was it"

The next thing I knew, all hell breaks loose. There were dive bombers coming down—torpedo planes coming in—and, naturally, everybody opens up. And we were hittin' each other: firin' low at the torpedo planes we were hittin' our own ships, killing our own men.

And that's when ships started blowin' up: tankers were blowing up, and freighters were being sunk.[7] We had a submarine come up right in the middle of our convoy, and everybody was firing at him. Everything was a mess; all you could see was smoke, smoke, smoke.

On the bridge of the ship we had two 30-calibers—one to starboard and one to port—and we had a 4"/.50 on the stern. That's all the guns we had. The .30 calibers—they were firin' like mad.

SS *Pan Atlantic*, 18 November 1941, showing typical United States (then noncombatant) identification of pre–Pearl Harbor period (Mariners' Museum, Newport News, Virginia).

I remember the Navy armed guard crew, they was doin' the firin' and pointing. I was loading on the 4"/.50. We was at the gun, loaded, but we couldn't fire at the planes. The Armed Guard officer told us to hold fire. But when the submarine come up, then we opened fire on the submarine.

We were just kids—excited and everything—and didn't do too good. We were hitting abaft of the submarine. Other ships was firing at it too. Now he wasn't completely surfaced, he was just up breaking the surface a little bit. And I presume he sank some ships because they were still going up all around us.

Then we got word—by flag hoist—to split up the convoy: disperse. Every man was on his own. The reason why was because the commodore had gotten word that the German pocket battleship *Von Tirpitz* and a couple of other German ships was looking for the convoy, was gettin' close. They could've wiped us out—one by one—by sittin' off 20 miles.[8]

So we got the word to disperse and proceed to destination the best you can. So we did. The captain told everybody what we was doin' and where we was goin', and we dispersed.[9]

We was gone—I would say about two days when we spotted this

reconnaissance plane.¹⁰ We were all by ourself, nobody was around us. We knew we were gonna get sunk. So we seen this reconnaissance plane. He flew around us, and then he took off. Then we knew we was in for it then.

The next thing we knew, we spotted this dive-bomber; he was comin' out of the sun. We fired the 4"/.50 and everything at him; everything we had, we fired at him. We even took the 37-millimeters from the tanks and stripped them, and was firin' them. But the plane hit us; I think it was in #2 hatch. He hit us in #2 hatch and the ship just shuddered, just lifted us out of the water. It knocked everybody down, and then we started running to the lifeboats.¹¹

As I was runnin' towards #2 lifeboat, I seen the gunnery officer with a .45-caliber machine gun in his hand. He jumped down from the bridge to the main deck, and that's the last I seen of him. He may've killed himself, I don't know. But we were talking about it later on, when we were in Archangel, Russia, and a couple of the guys said he broke his legs, which I don't know. Anyway, we all headed for #2 lifeboat.

The ship was on fire. I seen one of my shipmates—his name was Marshall Emanuel—he was from Mobile, Alabama. And he was burning: his lifejacket was on fire. The last I seen of him he was running forward.¹²

We ran to #2 lifeboat. They more or less threw me into it, and I got in there and—we got the [drain] plug in and everything. And they started lowerin' us down. In the meantime the ship was sinkin' and the next thing I knew—wham! Boy, the front end goes down and we were all dumped in the water. I went down—I'd say—it must've been a hundred feet. It was like I never would come up. The suction of the ship pulled me down. I opened my mouth, and I thought that was it, but I come up.

I had a cork life preserver on, but I just kept going down, down, down, down, but the next thing I knew I started comin' up. All I could see was water, water, water, but I finally popped to the surface. And the first thing I noticed after I got up was men in the water. They had a life raft, a wooden life raft with, like, drums in it. Evidently when the ship went down the life raft come loose; they were designed to do that. You could either do it manually—like [with] a pelican hook [for] releasing 'em—or they would release itself.

But anyway, the life raft was there, and we had a bunch of men in the water. And I got to the life raft and looked around. As soon as the other men got to the life raft I jumped up and tried to pull them—the older men–up onto the life raft. I think I pulled about five aboard. And we was on the life raft I think for a few hours when we spotted the lifeboat. And the lifeboat comes over and took us off the life raft. And we get in the lifeboat and the captain is in there. We got all the rations from the life raft and put them in the lifeboat.

And we was in the lifeboat—I'd say about nine days. While we was in the lifeboat a German submarine surfaced. That's why I thought we might've got torpedoed too. I remember there was two explosions. I definitely remember that: the first from the dive bomber—and that's when we all started running for the lifeboats—and then after that we got hit again. So, I have never heard of a dive bomber dropping a bomb and then comin' back that quick and dropping another one. Between you and I, I think it was [from] a submarine. I really do, because it was—when the torpedo plane hit us—the length of time—it was maybe like 15 or 20 seconds before we got hit again. And I believe that was the submarine, because it surfaced shortly after we got into the lifeboat.[13] Anybody that got injured in that ship, they was dead. The ones that was alive was the ones that was on the stern, and the ones that—some of 'em was on the bridge, you know, and in the engine room got away.[14]

And the submarine commander, he give us what the closest distance was to land, and he offered us water, and bread, and baloney, and then we was on our way. He asked where the captain was, and we had the captain underneath the canvas on the floorboard. We told him he was still on the ship.

And the submarine commander said, "Sorry we had to sink your ship, but that's war." And he said the closest land was—I think it was Spitzbergen or something like that, in that direction. He told us, and he gave us baloney and bread and stuff. He was a gentleman. A lot of the stories you hear about machine gunning and stuff, it's—I don't believe that, because they treated us all right.

[I had on] plain shoes, a little jacket, pants, and a shirt. And the water was—cold. It was very cold, even in July 'cause we was way up north there. And we was told to be on the lookout for icebergs and things, you know, after we dispersed from the convoy.

But we was in the lifeboat about nine days.[15] We got picked up by His Majesty's ship *Lotus*—it was a corvette—and when I went aboard the corvette I was a shell passer for the pom-pom. And after we got aboard the corvette, they sunk the lifeboat; they didn't want it floating. And about an hour or two hours after that a German dive-bomber come and attacked the corvette. We fired, and we got away from it. And I was a loader on the pom-pom.[16]

But after we got picked up by the *Lotus* and they took us into Murmansk, Russia, we didn't even go ashore there, just long enough to make the transfer. Everything was so fast. I mean, they had been bombed and everything. And then they transferred us to a British destroyer; the name of the destroyer I don't know. And they took us down to Archangel, Russia.

Well, anyway, they brought us to Archangel and they put us ashore in the Intourist Hotel. If I had to do it all over again, I wouldn't want to go to Russia 'cause they put us all in the Intourist Hotel, and they had two or three of us in one room, and we had straw mattresses. And the girls would come in to clean the rooms up in the morning; they would use a rag to swab the deck. And they used—it looked like straw on the end of a stick for sweepin'. That's the way they lived out there: it was very, very backwards. And they didn't treat the Americans very good at all. The food we had—the water had to be boiled. They'd give us hot tea—no cream, a little sugar; it was brown sugar. And they give us what's called "croquets." It was horse meat. Like I said, they didn't care for Americans. They liked the British pretty well, but they never cared for Americans.[17]

And while I was in the Intourist Hotel I had trouble with my feet, so they sent me to the hospital, and they worked on my feet for me. They massaged them, and they took electric needles, you know, to get the blood circulation going back again. So it took me about a week before my feet were better. Some of the guys had to have their feet cut off—it was that bad: they had gangrene.

Now, while we was in Archangel we weren't working with anybody, we was just waitin' to get out of there. And the naval attaché in Archangel was Commander [S.B.] Frankel. And the Armed Guard went to him, the Navy boys. While we was there in Archangel we'd go over to help—fool around the headquarters, painting and things like that. You know, helping him out a little bit.

And we had a lot of air raids while we was there—the German dive bombers would come down, you know—and we helped the Russians fight the fires. And the British, you know. We had to go up on top of the roofs and fight the fires, tear the shingles up, and do everything like that.

We'd be at the Intourist Hotel and hear the sirens, and a lot of times we hit the deck right there: lay down and cover our heads, you know. We'd stay right there, and they'd be bombing all around us. After the bombing was over we'd run out and fight the fires, you know, for the Russian population. We had some hoses, and they had fire extinguishers—water squirted out. And we had axes and things like that. The British were very good about fightin' them fires because they had a lot more experience than we had. But we helped them.

And another incident while I was in Archangel was—there was a trolley, you know, a streetcar. And it was packed: people were jumpin' on. And we was in town that day and we happened to notice this trolley. And this little girl—about 12 years old—she went to jump on the trolley, and she missed. She got underneath the trolley and it cut her leg off, her right leg. And we—the Americans—went over and pulled her out. And one of the guys took his jacket off and put it over her leg. And the Russians didn't even attempt to help her or nothing. We took and covered her up, you know, and everything, and tried to talk to her. And we kept waiting, and waiting, and waiting, and they finally brought a stretcher, and we was carrying the stretcher to the hospital, where we thought it was, you know. And while we was doin' it the Russians grabbed the stretcher, real sarcastic like, and pushed us out of the way. And they carried her on her way. And that was the last we seen of her.

We were in Russia about six weeks. As far as the Russians go, the way they treated us, I have no use for them, none whatsoever.

We got word to go aboard the *Bellingham*, a Waterman freighter carrying iron and steel or something in the holds.[18] We got one egg for breakfast. You know, they was short on food and everything. And we left Archangel, I think it was sometime in September.

And about two days out of Archangel we got torpedoed.[19] There was one explosion, and she didn't settle right then. She was making headway there, a little bit, and she kept going. In fact, the way I understand it, they had to sink the *Bellingham*; I think a British destroyer went back and sank it. As far as I know nobody was killed on there. Even the Armed Guard officer and one of the guys that was trying to get that life raft off, I understand that they got away all right too.[20]

We got torpedoed on the starboard side—#1 lifeboat was ripped apart 'cause I seen it. I was workin' the mess hall, port side, and when the torpedo hit I was workin' as a messman. It was about six o'clock in the morning when it hit. And I took a look out on deck and #1 lifeboat was completely gone.

So we all got in #2 lifeboat and got the lifeboat away. I do remember—as we were getting in the lifeboat they were trying to get the life raft—it was all frozen up with ice and everything. And the gunnery officer had his .45 and was trying to shoot the life raft loose. I don't know whether they got the life raft loose or not. All I know is we got in the lifeboat and we got picked up by a British rescue vessel.[21]

After we got torpedoed everything was smooth—we all got in the lifeboat and we got away. And the convoy kept on going and we was way behind. And this British rescue ship come on by and picked us up. They took us into Johnstone, Scotland, and in Johnstone, Scotland, they took us—all of us survivors—and put us in a place there, and they treated us really, really good.[22] They gave us clothes—big coats—and things like that.

And we were in Johnstone for about a week. And in the meantime now, we kept our life preservers with us all the time. Then they put all of us survivors from the Russian convoy onto the *Queen Mary*. They sent us back to the United States in the *Queen Mary*. If I'm not mistaken it took us about two and a half days, and then we put into Boston. And the Red Cross come out and gave each of us 50 cents apiece.

While we were there they took movie pictures of everybody, out of the convoy and everything. They had a couple of the guys on the newsreel, you know, talkin' and explaining about the convoy and things like that. And they showed it all over the United States in the movies.

Then I come back to Mobile. I took a train and I got back to Mobile. They all thought I was dead; they thought I'd been killed, see. Anyway, I got back to Mobile and they thought I was killed on the *Pan Atlantic*. They didn't believe I was alive.

But anyway, I stayed in Mobile until November the 2nd [1942] and I joined the U.S. Navy: I wanted to fight back. That was the whole thing: I wanted to fight back.

*And fight back he did. Unlike many others who were advised in those early goings to remain in the Merchant Marine (see Chapter 5, for example), Lawrence seemed to make the transition easily and quickly. After having had some experience with guns on merchant ships as an ammo handler and loader in support of Navy armed guard crews, Lawrence became a gunners mate in the Navy, initially back—assigned to the Armed Guard—in merchant ships such as the tanker* Pat Doheny *and freighter* William Glackens. *He was later a gun captain in the rocket ship LSMR 189 at Okinawa. Lawrence served for the duration of the war and several years into the postwar period in the Navy. He later resumed service in the Merchant Marine, sailing as AB and Bosun. Working as Bosun in MV* Rover *in the South China Sea in 1981, he was involved in the rescue of Vietnamese "boat people." He retired soon after, and passed away in Mobile, Alabama, at 72 in 1997.*

## CHAPTER 10

# John M. Le Cato: "*Norluna*, you're supposed to be sunk!"

*John M. Le Cato was born in 1917 and spent his boyhood on the family farm near Baltimore, Maryland. After graduating from high school in 1936 he attended the U.S. Naval Academy in Annapolis for two years, then went to work for the Merchants and Miners Transportation Company in 1939 as a cadet in SS* Berkshire.[1] *On December 7, 1941, he was home on leave from duties as quartermaster in SS* Chatham, *a coastal passenger ship, when news of the Japanese attack on Pearl Harbor was received.*[2]

I was visiting my fiancée in Washington at an exhibit of Japanese woodcuts in one of the museums when we heard the word that Pearl Harbor had been attacked. We began hearing words—sort of rumors. Nobody seemed to know what was going on, but they beefed up the security guards very quickly around the exhibit. It seemed to me this was early in the afternoon.

My fiancée lived in suburban Maryland and I had my clothes and stuff there. So I went back to her house. It was early evening when I arrived at Union Station in Washington, and it was in a shambles: all sorts of military were trying to get back to their duty stations. The ticket clerks were reluctant to issue tickets to civilians, and I was not in uniform. But I showed them my seaman's papers and told them I had to get back to my ship in Baltimore. The *Chatham* was on Pier Two, Pratt Street, in Baltimore.

We went immediately the next morning down the bay into Newport News Shipyard [Virginia]. I don't think there was anything that approached panic: nobody said, "I'm paying off when I get to Norfolk" or anything like that. We went about our duties just about as usual.

**Second mate John Le Cato on wing of ship's bridge, Atlantic convoy duty, late in World War II (J.M. Le Cato).**

Newport News spray-painted the ship gray from the stack to the waterline in about three or four hours. It was very quickly done. Of course, as a passenger ship she had a lot of windows—in the dining saloon and elsewhere—and all of those were painted over heavily. I think that was all that was done at that time. There weren't any blackout curtains or anything of that sort installed. The ship, I can still remember, was black as anything. I made about four turns around the deck trying to find my way into the mess room after I got off the wheel at midnight. It was pretty dark.[3]

*After receiving his third mate's license from the U.S. Maritime Service Training Station, Ft. Trumball, New York, in May 1942, John Le Cato shipped as third mate in the SS* Norluna, *which joined Atlantic Convoy SC-95 for Iceland.*

## "Norluna, *you're supposed to be sunk!*"

Some days out of Halifax—maybe more than a couple of days because we were only steaming at about eight or nine knots—the Iceland portion of the convoy broke off. That was four American ships about the size of the *Norluna*, which was a Laker.[4] These four ships broke off for Iceland [and] were escorted by an old four-stack destroyer and one of the big Campbell-class Coast Guard cutters.

The first night after we broke off, which was the fifteenth of August, I believe, a submarine surfaced right in the middle of the convoy, just at sunset. We were in a square, with the escorts steaming well ahead, and the submarine evidently came up from behind and fired one or two torpedoes off. Our lookout thought he saw one, and some of them thought they saw two, which missed.

This was apparently a rather incompetent U-boat skipper, because after discharging his torpedoes he did not ballast properly but came to the surface like a trout! He lay there on the surface and actually was so close that nobody could bring a heavy gun to bear on him [because of the angle required].[5] Our 50-caliber bullets and the bullets of the other ships were just bouncing off his deck and flying over in the direction of the other ships in the column. It's a wonder we didn't kill ourselves!

We signaled the escort and sent up rockets and signaled by light, and the escort sort of implied that this was just a bunch of trigger-happy civilians, and they didn't even alter their search pattern to come back. They could've come back and dropped a few depth charges, and they might've gotten him then.

Then around midnight there was an explosion, and the last ship in the column got it and sank quite rapidly. We were the aft ship in the starboard column, and the aft ship in the port column was the *Balladier*, and she was the one that got it.[6]

We fired signal rockets with no proper device for launching them—the second mate had built some sort of a launching tube. But we were rolling a bit, and the first rocket, instead of going in the air, went in the wheelhouse door and ran around and finally exploded in the corner in a bunch of red stars.

The *Balladier* got one of its boats off and, of course, in the Arctic it's not really dark any time, so we could see the people in the water. And we rescued quite a number of the crew members. At that time I believe it was official orders, in the absence of a specially designated rescue vessel, that the last ship in column would do what they could to pick up survivors. It was also assumed by us that one of the escorts would come back and cover us anyway. They may have dropped some depth charges. I don't remember.

SS *Norluna*, outbound on 3 May 1942 (U.S. Coast Guard/Mariners' Museum, Newport News, Virginia).

Anyway, the next morning at daylight all we saw was a big pool of oil with a lot of telephone poles and other deck cargo floating in it. And the *Norluna* was on one side of this pool, and about a mile away on the other side was the submarine. And just before that we had seen what we took to be a big, black Negro in a little donut raft. We got him aboard, and got the oil off him, and found out he was the skipper of the *Balladier*.[7] He was just oil-covered.

After we sighted the submarine we went ahead at our full nine knots in the direction of—Iceland. The submarine apparently thought we had a rendezvous with the rest of the ships, and rather than waste a torpedo on us he'd do better to follow us and get the whole hog.

It started off the weather was fairly calm with just a low groundswell, but it rapidly got worse. The submarine would sometimes come up within a half mile or so, and we would drop a 3-inch shell back in his direction, and he would drop back just keeping well out of our range, but keeping us in sight.

In that part of the world there are a lot of killer whales and marine mammals of that nature that look very much like a torpedo. So every so often somebody would sight one of those and we would put the rudder over and try to take evasive action. Our steering gear consisted of a steering engine in the upper engine room and a system of rods and chains which ran back to a quadrant on the fantail. Well, this wasn't intended for this kind of maneuvering and eventually one of the chains gave way. And our rudder jammed hard over and we turned around back in the direction of the submarine! I don't know whether he thought we had sighted reinforcements over the horizon or just decided we wanted to come back and fight.

Anyway, he immediately submerged and we never saw him again. Eventually we got into Iceland without any further incidents [and] we learned the escort had reported both the *Balladier* and the *Norluna* sunk. So there was some question [and] as we came up to the guard vessel she said, "*Norluna*, you're supposed to be sunk!"

We actually made it in before the convoy. With that submarine behind us we went the most direct route. The convoy had gone way up to the north, and they didn't arrive until the following day. I never knew what happened after that, but the Navy officer—the convoy commodore—came over and was closeted with our skipper for a long time. And our skipper was told not to discuss anything that was said.

Later on in the voyage we got the idea that the command in Iceland had told this commodore to come over hat in hand and apologize for his actions. That's unusual for the Navy to send an officer over to apologize. We thought they might have summoned our skipper ashore and had everybody ashore, but I guess they thought that by going to him there'd be no notes or anything else.

We stayed there about a week, discharged our cargo, and were sent to a place in Greenland to load cryolite ore, which is an important ingredient in making aluminum. And we got about 200 tons of cryolite aboard and a message came: "Stop loading and proceed to Port Churchill in Hudson's Bay."

So, the authorities around there found us some kind of charts that had been used for one of the expeditions that was searching for Sir John Franklin, and [which] were only approximate in the location of islands and that sort of thing.[8] But anyway we made do with that and eventually found Port Churchill. And then we acted as a supply ship for the Arctic bases.[9]

We had a weird fleet up there. They had Admiral Byrd's old ship, the *Bear*,[10] and Bob Bartlett was there with the *Morrissey*. There was a Danish reefer ship that [had] supposedly defected from Denmark when the Germans came in, but nobody really knew whether he was a German plant or not. But they decided that the damage he could do, if they kept an eye on him, was worse [sic] than losing the services of the ship. Also, we had a hopper, a self-propelled hopper dredge with a door in the bottom for dumping the dredged mud out. Somebody opened the bottom once—thought he was working the bilge pump—and dropped the tractor into Hudson's Bay!

We stayed up there until the bay started icing up, and then we were supposed to make a final voyage to Fort Chimo, which is on an arm of the bay.[11] And they loaded us up with—*over*loaded us despite the captain's protest. They gave him two or three bottles of Scotch and appealed to his patriotism, and we set out with a big rock-crusher on the foredeck and all kinds of construction machinery aft.

And the first night out we got in a blow and some of this [cargo] shifted, so we had about a five or six degree list from then on. [But] we got into the Koksoac River on which Fort Chimo is located. That was one of a series of air bases being established. And the ship was discharging there—we were there for some days—and finally dragged anchor and grounded on a rocky island, and we had to abandon her.[12]

And we were taken ashore to the air base, which at that time was more a construction base than anything else. And because of the secrecy of the base nobody wanted to let us go home. And ultimately we got a—somebody from the War Shipping Administration up there on an entirely different matter put things right. He got back to Washington. I sent a letter back to Captain Merrill, who had been operating vice president of Merchants and Miners [Transportation Company] and then was on active duty with the Coast Guard.[13] I managed to get a letter back to him [and] to this War Shipping man. And a week or so later we were loaded on a transport plane and flown home.

*By that point—December 1942—Le Cato and his wife had moved to New York where he could be closer to shipping, upgrading and training opportunities. He did receive some training in such things as wartime signaling but was lacking enough sea time and was unable to upgrade to second mate. After being ashore in New York for about a month and receiving some training, Le Cato shipped out again on 13 January 1943 as third mate in the Liberty ship* Thomas Hartley *in what would become known as the "Forgotten Convoy."[14] None of them could have imagined how long a voyage to a North Russian port could be, but during the next eight months they would find out.*

## *The Forgotten Convoy*

I shipped out on the 13th of January '43. I went out on the *Thomas Hartley*, still third mate, and that was the "forgotten convoy" [in which] we were well escorted: destroyers, rescue vessel, antiaircraft cruiser.[15] She had made one trip to the West Indies and had [carried] a load of bauxite, as I remember. The captain was a Captain Callous, from Matthews County, Virginia. The [Liberty ship] was the biggest thing I'd ever seen![16]

There were some submarine alarms on the way up, as I recall, [but] none of our ships were hit. And we went on up till we got to North Cape, and then we spotted a German reconnaissance aircraft, very high in the sky. And he made a peculiar mark: sort of an "O"-shaped or "Q" maybe, with smoke in the sky, which evidently was a signal either to submarines or to someone else who was watching.[17] And from then on the Germans really started working us over. They had high-level bombing and had submarines simultaneously. And again, as I recall, we did not lose a ship.

The antiaircraft cruiser when she opened up was just a solid wall of fire from bow to stern. And of course at that time our ships were much better armed. That was one of the first convoys where the .50 calibers had been replaced by 20-millemeters. We had an antiaircraft gun—a 3"—on the bow, a 5"/50 on the stern, and eight 20-millimeters, so we could put up a pretty formidable barrage ourselves. We had about 20 ships all doing the same.[18] And I didn't see any Germans coming in. I didn't see any torpedo bombers.[19]

We made it into Murmansk, and from then on [there were] continual air attacks.[20] And we waited our turn to get into dockage; they could dock about three ships at that time. A British ship named the *Ocean Freedom*—one of those coal-burning British Libertys—was directly across the pier from us. And it [took] a bomb in number two hatch [and] broke in half at the pier, without any loss of life.[21] But the piers were continuously getting holes blown in them, and the city of Murmansk was rapidly being leveled. They had a hotel there called the Arctica that got hit and lost about a quarter of it.

And there was just one air alert after another. The Germans had an airfield right over the mountain in Finland, so they could come and go at their own pleasure almost. They'd be over the mountain and on top of the ships with the dive-bombing before you even knew they were on the way. And one incident, a German seaplane apparently mistook Murmansk for [a port in] Finland and came in and landed in the harbor, saw his mistake,

**Members of merchant crew in a serious mood, SS *Crosby Noyes*, 1945 (J. M. Le Cato).**

and tried to take off. And just about the time he took off everything in the harbor had a bead on him, and that plane just disintegrated.

But ultimately we went out to anchor with the expectation that another convoy was gonna come and take us home. But the convoy following ours had taken a shellacking either from the Germans or the weather, or a combination, so they did not—they avoided that convoy and when we came into Murmansk another convoy was coming out, and their escorts went with them.[22] But there weren't any escorts. Since there was no convoy, there were no escorts to bring us back. A British cruiser came in once, and brought some supplies, but—we just sort of sat. And the Germans would come over once a day or so and try to get the ships out at anchor.

The ice finally cleared up enough in the White Sea, and our ships were sent over to the vicinity of Molotovsk, which is the port at the mouth of the Dvina River which leads up to Archangel. This was around the first of May. Some of the ships were scattered—[in groups of] twos or threes—all around the area.

That's where we spent the summer.

We had back-loaded some cargo: a little bit of timber, and some chrome ore, and a few things of that sort. Quite a bit of chrome ore.

We did various things to amuse ourselves. It was daylight around the clock. We had a baseball league, and they had to make their own bats.

One of the ships had a lathe on it, and they picked up timbers in the White Sea and turned them into baseball bats. [They] used the gunners' hot-shell mitts for catchers' mitts. And they used to—had a mud flat alongside the pier and laid out a baseball diamond and sort of a sports field. I was never any good at baseball, but I had played soccer a bit. So I played on a soccer team [for] one of the British ships.

The Germans weren't getting over that far. I don't think we had but one alert the whole time we were in Molotovsk. The Dvina River has quite a delta with a number of channels, and Molotovsk is where one of those channels opens out into the Black [sic] Sea. The Russians at that time had a shipyard there, and commercial facilities, and a one-track railroad that ran up to the river opposite Archangel, and then a ferry across in good weather.

We began running out of food, and we had—the Russians had practically nothing themselves, but they gave us half of it. And a number of us contracted the first stages of scurvy.

I started losing hair there, which I've never regained. And people say you didn't get scurvy in the 20th century, but we damn well did.

But we were running out of food, and consequently, to conserve food, the ships were encouraged to give their people as much liberty [shore leave] as they could. So we would. The three American Liberty ships were there—the *Thomas Hartley*, the *Francis Scott Key*, the *Samuel Putnam*, and a Lykes Brothers West Coast ship similar to a Hog Islander—the *City of Omaha*—another ship called the *Bering*, and I believe there was another one.[23]

We got quite well acquainted with the Russian populace. We were treated very well by the local civilian population. We were not encouraged to do too much fraternizing, but did just the same. Also, there was a thriving black market, selling farm produce mostly, but all sorts of other things—the odd bits of jewelry, and pins and needles, and buttons and whatever. The ships set up—they had open stalls there which most anybody could move into.

So the *Thomas Hartley* set up its own little black market enterprise. And we sold cigarettes, and soap, and bits of clothing that we felt we could spare. And one of the cadets on the *Thomas Hartley* was a man from Atlanta named Harry Marshall. And he was extremely enterprising and shrewd in his business dealings with the Russians. There's a Russian word—*hetri'*—which means "foxy" or "sly" so the Russians all called him "Hetri" Harry.

And he discussed the principle that you can wash your hands three times with a bar of soap without wearing it down to the point that you can't sell it as brand new. And incidentally, he put his business training to good use and ultimately was president of a small American shipping company. He ran the stall, and we got melons, and blueberries, and cucumbers and potatoes, and cabbages—a lot of cabbages.

Well, after Molotovsk, Archangel was a big town.[24] In Molotovsk I don't think there was anything but log houses. But Archangel had a really nice bathing beach and the Dvina River got quite warm. And we used to go there and stay at the Intourist [Hotel] and go swimming every afternoon. And the hotel meals were pretty sparse but they were a lot better than what we were getting aboard ship, or at least a change. Plenty of cabbage soup, and a couple kinds of stew, oatmeal porridge and smoked salmon for breakfast.

Ah, yes [and then there was vodka], some of which wasn't vodka. We—There was a belief that if it would burn with a blue flame it was all right to drink. A couple of us bought a bottle on the street and poured it out—a half an ounce or so—in an ashtray in the Intourist and lit it, and there was a flash of fire, and a great mushroom cloud rose up to the ceiling. The ashtray shattered, and I don't know *what* that stuff was. But we didn't drink that.

There were dances. Somebody formed a theatrical group from the ship's company, and we put on a musical comedy, some of which parodied life there, and others were typical American theatrical acts. And we had picnics. The Intourist people had several young women who acted as interpreters and guides and organized picnics. And once we went on a tugboat ride way up the river. But, as far as social life was concerned, we were well taken care of.

The Russian army, it seemed to me, were a pretty mean bunch. They were on duty in the streets in Murmansk and were very suspicious of all foreigners, always. They had sort of a chip on their shoulders. But the Russian navy had some very fine people in it. They were more sophisticated, more worldly and willing to talk about ports where they had been.

We were there until the first of November. We were getting into our second winter, well into it. The problem was, with the aerial bombing, and the 24-hour daylight, that's the reason no convoys were set up because by the time they could've gotten the convoy re-formed after the one which we did not make, you were starting to get a good bit more daylight than darkness, and that run around North Cape would've just been suicide.[25]

As I recall, we had very little advance notice [of departure]—maybe a day or something of that sort. And we had a Russian navy escort [which] took us out—all except the one that was lost alongside the pier in Murmansk, the *Ocean Freedom*—and on around to Murmansk—not actually Murmansk but to the Kola River—and then we picked up the British escort.

We went back and anchored in the Clyde in Scotland. That was our first Scottish port. Maybe [we were there] four of five days, not more than that. Ships, of course, had to be fueled, and you had to kind of wait your turn for that. Had to take stores [aboard]. And some of them may have had medical problems that required treatment. And we got some food: there was an Army transport in there, and they sent us over a boatload of food.

About the only meat that we had had—besides a little Russian seal meat or something of that sort—was Spam, which we were thoroughly sick of. And on Thanksgiving the steward was in more danger than he had been all the whole voyage because he had the audacity to serve the Thanksgiving turkey with Spam stuffing! Why anybody didn't kill him, I'll never know!

They re-formed another convoy in the Clyde, and I think all of our American ships came back together, and most of them went to Baltimore. After we got off, paid off in Baltimore from the *Thomas Hartley*, I went up to New York. I went to school, raised my license, used up leave and stayed ashore till the draft board began looking at me [laughs]! Then, on the first of March in '44, I went out as Second Mate on the *George Walton*—Captain Ernest Lewis is also another Matthews County man—and we went from Baltimore to Hull, England, with a load of general war supplies. [We] had several air raids while we were in there, also saw some of them thousand-plane raids going across the Channel, which is quite a sight to see.

And we got back, went over to Bristol Channel, took some ballast, and went back to Boston. And [from there we] went to New York and loaded ammunition and general cargo for the Normandy invasion.

*After returning from his experience with the "forgotten convoy" to Russia, John Le Cato shipped out again in early 1944, as second mate in the Liberty ship* George Walton, *in support of the Normandy Invasion of June 1944.*

## *Normandy: D-Day Plus Ten*

We went over to the Clyde,[26] and then up to Oban, Scotland. We waited a week or so there while they were—getting started. We were not involved directly, but we went in finally to Utah Beach maybe 10 or 12 days after the initial landings.[27]

Well, everything by then was swept channel, the sky was full of barrage balloons, there were landing craft of all sorts. We unloaded into DUKWs mostly, but there were all sorts of LSTs and things of that sort.[28] A number of ships were sunk on the beach to make breakwaters.[29] They had those artificial off-loading piers—"mulberries," I think they [were] called.[30] Anyway, we unloaded there without any serious incidents.

The fighting was still close enough that you could hear gunfire, and see flashes of gunfire at night, but we bummed rides ashore in the DUKWs and wandered around the countryside picking up souvenirs and observing the situation. But we didn't see any casualties. I'd say that while we were there perhaps four or five bodies [of] American GIs floated by and were retrieved.

That was of course really an agricultural area, so there wasn't too much—a good bit, yes, of craters alongside the roads, and farm buildings had been demolished. But farmers were already back at work.

We came back to Boston. And I again got off, and raised my license. And on the 21st of November I signed on the *Crosby Noyes* in New York, as chief mate.

## "Burn lights at full brilliance"

On the twenty-first of November 1944 I signed on the *Crosby Noyes* in New York as chief mate. And we went to Scotland, Molotovsk, and back to the Clyde and New York. That was the convoy that took such a shellacking [but] we'd got separated from it, which was fortunate, so we were not hurt.

The surrender [in Europe] had taken place before, just as we were leaving New York. I think the last day or so, and nobody was sure whether all the Germans had gotten the word or not, or if they got the word whether they had chosen to observe it. [We had] visions of some U-boat skipper saying, "Heil, Hitler, fire everything!"

Anyway, it was the last night out from the Irish Sea, last night before we approached the Irish Sea, that we got the word to "burn navigation lights." They sent a signal from the code book: "Burn navigation lights at full brilliance." So everybody turned on everything we had, and it was terrifying: the whole ocean was lit up! You'd look like you were going to run into the stern of the ship ahead of you, and the one behind you was about to run over you, and ships crowding in on all sides. Nobody really seemed to know how to handle himself.

[Before this] generally everybody carried a small blue light, but it was so dim as to be practically invisible if there was bad visibility, and they towed a fog buoy in areas of low visibility. You kept always changing your speed. You'd call the engine room: "Up two revolutions, down one, up three" [and] the engineer did nothing but work the throttle, and the mates [did] nothing but work the phone.

I don't know that the [the order for lights] bothered anybody but the skipper and the mate on watch. Everybody else was extremely jubilant.

## Poison Gas

I went back as chief mate on the *George Walton*, and we made two trips: one to Rotterdam with a load of coal, and another one to Cardiff [Wales] with general supplies. And we came back from there to Charleston with a load of German poison gas. The people wanted to make a chemical analysis of this and account for it. And we got to Charleston and nobody wanted—we couldn't find a pier that would take 'em, and the longshoreman wouldn't handle it. And we were at anchor there for about a month.

And they finally unloaded it up at the Charleston Army base. But it took forever to load the stuff in Cardiff because they'd have about six layers of bombs in one of the holds, and then one in the bottom would start to leak and they'd have to unload and find that one. And unloading her was quite a bit of trouble.

We had an Army chemical warfare officer with us, and after about six weeks in Cardiff and an equal amount of time in Charleston, they loaded it on rail cars at the Charleston Army depot and took it to St. Louis, where they unloaded it, studied it, and then they loaded it on another train, took it down to Biloxi and put it on an LST, and took it out to a deep spot in the Gulf and shoved it overboard.

They could just as easily [have] shoved the stuff off somewhere in the middle of the Atlantic in the beginning.

## V-J Day

I was on leave. And in fact I was on leave and I had bought a sailboat. And my wife [Maureen] and I were sailing in Delaware Bay and we put into a little town called Smyrna, Delaware. And that's where we got the news about what was going on. It sure did [feel good] because the next thing, I suppose, I would have been back on my way to Japan on something when my leave was up.

At that time Merchants and Miners [Transportation Company] was cutting down their operation very sharply. I spent some time relaxing at the beach, and then went up to New York and got my master's license.

*Le Cato continued his service in the Merchant Marine for many years after World War II, including during Korea and Vietnam. Shortly before his retirement, as master of USNS* Victoria, *he went aboard a U.S. Navy submarine tender in Scotland for lunch one day, where the subject of his service in the Atlantic during the war entered the conversation.*

For the last years before I retired, I worked very closely with the Navy—the Polaris submarines—and I developed a healthy respect for most of the naval officers. One of the things I particularly remember [was] having lunch aboard a submarine tender in Scotland [where] there were a couple of submarine captains, captain of the tender, and the commodore of the submarine squadron.

And we were having lunch, and one of the naval officers was wearing some sort of an unusual [service] ribbon. They were all decorated, you know, about four rows of ribbons, and I had a puny little row across my pocket. But anyway, somebody asked what this was, and the man told him. And the conversation of campaign ribbons, and whatnot, was going around.

And the commodore leaned over and tapped me on the chest, and said, "I envy Captain Le Cato. With these two decorations—the Merchant Marine, Combat [Bar] and the Merchant Marine, Atlantic [Bar]—he can hold his own with any of us with these."

I [also] had a Vietnam ribbon, American Defense, and should have had the Korean, but for some reason I never got it.

*After retiring from a long seafaring career in 1980, including command of ships providing logistical support for the wars in Korea and Vietnam, Le Cato moved to Charleston, South Carolina, where, for many years, he was editor of* The Best Friend, *Charleston chapter newsletter of the National Railway Historical Society. He passed away in Charleston, at 87, in 2004.*

CHAPTER 11

# Edward A. MacMichael: One Step Ahead of the Japs

*Edward A. MacMichael was born in Philadelphia in 1914 and attended high school in Lansdowne, Pennsylvania. A self-described "rope choker," he first went to sea in 1933 and served in deck ratings with United States Lines. He then entered the Pennsylvania Nautical School (Pennsylvania School Ship) in 1934.*[1] *Soon after graduation in 1936, he returned to U.S. Lines and shipped out as cadet officer in SS* President Harding *and extra junior third officer in SS* Washington. *Prior to the entry of the United States in World War II he had also worked as chief mate and obtained his master's license. Mac-Michael shipped out as chief mate in the MS* Sea Witch *in October 1941 for a voyage to the Philippines, Shanghai and Hong Kong.*[2]

I was chief mate when we took off—departed from New York—October of '41 and were bound for Manila, Shanghai, Hong Kong, and back to Manila. We never got any farther than Manila: we were diverted into Manila. This would have been in November. We got in and sat there and sat there and sat there.

We were fully loaded. Matter of fact, we had the—I guess you could call it Lend Lease cargo, for the Canadian troops that were in Hong Kong.[3] Come the day the Japs bombed Pearl Harbor we were very much upset around Manila because they were also bombing Manila. And I think between then and the 24th of December when we finally got out of there we made something like 48 trips from the dock out into the harbor and back to the dock again.

My own feeling was that it was going to happen, but we didn't know when. My first indication was—this was on a C-2 the master's cabin was here, and right abaft of it was the chief mate's room—and about 4 o'clock in the morning I heard this pounding on the Old Man's door, and I charged out of my bunk, and here was a Navy lieutenant with whites on top and blacks on bottom. And he said, "The Japs have attacked Pearl Harbor" and we were to get away from the dock immediately.[4] Being a diesel, we cleared the dock in under a half-hour, from a cold start, getting everybody up.

In the meantime, all this military cargo we had for the Canadians, it was commandeered by the quartermaster, U.S. Army, and it all had to be discharged. So we finally got out of there and we were having a little trouble with fuel oil—we were low of fuel oil—and we dropped into Balipap [for] fuel oil.[5] And we were picked up at Balipap and, with the marshall's yacht—which was allegedly carrying the Philippine treasury—and a couple of destroyers, and went down to Surabaya.

Well, we started painting things gray: we just happened to have a little gray paint. The chief engineer put some drums of diesel—half-drums of diesel—on deck. And whenever we thought we were about to be plastered we would light off a diesel and we would make smoke so they would think we were on fire and leave us alone. In addition to which, he could throw a 10-degree list in the ship in a couple of minutes by shifting the fuel oil. We did that several times.

We made preparations for blacking out. This was no big thing, just a case of painting the portholes black. And when we were underway the ordinary seaman was constantly roaming around to make sure nobody was—I didn't mind them opening [portholes] of course but I didn't want anybody opening them and turning the lights on.

We left Manila on Christmas Eve of '41. And as I say, we proceeded down to Balipap and from there to Surabaya, and from Surabaya down to Fremantle around to Melbourne [Australia]. And we loaded boxed aircraft on the ship. A bright and shining lieutenant came down and wanted to know what the cubic capacity of the ship was. So I told him four hundred and some odd thousand. So he worked out his little slipstick, and he said, "Well, you could get 92 aircraft on there."

Well, my common sense told me that the [aircraft carrier] *Lexington* and *Saratoga* only carried about 80, and they were a hell of a sight bigger than we were. So I asked him how he arrived at that figure. He said, "Very simply." He said so much cubic, and a cube is a whatchyoucallit, and just divide into it."

So I said, "It's not quite that simple. What's the dimension of those cases?"

Ed MacMichael as third mate in SS *Washington*, circa 1937 (courtesy Capt. John L. MacMichael, Sr.).

So he told me, and I did a little doodling, and I came up with 27. And that's what we took out, much to his chagrin.⁶

We backed and filled, and went from Melbourne out to Fremantle. And they took all the planes off today, and they put 'em back tomorrow, they took 'em off the next day, they put 'em back on tomorrow, and the next day we sailed, allegedly for Colombo, Ceylon. We were with the convoy including the aircraft carrier *Langley*—this was the old *Langley*. And she peeled off around midnight, and the next morning, why, we were told to peel off and go to Tjilatjap, Java [Netherlands—Dutch East Indies].⁷

This is February, now. We didn't have a chart, but we looked it up in the sailing instructions—no, we didn't, we had a *Rand-McNally Atlas*—that was it. And we found Tjilatjap and what the *Rand-McNally Atlas* didn't mention was the fact that it was 10 miles up a river. So we floundered along and the next thing you know, why, we heard the *Langley* had been under attack and sunk, and Tokyo Rose advised us that we were next.⁸ This was a very nice way to have your watch, when you get the news like that.⁹

So be it, they didn't find us or something. But we proceeded up. We could see the haze of land, we sort of snuck up on it, but we didn't see anything that looked like a town. And the Old Man said, "What do we do?"

I said, "Let's toss a coin: heads, we go left, and tails, we go right." So we went left for an hour, and nothing happened. We went right, and we were back where we started and continued on the right, and at about that time we were picked up by one of our old four-pipe destroyers and he led us in there. And we arrived in there at, oh, tied up at the buoy at about eight or nine o'clock in the morning.¹⁰ And the *Marblehead* and a couple of destroyers were there.¹¹ A friend of mine was on one of the destroyers and he come over to bum some ⅝ wire because they had the old tiller wires and he needed a replacement. And he said, "You better get the hell out of here as fast as you can."

So I wandered up and told the Old Man, and he said, "You better go and talk to whoever's in charge of this thing." The Old Man was not Navy, but he realized somebody [there] was in charge. So I went over to *Marblehead* and talked with the executive officer, and he said they were getting underway as soon as possible. And his strong recommendation was to get out as soon as it was possible.

I went back and told the Old Man. And in the meantime, a Dutchman had arrived and he says that they would discharge tomorrow, tomorrow being Sunday. The Old Man looked at me, he says, "Lift five cases with slip hooks, and if there isn't a barge underneath by 11 o'clock discharge them over the side."

And the Dutchman rather vehement said, "You can't do this" and so forth.

And the Old Man says, "You have your orders." So I made preparations for dumping the cargo over the side.

In the meantime, I had these things swung out over the side. And about 10 minutes to 11 there was a frantic scurrying and the barges come out. Well, we got rid of all cargo maybe by about 10 o'clock at night.

In the meantime, total blackout, and the Old Man said, "Well as soon as you're secure for sea we'll get underway."

I said, "Captain, are we gonna be able to get a pilot?"

He says, "Well, you got us in here, you better get us out of here, young man."

So I said, "Well, we need a boat to get our chain loose from the buoy."

He says, "Back it out and drive the pin out of the connecting link, and we'll take off." Which is exactly what we did [and] we sacrificed 15 fathoms of the chain, which is what it amounted to.

So we brought it out and started south, and in the meantime we picked up the USS *Isabel*, which was the flag ship of the China fleet back up in Shanghai. It was an old gunboat, which on a windy day in a swamp or creek would be making heavy weather. So you can imagine the problem it had in the south.[12] It had left before, and we overtook it, and he signaled that he would escort us. And it could only make about 10 knots, so it went straight ahead, and we zigzagged back and forth.

About the second morning out—I'd been up on the bridge all night—and the Old Man come up and relieved me. And I said, "Well, I think I'll go down and take a quick shave and wash my face." So he said, "Go ahead." And I was all lathered up and I remember shaving one side of my face when the third mate come in and he said, "You can finish that shave in Tokyo: there's a Jap cruiser comin' over the horizon."

So I dashed up to the bridge and put a pair of binoculars on, and I couldn't see the "pagoda" mast. We notified the *Isabel* by blinker light that there was an unidentified ship bearing such and such. And he said, "Proceed on such and such a course. I will go and challenge."

So here was this little thing about twice the size of our lifeboats here with a 3"/25 main battery. But by god he went over there. It turned out it was the *Phoenix*. This was a ship that was part of our escort when we initially left Fremantle, and he had delivered the rest of the troops up to Ceylon and was on his way home.[13] We made contact only by visual light. He suggested that we proceed on present course at maximum possible speed, which we were very happy to do. We were headed to Fremantle again.

And we got there with the *Isabel*, and we had a party to end all parties.

## "I'm sure you wouldn't want me to shirk it"

*In a letter to his family dated 21 March 1942, sent presumably from Fremantle, Australia, MacMichael recounted some of his time in* Sea Witch *in the Pacific, as follows*[14]

> For the last month we have been in Penang Bay [Malaysia]. Then the Jap parachute troops landed. [We] just skimmed out of there down to Surabaya with a load of aviation gas. We left Surabaya on "Black Friday" when the Jap battleships cleaned up our Allied cruisers and destroyers. What a sad mess that was. We managed by 'reef-hopping' to get around to the south coast of Java to pick up some evacuees.
> 
> We left the Japs 40 miles away and coming strong. About 20 miles offshore our convoy of eight ships, no naval escort, ran into a submarine trap supported by Jap destroyers. Of the eight ships we are the only one left to tell the tale. We took advantage of a heavy rain squall to get away. All this happened about dusk. The next day we were bombed on eight different occasions but suffered no casualties, although we had lost half of our rudder and had several small shrapnel holes put in us from a nearby mine. We were certainly glad to see darkness.
> 
> Next morning we were overhauled by a cruiser and I figured on a fishhead and rice diet for the duration, but it turned out to be one of our cruisers and took us into protection and brought us down into Freemantle. Needless to say we were glad to see Australia once again.
> 
> We are just about fixed up again and ready to put to sea.
> 
> Funny thing, though, after it is all over you forget about the tough parts and only seem to remember the little incidents that seemed tragic at the time, but humorous, as all goes on. Don't worry about me; I'll be all right. After all, this is my job, and I'm sure you wouldn't want me to shirk it.

*MacMichael had presumably been sworn into the U.S. Navy Reserve by this time and was called to active duty following this initial voyage in MS* Sea Witch.[15] *The ship was acquired under charter from the War Shipping Administration by Southwest Pacific Area Command and converted to an army troop transport in Australia. MacMichael remained as chief mate as the Ship was involved with movement of troops between Port Moresby, New Guinea,*

*Darwin, and Thursday Island, Australia. He eventually assumed command of* Sea Witch *for a period of time before serving for the duration of the war as executive officer in amphibious attack transports USS* La Salle *[AP-102] and USS* Edgecomb *[APA-164]—eventually taking command of Edgecomb—in support of landings at Tarawa and Okinawa.*[16] *Following the war, MacMichael worked for 18 years in maritime-related agencies in Washington, D.C., and California before resuming active service in the Merchant Marine. This included command of SS* Lane Victory, *with ammunition, to Vietnam from 1966 to 1968. He also served as Relief Master of the nation's only nuclear-powered merchant cargo ship, the NS* Savannah. *In 1978 he became Executive Director of the National Liberty Ship Memorial in San Francisco, and later served as Master of the operational Liberty Ship* Jeremiah O'Brien. *He passed away in 1982, and his ashes were scattered on San Francisco Bay.*

CHAPTER 12

# Edward C. March: Torpedoes and Molasses Don't Mix

*Edward C. March was born in Philadelphia in 1920. From an early age, he "always wanted to go to sea, never wanted to do anything else."[1] His first opportunity came in 1937 when he shipped out as a wiper in the Laker-type freighter* Nantucket *for a voyage from Philadelphia to Boston and back. As an engine department rating, however, this was not what he really wanted, and from then on he shipped out—in such ships as* Carrabulle, Marcidoc, *and* Dorothy Cahill—*on deck. He was at home when Pearl Harbor was attacked, and shipped out in March 1942 as ordinary seaman in the SS* Catahoula, *a molasses tanker, for a voyage into the Caribbean.*[2]

We sailed from the Delaware, from Deep Water Point, New Jersey, up on the Delaware, and everything seemed to go wrong in that voyage. We got in a big windstorm going down the bay and had to anchor. And it dragged. And then we got outside and the auto-alarm [signaling alerts of other ships in distress] was going all the time.

We were down around the neighborhood of [Cape] Hatteras. The Navy had us routed down the East Coast to the Florida Straits and across the south coast of Cuba and Hispaniola to Ensenada, Puerto Rico. And that's a long route and there's no sign of escorts or anything. Occasionally an Army bomber would fly around.

I think we were the only ship in the Cuba Distilling fleet that was armed. We had a four-inch or five-inch gun on the poop. And then we had two raised gun tubs on the poop with a 50-caliber machine gun in each, two on the fo'c'slehead with a 50-caliber machine gun in each, and a Browning machine gun on each wing of the bridge.

When we got down around Diamond Shoals, like around Nags Head somewhere off the coast of Virginia or North Carolina, we see some people in a lifeboat. But the beach is in sight, and we just kept on going.

We got down the Florida Straits, and the Navy had an antisubmarine school in Key West, and there was an old four-stack destroyer circling around down there. And we're proceeding along in the afternoon and somebody spotted a submarine periscope. So the Old Man turns the ship and heads direct for the destroyer on the other side, whereupon the periscope disappeared. So what was that? It was probably an American submarine out there exercising with the destroyer, but it caused a great deal of excitement.

But we proceeded around Cape San Antonio that evening, I guess— the west coast of Cuba—and we head east along the south coast of Cuba. And that night or the following night the lookout spots a light astern of us, and that caused a lot of commotion, of course. A course change was made, and the light changed [course] also. And another course change was made, and the light again changed course. But nothing came of it, just a lot of excitement, you know.

I think the morning after that a fireman was found dead in his bunk. Heart attack or something.[3] We sewed him up and stopped the ship that afternoon and buried him. It was the first and only time I did that. The Old Man didn't want to stop the ship in those waters, especially then, but he did, and we had a burial ceremony and did bury him at sea.

Eventually, we arrived in the Mona Passage, but we couldn't go into Ensenada at night; we arrived after dark. There were no navigation aids so you couldn't go in there at night. So we just circled around there all night. And that night a submarine shelled Mona Island, which was reasonably close to us.

War period portrait of Edward March in uniform showing Merchant Marine Combat Bar (ship engaged in direct enemy action), left, and Atlantic War Zone Bar (Audrey M. Ivey).

Then we went into Ensenada and started loading. We took part load in Ensenada, which isn't far from Guanica, Puerto Rico. And then we went over to La Romana, in the Dominican Republic, and we loaded some more there. There you laid out in the middle of a narrow river with lines out. You couldn't go alongside [a pier], you just laid in the middle of a river alongside a float. And [dictator] Trujillo's yacht was moored up ahead of us there.

And then we went to San Pedro de Macoris. That was an open roadstead: you laid out in the open Caribbean there and loaded from barges. We finished loading there. I don't recall what time we left, but it was probably late in the afternoon of April 4. And then we went through the Mona Pass and were on a course, I guess, directly for the Delaware capes. At least we weren't running along the coast; we were headed straight for the U.S. Northeast coast.

And then the ship gets torpedoed on Easter Sunday.[4] The wind was blowing, and there was a moderate sea running. It was a beautiful day. It was sunny and nice. The ship was deep-loaded. We had all four boats out, ready to lower away, but the seas were coming up very close to the boats. So we took three of the boats in during the afternoon. We only left one out: #2.

So at five o'clock I go up and have supper with my watch partner, Murray. There were two Scandinavians there. One of them was [Emil] Christensen, and I can't remember the other one's name.[5] But the other one was a real big man, and an old man. They were real good seamen, sailing ship men.

But at any rate, Murray and I came back on the catwalk and sat on a cot on the poop. And I took my shirt off, and all I had on was a pair of pants, sitting there in the sun. Dungarees or khakis, I forget which. And both of the Scandinavians were sitting on another cot next to us. We were sitting on the poop facing the port side.

And all of a sudden we get a terrific explosion, and this torpedo hits.

Where it actually hit [according to] the Navy report was wrong. There was no number four hatch; it was a tanker. But it was where number four hatch would have been if it had been a cargo ship. Where it hit was in the pump room, or maybe the bulkhead between the pump room and the adjacent tanks. But all of this is close to the engine room bulkhead too.

It really was a terrific explosion. I'll never forget that sound, a metallic sound. A terrific explosion, and a terrific column of smoke and molasses and everything and water went flying up. We got blown across the poop, and Murray and I landed against the rail on the starboard side. The big heavy AB was one of the casualties; he went sailing right over the side and nobody ever saw him again. I don't think Christensen went over the side, but I think he was one of the ones that was killed.[6]

So we headed down the companionway immediately to get our life vests. We were all right except my knee was bad, and I've still got scars here [over left eye]. My knee was injured but I could get around. You don't think about it, you know, you can do things in circumstances like that, that maybe you couldn't do otherwise.

But we started down the companionway to get our life vests, which were down in the fo'c'sle, only to discover the water was almost up to the deck. Maybe two or three steps down. So we didn't go down. And the catwalk was all torn up and everything, molasses everywhere, just slippery as hell.

We dragged ourselves forward over that catwalk, and then we got midships. The whole afterdeck of the ship was under water then. The poop was sticking out and the catwalk was above, but the afterdeck was under. There was a tremendous hole in the deck there; you could see right down into the tanks. The hole must have been about 25 or 30 feet across.

When we got midship the smell of ammonia was very strong. And that was from the refrigerator plant. You had to walk past the galley, and there was the—I think it was the chief cook, but it may have been the second cook.[7] I don't remember, but he was there pinned down. The beams overhead had come down, and he was pinned under those heavy steel beams in the galley. There was nothing you could do for him. He was probably dead. The galley was a shambles; it was only a few feet from where the torpedo had hit. It was just a mess.

The antenna was down, and the radio operator and the chief mate were up there. We had to get the emergency antenna up before we did anything. So we got [it] up, and then we got the boats out. And the operator proceeded to send off a message.

Number four boat was gone, blown up. We got #1 and #3 out as fast as we could. And just about the time we got them out, the second torpedo hit, just forward of the bridge somewhere on the starboard side. One of the sailors had just gone forward to let go the raft on the foredeck, and he was right there where it hit. So he was killed in the explosion for sure.[8] That took care of the raft and him.

The ship went [down] so fast then. The radio operator wanted to go back in and get his cat, and he was dissuaded from that. But we got that

#1 and #3 out as fast as possible. Everybody piled in and we lowered them away. And the guys that lowered away [then] just came right down the falls right away.

And she was going *fast*—she was going real fast. The ship was starting to roll over to the starboard side, toward us. By the time we got that boat in the water, it wasn't more than seven or eight feet below the boat deck. And she was just rolling right over.

I was in #3 boat, which was the second mate's boat, and I remember the first assistant [engineer] ran down below to get his license out of his room. He lost his life as a result.[9] He came tearing back up on the boat deck and jumped for the boat, and got caught up in the—I don't know if it was the boat falls or what. Maybe it was the boat painter. But the ship was just rolling right over on us [and] the stack was coming right over on us. And at the same time the stern was lifting up in the air. I don't know whether the stack hit us, or the topmast; one of them did. But she just went real fast after that second torpedo hit. It couldn't've been a minute. It couldn't've been a minute.

I remember the Old Man standing on the starboard wing of the bridge, when she was rolling over, looking at us. And the second mate was ordering us to get the oars out and row for our lives. But we didn't have time to get the oars out—we didn't have time to do anything. We got the boat in the water and she was rolling right over on us. And that was it. I saw that stack coming down on us, and I saw that topmast coming down; it was way up in the air and coming down. And the ship, she was rolling over and also standing up at the [same] time.

The next thing I remember, I'm way down in the water and coming up! I didn't think I was going to last, until I got up to the surface, you know, air wise. But I popped out, and most of the others did.

One of the boats came back up—just one end up, upside down—out of the water. It was almost all submerged with one end of the bottom sticking out of the water. The pumpman was under the boat. Somebody swam underneath to see if anybody was under there, and the pumpman was under there. He was in an air pocket, and he *wouldn't* come out. Two or three of us went under there and tried to get him to come out, and he would *not* come out. So he was one of the casualties, and the boat eventually disappeared.[10] We had been hanging on the boat.

Meanwhile, there was a raft floating around, a damaged raft that had just floated off the ship. The gun crew were rowing around in #2, and by this time they had some other people in the boat with them. I don't know

The molasses tanker SS *Catahoula*, November 11, 1941 (Mariners' Museum, Newport News, Virginia).

how many, but that boat was damaged too; it had been over there not too far from where the first torpedo hit. Anyway, they towed the raft over to us, and those of us who were from number one and three boats were hanging on— sitting in or hanging on the raft. The raft was damaged; it was awash, and it was totally overloaded. You know, the rafts at the beginning of the war were kind of rough affairs; they weren't so nice as the later ones that came out of the factories. This was something the shipyard just put together with oil drums and whatnot. There were food compartments there, but we couldn't get into them because that was what was keeping us afloat; the openings were submerged. So, fortunately we weren't on the raft too long.

We had a fellow on the raft who was an AB. I can't remember his name—we called him Whitey. And he had a rivet in his eye; there was just a hole here, and the rivet was there. I don't know what kept him alive, because he was in terrible shape. A lot of people were banged up to a degree, including me, but he was bad.

So we were bundled on that raft. Murray and I were still together. Sometime during the night, there was about a six- or seven-foot sea running; it wasn't real bad. But sometime during the night a PBY [flying boat] just happened to fly by, and with navigation lights on. The Old Man was in the boat and he fired a flare. And then the plane circled us. We probably wouldn't've survived—at least not on the raft—if that hadn't happened.

The next day the USS *Sturtevant* [DD 240],[11] a destroyer, picked us up. Well, [it] comes alongside the raft. They picked the people up off the boat first, then they came alongside the raft. She was rolling pretty good in that sea. They had a wooden rub rail running along her at the waterline, you know, to protect her from damage against piers. And every time she rolled up it caught on the raft and tried to upset it.

They had this net over the side and everybody's climbing up, except Whitey, who had to be hoisted up. A fellow named David "Casey" Jones, a messman, and I were holding the raft away from the side of the destroyer while the others climbed up. And after everybody was up we stopped holding on and reached for the net; we were waiting for the opportune moment to go up ourselves. And there were sharks swimming around the raft now.

Well, the rub rail [of the destroyer] caught on there and Casey went flipping off the raft with the sharks swimming around. And I don't know, the things you do at a time like that. I just reached over—I had my hand on the net and my foot on the raft—and I reached over and took him by the hair of the head and lifted him out of the water! But he had a shark bite on his thigh. And that's what we got ourselves in the paper about later on. It doesn't mean he would've lost his life; he probably could've scrambled out. But I did hoist him out of the water without, you know, where do you get the strength? And he was a fat man, too. I just pulled him right out of the water by the head, by the hair with one hand, and it didn't seem to be any effort at all.

The water was warm but the air wasn't. And I didn't even have a shirt on. When I got aboard the destroyer I was just shaking uncontrollably. They gave us coffee and blankets, wrapped blankets around us. And I was down in the fireroom—one of the firerooms—with a couple of other people, on the deck wrapped in blankets, drinking coffee and talking to the fireman. I was all right after a while.

Because of Whitey with the rivet in his head, I guess, or maybe because this destroyer was just in a hurry, she took us into San Juan doing 30 knots. That was really a ride, and with a good sea running!

They had us down in the crews' quarters patching us up. My knee was bad, and I was bleeding from the back, and had—Well, you can still see that scar if you look closely. I guess I've still got a scar under the hair here over my left eye. It was visible for years. They put that purple stuff on it and the purple stayed for 20 years.

Well, anyway, they took us up to San Juan. There was somebody there to pick up the Navy gun crew and take care of them, but nobody for us. Eventually the Salvation Army took us uptown and to the hospital for a while in San Juan. Then in a hotel in old downtown San Juan.

The Old Man got some money somewhere. I think he gave us each five dollars each or something. But the Salvation Army gave us each a suit of clothes: a shirt, and a belt, and a pair of pants, and a pair of shoes, and a pair of socks and underwear. I think I spent my five dollars on a sweater. And they gave us a toothbrush and toothpaste, and a razor and a comb, which was, you know, that was nice. And they came to the hospital and wanted your sizes, and then when you left the hospital they brought you the clothes. Very nice.

So ever since, I've donated to the Salvation Army.

*For injuries sustained as a result of the attack on SS* Catahoula, *March was subsequently awarded the Mariner's Medal. He returned to sea soon after, as AB/quartermaster in the SS* Badger State *during the winter of 1942. He continued to ship out for the duration of the war. At one point he went on leave for additional training and upgraded to third mate. In that capacity he took a new T-2 tanker—SS* Kettle Creek—*out of the shipyard from Chester, Pennsylvania, in July 1944.*

## Convoy Procedures: "Three-two, what are you doing?!"

I was in a T-2 tanker named *Kettle Creek*, and took her out of the shipyard—Sun Ship—new, in a 15-knot convoy going to England. And they [were] all fast ships. And you zigzag from dawn until sunset, and then at night you *don't* zigzag. And then in the small convoys you got all these "Christmas tree" lights and sound signals for course changes and orders, you know, [but] you didn't use them in fast convoys. They had a voice radio which they called PBY. But the voice radio was manned only during daylight hours—sunrise to sunset—because it had a much longer range after dark. So your orders for the night were given before PBY was shut down for the night. And unless there was an emergency during the night, and then the "Christmas tree" lights did come on. But unless there was an emergency nothing happened, except if there was a course change the commodore's ship would blow a "turning" blast, and everybody turned. They already had the orders, which was all in the convoy procedures. MERSIGS, they called it, and WINS, were two books of convoy signals: Maritime Instructions for Merchant Ships, I guess, and the other was MERSIG—Merchant Ship Signals, I suppose.

So we're going to England, and we've got the *Empress of Australia*

## 12. Edward C. March

alongside us on the starboard side, which is full of troops—a big three-stack passenger liner. Nothing less than 15 knots in the convoy. They always did have a couple of C-1s in the convoy [but] they couldn't keep up; they were stragglers—they were *always* back there.

The T-2 was a 14 and a half-knot ship but can easily do 16; all you have to do is put on the revolutions, and you just burn more oil—a lot more. But you can do it, no problem maintaining 15.

So now, when you get in fog in a convoy, you—nobody's got radar—you had a "fog buoy" and you towed the fog buoy. And the ship astern of you he's got the fog buoy right next to the bridge and kept it there. And that's how you maintained station and how to avoid collision.

So I go on watch—we're up on the Grand Banks somewhere—and I go on watch at 4 o'clock in the morning, relieve the second mate, and it's so thick you can't see the fo'c'slehead. And he's got that fog buoy right next to the bridge, about 30 feet off, you know, and it's shooting up a flume of water. And it's right there on the port side, and it's shooting. I bullshitted with him for a while, and then he goes. And it's one man in the wheelhouse, you know, at the helm, but he can use the phone. So you're calling "right one [degree] or "left one" to keep that buoy there, or "up one" or "down one" revolution, then he had to call the engine room.

And we've got a 20 degrees course change to the left at 0600, which will happen when the commodore blows a "turning" blast and everybody turns 20 degrees to the left.

We're on the left side of the convoy. There's nine or 10 columns, numbered from left to right. We're in the third column, and we're the second ship [back] in the third column, so they're all behind us too, mostly.

And, all right, so we keep the fog buoy going there, and everything is going fine, it's blacker than hell, and I'm pulling my flashlight out once in a while, looking at my watch to see how close we're getting to [course change]. And all of a sudden the helmsman calls out, "Mr. March, the wheel won't turn!"

It's about two minutes to six, maybe less. I was waiting for the signal, and "Mr. March, the wheel won't turn." And I go dashing into the wheelhouse and grab the wheel—and it's all dark in there except for the light on the repeater [compass]—it won't budge. So I pulled my flashlight out of my pocket and looked. Well, this guy at the wheel had gone through Sheepshead Bay, and he had one of them Maritime Service blue wool sweaters. I still have mine. And it had gotten warm in the wheelhouse [so] he took his sweater off and he thought he was hanging it on the binnacle ball. Instead, he dropped it into the telemotor gear. The T-2 when they came out, there was no cover over the telemotor gear; they were exposed. He dropped it right into the gears. And every time he turned the wheel, he pulled the sweater farther into the gears, and there was little pieces of wool all over the deck, come off, and it was jammed.

And just about the time I discovered it, the turning blast goes. And the convoy turns, and I keep going. We're 3-2—the second ship in the third column from the left—and there's another column off to the right turning ahead of us! And the one right next to us is a trooper, and we're loaded with gasoline! And fighters on deck, fighter planes—P-51s.

So there was nothing I could do but call the Old Man. So I call the Old man right away, then I called the engine room right away to get up and get emergency steering hooked up aft. And I can't go until he comes up—the Old Man comes up—and then I get aft.

Well, the radio comes alive in the meantime—the escorts are watching everything on radar—and, "Three-two, what are you *doing*?!"

So. But three-two kept going for a while, because it was quite a while before we got on the emergency wheel, and I was back aft. We never saw anything or heard anything except what came on the radio before I left the wheelhouse.

And when it cleared up several hours later, we were way off on the starboard side of the convoy [laughing]! We got it fixed up, but by the time—the whole convoy is going 15 knots, over *here*, and we're going *this* way.

## *The Cadet*

Another time on the same ship we had a Merchant Marine Academy cadet—two of them, one engine and one deck cadet—and we put the sailor on day work and the cadet on my watch, because cadets should learn to be a sailor, and they don't today. But a cadet should be put to work and do sailor work and learn things. He shouldn't be an officer unless you've done what you're telling people to do. At least that's what I think.

But at any rate, we've got this cadet on my watch—the cadet's name was Bishop—and his father was master of [a ship] up on the Great Lakes at that time. But he was a nice kid, and it was his first trip at sea.

We went down to the Gulf and back, unescorted. We went down to Texas, unescorted, loaded, went back to New York, unescorted, and then took the convoy from New York to England, see. And he learned to steer on that ship, the coast-wise leg—legs, I should say—of the voyage.

And so, he relieves the wheel at 4 o'clock on this afternoon, and I'm relieving the Second Mate, and we're on the port wing [of the bridge], chatting, before he went down. We'd passed Londonderry shortly before, and the escorts were based in Londonderry and [they] all left and were heading into Londonderry—they were in sight—but were heading. Well, they weren't far away—only a mile or so—they'd just left. And the Loch Ewe ships were breaking off to the left, and all of the other columns are turning down the North Channel.[12]

And the phone rings, and I dash in the wheelhouse, and it's the gunner on lookout on the bow, who reports, "A torpedo has just crossed our bow!"

And then I go running out to the port side just in time to see it hit the *Jacksonville* right next to us.[13] And she just went [makes sound]—just like that. In two seconds there was nothing to see but flames; she had a load of aviation gas, same as us, identical ship.

And those T-2s had a *big* gun crew in 'em. The total men in there at that time was about 85. They had a communications officer and a gunnery officer. And they had a lot of gunners—I forget how many, 28 or something. And she just went—swoosh—just like that.[14]

And my cadet fainted at the wheel. I don't blame the kid. I just left him lay there. I had to go and steer.

Some of those convoy experiences were real hairy. Keeping station on a pitch-black night—huh, can't see anything!

*March upgraded to Third Mate in 1944, shipping out for the first time in that capacity in the T-2 tanker* Kettle Creek, *and for the duration. He continued to ship out after the war until 1952, when he began a long career of maritime-related government service, retiring from that in 1980. He passed away, at 91, in 2011.*

CHAPTER 13

# John S. "Jack" McCusker: "Did you ever hear a ship die?"

*John S. "Jack" McCusker was born in Seattle in 1915 and first went to sea in 1932 as wiper aboard a tanker.[1] After two years in the Coast Guard, in 1937 and 1938, he continued to ship out in the Merchant Marine and was an AB in the SS* Brazil *in the Caribbean at the time of the attack on Pearl Harbor. Upon returning to New York in December 1941, he upgraded to Third Mate, and shipped out in the SS* John Witherspoon, *a brand new Liberty ship, for PQ-17, the ill-fated convoy to northern Russia.[2] After proceeding in small convoy from the shipyard in Baltimore to New York, the SS* John Witherspoon *steamed to Halifax, Nova Scotia, then proceeded in convoy to Reykjavik, Iceland, where it sat for 29 days waiting for Convoy PQ-17 to shape up before departing for North Russia.[3]*

So we finally got underway, went straight up the northwest side and we laid up just north of the Cape—North Cape. So everything was fine. Meanwhile, it's the Fourth of July, so like you never saw before, everybody broke out the flags that they could get, they run up their flags. Everybody was in the game. So with all the bunting [and] flags flying, sometime that evening—8 o'clock or so—there were about 25 torpedo planes, from the starboard. And they were regrouping, getting ready to hit. We had Stukas, we had Junkers [and] the ones on the starboard side, aft, they sneaked in and they hit the *William Hooper*—an American Liberty ship—and the *Navarino*, a British ship.[4]

And the *Azerbaidjan*, a Russian tanker way off on the port, she got hit. She was hit, I don't know how badly, but there was a fire, and smoke. And she got it—they didn't abandon—they got in. I was watching the whole scenario through the glass, this *Ajerbaidjan* after the smoke cleared.

And the women crew members are piling out of a lifeboat, where they obviously didn't want to be in the first place. They didn't want to be in that lifeboat and lowered over the side. And the last I saw, they had disappeared into the smoke; they never got off the ship.

That was like at 9 o'clock at night—again, on my watch.

Well, then we were really feeling pretty cocky, and then we got this bombshell [signal] to scatter. That was about 10 o'clock. I don't recall how the signal came [but] we had a Navy Armed Guard signalman who was—just about adequate. But between the two or us we put together the signals that were going between the cruiser force—which had suddenly appeared, aft. All of a sudden, here's the cruiser force!

And one of the escorts [signaled]—I don't know how he signaled, whether it was a flag or other signal by lamp. But apparently our [convoy] commodore—he was in the *Lord Ashton*—didn't hear it or couldn't believe it. None of us could.[5] We were absolutely—this was unbelievable! [And then we received the] commodore signal: "scatter."

And that's the only time that you finally got it—or heard it—visually. So, and that was a little back and forth down the line, to scatter. The cruisers were heading west, to Iceland, which was the last we saw of them.

The Old Man [came in and said] "What's happening, what's happening! What's going on?!"

I says, "Hey, we just lost everything. We just got orders to head for Archangel—alone."

We were dead abeam—at noontime—of North Cape. At this point, 240 miles actually. And we couldn't go any further north because of the ice. So what to do when you scatter? It's like, everybody does a fan job, but it doesn't quite work out that way, you know. And the confusion and near collisions, and hugging together for some kind of protection. I mean, the idea of a convoy is like you stay together and have firepower, right? But now there wasn't going to *be any*. There wasn't going to be an escort.

Anyway, a submarine appeared on the starboard quarter that afternoon. It must have been the 6th [of July] because we got it on the 6th. He shadowed us for a while, and we fired the 5" at him—about 20 rounds—and he disappeared. He just ducked. That evening on the 12 to 4 watch—on the second mate's watch—we got hit, on the starboard side. It was two, three or four torpedoes, nobody's sure. But I mean, he really plastered us.[6]

I was asleep, but I was ready. I'm not brave, believe me. I was shaking like the rest of the guys, but I also knew we were going to get hit; there wasn't any question about it. So I had my papers—my license—and a toothbrush. I think I ended up as the only guy on the beach in Archangel with a toothbrush. And I had my clothing on, plenty of clothes on.

My lifeboat was #1, all the way forward on the starboard side. But it got hit; it was a fuckin' tangled mess. It was smashed, totally, hanging off the davits. Both [lifeboat number] one and three.

The hit from the torpedo—the wave from it—hit the side like a tidal wave. It hit my porthole and the outer way. I was washed right out of my bunk. I was on the starboard side, and was washed all the way to the port side, right out onto the port boat deck: POW, Slammed up against #2 boat! This was the Old Man's boat.

But anyway, we get into number four, and the ship was still going ahead, under way. There was a valve on deck, on the boat deck, and somebody had the good sense to shut off the steam, but it was still going ahead pretty good. We still had no trouble launching the boat.

So Lind [second mate] yells over, "I'm gonna come over and pull you out of here." He's farting around with the [lifeboat] engine, and pretty soon he gets it going, and it shot into a fog bank, and we never saw him again. And I said, "Jesus, this is really a lot to lay on a third mate on his first trip out!"

So Lind is gone, and here I am. The ship is still afloat, creaking and groaning. Did you ever hear a ship dying? It's really, like a wounded dog out that door howling and screeching and carrying on. Everything is coming apart, beams are splitting, cargo holds are collapsing. You know, the whole thing is really—You sit and watch that thing that just five minutes ago was your home. And it's just, really in agony.

I was thinking, "This is how it ended? After all this preparation, all this struggle, all this fight, all this protection, all this hope, and this is where it ends—there—without even a fight, gone? Seventy-five hundred tons of cargo? I later learned that the amount

Jack McCusker as a new third mate, 1942, photographer unknown (Michael Gillen collection).

of cargo lost in the convoy—the amount of planes, tanks, equipment and food—was enough to equip 50,000 Soviet soldiers. Fifty thousand!

So, the ship wasn't going anywhere, yet, until I see some pecker tracks, and here's another torpedo—I could see it coming—that slams into the midships section. And WHAM, boy, and then she really shrieked when that one hit her. The boiler went, the bridge collapsed, and what was left of the lifeboats and davits went over the side. The potatoes—she had a coal stove in the galley and a coal locker up on the boat deck—the coal locker and the spuds were rattling over the side.

And we sat and watched her go. She just, the ass end—stern—went up, but the wheel was still going, barely. And at about that time up popped the submarine. We had been alerted to look out for submarines with polar bear markings. But this was not white with those markings; this was a sleek little gray job, man, like you never saw. It was beautiful, right out of the yard. She didn't have a blister on her. And she bore down on us.[7]

And I told the ensign, who was wearing his high-pressure hat, "Hey, take it off." You know, at this point about ensigns, I've got sort of a composite of them; there were so many of them, and I can never remember which one was which. But this guy, a nice, mild little guy, was really all right: he, by god, he came through.[8] He ended up in my boat, too, along with the steward, and Manuel. I had a nice gang.

But, meanwhile, stuff started to surface from the ship: hatch boards, rags—everything—and hams. Huge fuckin' hams! Paper wrapped, right? They came up by the dozen. And the submarine was laying off, and he ain't heading for us; he's got the periscope on the hams. And the first thing we see is these guys crawling out of the conning tower, and they're heading not for the machine guns, but for boathooks to spear some hams. By the way, a couple of them floated by and we put them in. I said, "We'll take them to have when we hit Novaya Zemlya. We're supposed to be 30 miles off Novaya Zemlya." So I figure, this is a snap: we can row that. We've got a sail, but we can row that.

We lost one guy, an ordinary seaman. I don't know who this kid was, but he was lookout in the crow's nest.[9] I don't know whether he was blown over, jumped over or what. But if he had stayed where the hell he was and climbed down, he wouldn't've been lost. The last we saw of him, he was floating face down. And one of his shipmates said, "Let's take him aboard!"

I said, "Jesus, man, he's gone! I mean, this is a sad situation, but, you know, he's gone. What are we gonna do, bring him in here, and look at him, and then throw him over again?"

The guys were really pissed off at me. "Well, he may be alive!" some said. I almost had it out with a couple of them, you know, because one guy was a pal of his from ashore. Well, they finally got the idea that he was gone.

Anyway, we had pulled up two hams. After this guy in the submarine got all he could, he slid alongside, and he said, "You have hams there?" And I thought to myself, "How will these fuckers ever lose?" I mean, nobody ever doubted that we would eventually win the war—the American has the idea that he's never gonna lose anything. But at the moment these guys were on top, right? And not only were they on top, but they were going to take our two hams!

"So hand them up, please," says this, you know, Aryan, young, healthy-looking specimen who's been doing nothing but fiddling in the fjords there, you might say. So we handed them up. And in return [he gave us] two bottles of "Courvoisier" [cognac]. It wasn't a bad exchange! And he had cigarettes, and we had plenty of cigarettes. So we got our two bottles of Couvoisier and he said, "Land—30 miles east." So that sort of coincided with our noonday position, right? And then off he went.

So we hoisted our red sail—we had a nice red sail. We passed the brandy around, and everybody's feeling pretty good. I figured, "What the hell, 30 miles, what's 30 miles?" We had a compass—magnetic compass—[but] it was absolutely haywire up there in those latitudes. A magnetic compass is about as erratic as you can get.

Anyway, we were going along pretty well and all of a sudden the weather changes. It started to rain, bitter cold, sun blocked out. The wind dropped and we were dead in the water, surrounded by pack ice. We were *stuck*, I mean stuck, forever.

Oh, how do you keep these guys—and myself—keyed up? I mean, there's no way that you could get your way out of it. So, there we sit. And it's cold: it's *cold*. This is the sixth of July, But it's cold. I was warm enough, and most of the guys, you know, had blankets. But the sitting there—the inactivity of it. You couldn't row; you couldn't put an oar in the water. So, what to do? But we could see.

Then we heard—what appeared to be the most gigantic iceberg you ever saw, coming out of the fog. I mean, a city-block long! And it's gotta be 10 stories high. All shapes and forms, growling and grinding, cutting through the pack ice. And every once in a while a huge slab would fall off: I mean a slab that—there was all kinds of 'em! A whole convoy of icebergs. So we figured, Jesus, maybe they'll break up the pack ice. But as soon as they passed, it just closed in again, and there we were. How long we laid there, and wondered and thought about what was happening, I don't know.

But Manuel was muttering to himself, praying and carrying on. We were sort of dozing off, but you wondered: if you fell asleep how long would it take to wake up because it was *really* cold. And when those icebergs came though it *really* was cold! Jesus, it was like in the bottom of the Grand Canyon, and howling and bitter. Weird! You know, and this was on the sixth of July. Jesus, what's it like in New York? We could use one of those on 42nd Street.

So Manuel shook me and says, "Senor Pilot, I hear something!"

I said, "Yeah, keep listening, Manuel, Jesus Christ, whatever turns you on, man." So I said, "OK, keep listening."

He says, "Senor Piloto, I *see* something."

But first of all, we hear something: here was this cacophony of sirens, bells, whistles! He said, "Jesus Christ, what is it?" And then he said, "I see something."

Before that we started blowing our whistles, you know, the little lifeboat whistles. And the sail was up because I had [ordered] it up for, you know, a windbreaker. And then Manuel said, "Now I see something."

The darling of the convoy, as far as I was concerned, and I make her a little hero—and she was—was the *El Capitan*. The *El Capitan* was an old Southern Pacific Morgan Line ship, built in 1906 of iron.[10] She was about 6,000 tons, and there used to be maybe a dozen of them around for the old Morgan Line out of New York, [which ran] down to Houston and New Orleans, I think. And she was still burning coal, under the Panamanian flag—she had long since ditched the American flag. She had a mixed crew, and as we found out later she had made this same run the year before and had been stuck in the ice in Archangel and had got out and got back, had gone to Greenock, England [sic], after the ice cleared in Archangel. And the whole crew deserted, from the master on down—like deserted, abandoned the ship. They got her back in time to load her up, and she was going again.

Anyway, here she came: she had heard our whistles. She was in convoy—some kind of a little convoy with some rescue ships—and they ran into the ice, the pack ice. The rescue ships, which were leading the group, saw the ice, slammed it into reverse—went full astern—started blowing these damn sirens and everything down the line, you know: the signals for "full astern" and the whistles and the bells. And this is what Manuel heard. And the mate [of *El Capitan*] put his head out the door—the starboard side door—at the lull when there was no noise whatsoever, when everything was dead still, and he heard our little "peep-peeps" and then he saw our sail.

And then the *Capitan* came charging over to us, which was beautiful.

And we went aboard her, and had bacon and eggs, fresh biscuits, and sausage. Now I don't know how many hours we were aboard her, but as soon as we had that first feeding the "Condor" was overhead and started laying the bombs on us.[11] She broke all the steam lines, and so the *Capitan* sat there: dead. They killed the *Capitan* right there.

So we piled off her and onto a [rescue vessel], I guess, and they laid a couple [rounds] into her midships, and that was the end of the *Capitan*. And there [close by] was the fuckin' *beach*! That really pissed me off.[12] I don't know what happened to the rest of those ships: I never did see or recall any of them.

Well, from then on it was a whole another story about the beach and all that, the interrelationships of the various ideologies, let us say, and the personalities and how people reacted to what was really deprivation: it was terrible, terrible!

Well, we were in Archangel for about two months. And the reason we got out, they drew lots. Two ships' crews were going to be taken out on the *Tuscaloosa*, which was laying down by the entrance of the White Sea.[13] And we drew a lot. So we went back on, let's say, FDR's ship. And in the toilet there were hand rails, you know, because of his paralysis. We left in September for Greenock [Scotland].

In Archangel I had a fine time. I *knew* what these people were going through. And, you know, I have a whole thing about being on the beach; I've been on a number of beaches. This was a beach [un]like any other beach in a lifetime. There were 1,300 of us there, including 680 some Americans, of every belief—and disbelief—that you can think of. And there were some really unhealthy, unpleasant confrontations. Some guy from the SUP [Sailors Union of the Pacific] who'd been in the NMU [National Maritime Union] and who had been a Communist and had his fuckin' teeth kicked in and he was now anti. And you've got this little antagonist laying off against all the others. It makes for a good little drama: how they reacted to the "workers' paradise." I mean, what the hell the people went through, man, was pretty admirable. They were terrific and they treated us real well. In other words, free haircuts, free shaves, steam baths, and they gave us whatever the hell they had. And they didn't have very much.

I stayed at the Intourist Hotel. The unlicensed guys stayed in the International Club. But they both had fare, if you could buy it, for $25, all you could eat. Me, I never—I haven't gotten the story on that one. It was an oasis! It was a fuckin' capitalist oasis of food. All you needed was the money. The rubles around there, you could burn them: they weren't worth a shit.

They were paying these kids, you know, setting up these kids to pick pockets. But pretty soon there weren't any pockets to pick. So they were out of business.

**Launched at North Carolina Shipbuilding Company in November 1942, the SS *Collis P. Huntington* was one of three Liberty ships on which John McCusker served during the war. The first, SS *John Witherspoon* (no photograph available), was torpedoed and sunk while en route to North Russia in Convoy PQ-17. McCusker shipped on the *Huntington* for an intended voyage to Russia via the Persian Gulf route, but, as luck would have it, the ship was in a collision with a Dutch freighter and just managed to limp back to New York.**

But it was terrible. I mean these people were living on less than we had. And what they had, we were eating. Thirteen hundred guys to descend on a little village like that, and you have to take care of them. Somebody had to take care of them.

The naval attaché there was quite a guy, a real man. And he laid the law down too. He said, "You guys were fucking up. Watch your ass or I'll take care of it myself." You know, most guys behaved. But, Jesus, out of 1,300 there were a considerable number of gas hounds who used to think of nothing except "where do I get the next shot of vodka?" or chasing some poor, fucking woman down the street.

I got introduced to a nice family [and] I met a lovely young woman. Man, she was an olive-eyed beauty. And she had a roommate: the whole family. I never did know who was who, but they were all living together. And one other young woman, who was a second mate who was waiting for the *Ajerbaidjan* to come in, 'cause her old man was skipper. She was waiting for the second mate's job. And she was terrific. She said, "What did you have to do to get your third mate's license?" And I told her, you know. And she said, "That's all?"

I said, "Yeah, it was rough enough for me."

"Well," she said, "we not only learn how to *run* a ship, we learn how to *build* a ship." They can tell you a false keel from a—meridian altitude. They're amazing, the schooling they got. She spoke three languages, so there was no trouble communicating. This was the roommate of the other one. It was a whole family. I never figured out who the hell was who. It didn't make any difference. I spent all kinds of time there.

As soon as we hit the beach they insisted that we all go to the hospital. There was nothing wrong with me [but] I was all broken out from the sun; I can't take the sun. I was all broken out on my nose from the ice reflection and all that. But there was nothing wrong with the rest of the guys, except exhaustion. And we slept for about 24 hours, and then they said, "Ok, you there, and you go there" and that was it. So, make your own flight.

You know, they had reading rooms at the International and the Intourist—beautiful reading rooms. Yeah, I mean they had everything there to read, too. All kinds of shit, man. You know, the British were there and were quite an influence. They had a little mission there, they had a church. There were all kinds of activities, games. They tried to keep it up in kind of a YMCA style. They had a football, until somebody stole it. Can you imagine, somebody stealing a football?

They had movies. They had, oh shit, *At Dawn I Die* was one of them. They had an opera house! They had a British string quartet, and the Red Army and the Red Navy used to have—their choruses would come up to entertain us. You know, really stirring stuff with all the acting that went on with it. They did everything they could. They wouldn't let us work. There was a big, burly guy—Ted Reeves. He was a big, powerful guy and he wanted to help these women wrestle a log.

She said, "Oh, no, you don't get enough to eat, you don't have the strength."

And you know, she was pretty right, because we didn't: we were without much protein. But plenty heavy on the carbohydrates—the kasha and the black bread—which was great for a bowel movement but didn't do much to sustain strength.

The air was bracing and the weather was beautiful. I mean, it was clear, and like a nice fall day every day. There were no—I think we got two air attacks. And we ducked into some shelter and that was it. It was nothing.

They bombed the shit out of Murmansk, because there was one ship that came around [from there] and they were bombing them so badly in Murmansk that they came around to Archangel. I knew one of the guys on her because I'd been shipmates with him, a guy named Blackie Newell.

And he said, "Oh, Christ, everybody used to get off the ship and go up and sit on a hill. There was nothing you could do on the ship: you had to get the hell away from there."

One of the points that I want to make is that we didn't bring anything: we were *takers*, not givers, through no fault of our own. At the same time, if you thought about it, that had to have an effect on you, too. You know, I'd go to visit this lovely woman, and I had nothing to bring her. For a while I'd filch a chocolate bar from somebody off the ship, or something just to make a token gesture. *They* always had something for us: they had caviar, they had black bread, and they had vodka so we always had a pleasant evening.

But as far as I am concerned—and then they found out who we were, and I'm sure if some of the other guys had made some kind of an effort to—just to show that they were concerned—and then they found out that we were working, the working class of America. They knew about our struggle, but they wanted to hear more about it. They wanted to hear more about the American labor movement, and *we* were the guys who could tell them about it. We were, you know, we were welcomed.

A lot of the guys sat around and bemoaned the fact that they were stuck in this godforsaken hole, and for how long, and nobody loved them and—it was bullshit. The drunks became drunker, and everybody found his own level, somehow or other. I found mine, man. I didn't want to leave!

I said, "Why the hell do I want to leave here for?" There's this lovely woman who was waiting at—watching me go. I mean, shit, man, I've had a lot of women in my life—up to that time and after—but that one was really wonderful. No, they had been through it, and they were going through it, and they had really treated us right, as far as I was concerned. But anyway, I hated to leave, I really did.

And the Germans by this time were also announcing that the *Tuscaloosa* was at the entrance to the White Sea, and that they were going to get her before she gets out, or once she's underway. This was an announcement. Yeah, it said, "All you guys on the beach up there, the *Tuscaloosa*'s at the entrance—we'll get around to her. She's on her way to Greenock with you guys, but we'll get her!" They did take a couple of shots at us on the way up—some kind of a [battle] wagon we ran down and sank on the way back, in the middle of the night. I don't know what the hell it was all about. I mean, we barely saw it.

So we were eating Navy chow on the way back. It was about a couple-day run [from Archangel]. Beans for breakfast, beans for lunch. I don't know, but it was worse than we had up in Archangel! I said, "Jesus Christ, where did you guys get the menu? At least we had decent black bread [and] we had cabbage soup." These guys [merchant seamen] who were used to—really, the chowhounds—they couldn't adjust to this. They were doing the best they could, with soup and once in a while a piece of meat which was totally unidentifiable. They said yak, but yak is not indigenous to the area. Reindeer meat they said, but yak comes from Central Asia. I thought, well, maybe they were driven in this direction. I never saw tougher—the toughest damn stuff you ever saw! You couldn't eat this with a fire axe, But that was meat. But one of the ships that did get in came in with Spam. And now we had Spam for about a week, and I thought that was as good as chicken croquettes, man. It was something else. Yeah, we had Spam for about a week. It wasn't bad there. The Russians thought it was, I mean, Jesus, they were getting it too and, man, Jesus Christ, what a treat! But that's how you—looked forward to the things there.

Well, we went into Greenock, the port for Edinburgh, Scotland. We were greeted there like we had been—just won the war. The lord mayor of London came, with bagpipes—there must have been 40 of them—they marched around this huge auditorium, blowing those fucking bagpipes. After about two minutes of them I'm—I mean, I love music, I play the piano, but I couldn't take that shit anymore than two minutes. And brother—and then the lord mayor of London gave this grand speech! "We made the fight" and blah, blah, blah. I thought, "What fucking nonsense." Who the hell needed that! All we wanted was some money, which they supplied us, by the way. And Lind and I took off for Edinburgh where we each bought a sextant. He'd lost his; I didn't have one. We each bought a sextant, the last two that they had.

We were there maybe a week. We came back on the *Queen Mary*—beautiful [ship], and what food! She was army-fed, the U.S. Army fed her. I'm telling you, you know, eating kippers for breakfast, it was fantastic! Clipping along at 32 knots. Just the trip before that she'd run down a destroyer and killed I don't know how many hundreds.[14] We went straight into New York. Man, what a ship. You could hear the *Queen* creaking and groaning, which is the sign of a good ship, to me. I mean, she felt like a ship, man: just the power of her—beautiful![15]

Then I took off for my hometown, Seattle. I went by plane via Pittsburgh, Chicago, and a half-dozen towns in North Dakota, Montana. It was a hedge-hopper. I was only about 25, or 24—a good looking guy—healthy, with a roving eye. And this stewardess said, "Oh, you're just a boy!"

And I said, "If you think I'm just a boy let's get off in Fargo or whatever the fuck it is. Jesus, just a boy." I said, "Do you know where I've been, you bitch? Boy. I may have been a boy a year ago, but I grew up."

By the way, that's another thing: a *lot* of guys grew up very fast.

*After his experience in Convoy PQ-17 to Russia, McCusker continued to ship out for the duration of the war. His wartime voyages included another to the Soviet Union, but via the Persian Gulf, on the Liberty ship* Collis P. Huntington, *which limped back to New York after a collision with a Dutch freighter, and to Brindisi, Italy, on the SS* Augustus S. Merriman, *where he and his shipmates celebrated the end of the war in Europe in May 1945. McCusker was "blacklisted" not long after the war, and was no longer able to ship out. He was a self-described "bar mechanic" for many years. A founder of the Marine Workers Historical Society and editor of its journal* The Hawsepipe. *McCusker passed away in New York, at 89, in 2004.*

CHAPTER 14

# Harry E. Morgan: Walnuts and Bauxite for the War

*Harry E. Morgan was born in Fullerton, California, in 1914. After moving around with his "wildcat" drilling contractor father, he attended school in Piru and Long Beach, California.¹ From high school he took an unauthorized break, running away to sea in a Richfield Oil tanker bound for Corpus Christi, Texas. Fetched home to Long Beach by his father in the family Model-T, he finished high school and entered Pomona College. Six months later he left Pomona and went to work on a tuna clipper, where he began as an oiler and was soon put in charge of the plant. Later, to boost the family income, he took a job as a machinist helper in a local shipyard, and in 1931 shipped out as a wiper in SS Point Lobos, Gulf Pacific Line. Thus began a maritime career that was to last, virtually without interruption, for 60 years. On 7 December 1941 he was first assistant engineer in SS Julia Luckenbach, loading in Philadelphia, when word was received of the attack on Pearl Harbor.²*

## "Just one of those things"

We were in Philadelphia loading cargo, and when the war started we discharged the cargo we had been loading, and they shifted us up to Red Hook Basin in Brooklyn to put the guns on, and painted the ship gray, and got her ready for wartime.

We [had been] working the cargo as a matter of fact, and it was a Sunday if I remember it right. But we were working down below, and we got the word that Pearl Harbor had been bombed. We figured we were gonna get into it sooner or later anyway; we just didn't know when it was gonna happen. I thought that they would probably bomb the Philippines or something like that first, but I wasn't payin' too much attention to it, to be truthful.

We were in the yard for approximately four weeks, and then we went over to the Brooklyn Navy Yard and we loaded war materiel for Australia. And, of course, at the time we left we didn't know where we were going, we just loaded the cargo and we sailed on Friday, February the 14th [1942]. And I [was] with them on the *Julia* [*Luckenbach*] approximately a year, year and a half.

We went down the coast to Panama, through the Panama Canal, and then we went straight down the west coast of South America until we got to about south 40 [latitude] and crossed over and went to Auckland, New Zealand—we stopped there for food and water—and then we went to Hobart, Tasmania. And from Hobart we came back up to Brisbane and discharged all our cargo there.

Portrait of Harry Morgan, circa 1940, by unknown photographer (Joanie Morgan).

It was worse off the Jersey Coast because they were sinking ships left and right—tankers—and we could see ships on fire when we went down. It's just one of those things. There was no other way of doing it; you just had to go. We went solo that time: we had no convoy. The *Julia Luckenbach* at that time was considered a fast ship: she could do 16 knots, and we could outrun a submarine on the surface.[3]

When we come back we went to Chañaral in Chile. We went there for fuel oil—we were instructed to go there for fuel oil—and when we got there, why, they didn't have any fuel oil. So we had to go down to Valparaiso and get bunkers because we were just about out of fuel.

And then we came back to Chañaral and loaded copper ingots and came back up into New Orleans. Discharged the cargo there.

Then I was taken off of that ship as first assistant [engineer] and brought back to San Francisco, and [then] sent to Portland as chief engineer on a Liberty—the *William S. Rosecrans*. That was my first Liberty.[4]

We loaded ammunition at Beaverton—down the river from Portland,

I'm not sure of the name of it—and we sailed for Calcutta.[5] We went essentially the way we went on the *Julia*: we went clear down the coast and then crossed over at [latitude] 40, went through Auckland [New Zealand], stopped for fuel and water. We stopped in Hobart, Tasmania, and then we put into Fremantle [Australia]. But since we had a crew member—an able seaman—with spinal meningitis, we were quarantined in Fremantle for six days. And when that was cleared up we went on to Calcutta. And from Calcutta we came back down to Trincomalee, which was a British naval base in India, and we loaded walnuts, which is more common almost than peanuts.[6] But we couldn't figure what that had to do with the war, but peanut oil was important to the war effort.

And then we went from there up to Port Said—through the Suez Canal into Port Said—and into Alexandria, and we discharged the rest of our ammunition. We only had discharged half of it in the first port. And then we—shuttled: they used us as a shuttle ship between Alexandria and Malta for four months.

And they only worked [on Malta] at night.[7] During the day you had to leave the harbor and go out and steam around the island because they didn't want any ships sunk in the harbor. The Germans coming back from Africa—if they hadn't found their target—they'd always dump anything they had left on Malta.

And then we came across to Bahia, in Brazil, and that's where we waited a week to form a convoy. That's when we got into this 70-ship convoy. We came out of Bahia and we headed up for the East Coast.

And it was off Recife where we got hit by a "wolf pack" where they sunk 12 ships.[8] This must've been the latter part of '43. It was night—it was around two in the morning—and the submarines—they said there was three or four, maybe there was more, we don't know—but they came right up in the middle of the convoy.

They [escorts] got one. It was an Italian submarine. The others were German. But they just surfaced in the middle of the convoy and shot their torpedoes, and then shelled anything else they could see.

The *Jedediah S. Smith* was in position alongside of us on the port side.[9] She got hit in #3 hold and it blew the hatch off and the hatch beams. And one of the hatch beams landed on our deck. We were only about, oh, maybe 100 yards away. Of course we were on general quarters, and I was down in the engine room, and when we heard that damn beam hit the deck we figured we'd been hit too.

But when we got to Port o' Spain [Trinidad] we left that convoy and went up to the McKenzie River, British Guiana—at that time it was British Guiana-and we loaded bauxite.[10] And this was the first big ship that ever went up that river. We had a lot of problems, not so much going up but when they got loaded up there—almost half loaded, because the river wasn't deep enough to fully load it—but going down the river.

But we got down to Port o' Spain again and we topped off the bauxite, then we waited there for about four days. Then we joined another convoy coming up the East Coast to New York. And we broke out of the convoy at New York and went into Brooklyn again, to that Gowanus Canal to unload. We discharged into barges.

And at that time the company called me back home again to San Francisco and put me on another ship. Well, I'd been out 14 months, and I was ready to come home anyway. So I was home for a month and then I took the *Charles D. Poston* out—another Liberty ship—and we went to

**Prewar photograph, undated, of SS *Julia Luckenbach* (Mariners' Museum, Newport News, Virginia).**

Hawaii, and then down to the South Pacific islands for interisland [work]: you pick up cargo here, pick up a contingent of troops and move them to another place.[11]

I came back, and I went on the *Luis Arguello*, a Liberty ship converted to carry 350 troops, and I went right back out again with them. We made one trip to Hawaii, and then came back, and I thought this is great: we were only gone two or three months at a time.[12]

The second trip out we went, we took troops to Moro Bay, New Guinea, and we went to Port Moresby.[13] They sent us back through the [Panama] Canal to New Orleans, and there again I left the ship and came home. On that ship I was out about a year.

## *Waiting for the Invasion of Japan*

So I came back home, and then I went on a Victory ship, and I finished the war out on a Victory ship—the *Simmons Victory*.[14] We loaded ammunition up in Port Chicago. This was two weeks before they had the big explosion up there with another ship—and we steamed out and were in Leyte Gulf [the Philippines].[15]

And when the war ended [in Europe] we had been laying at anchor there for almost a month and a half. And when the war ended it was the closest we had [come to being hit] because all the people were so exuberant with their celebration. They were throwing up rockets and everything else—signal flares, parachute flares, everything that they could shoot off to celebrate—and the rockets were landing on our ship and setting fire to our hatch top and everything else. And here we were sitting on about 10,000 tons of ammunition!

And then we had been equipped to supply the Sixth Fleet when they made the invasion into Japan—the intended invasion. We had long lines on our winches, runners and everything, so we could transfer ammunition at sea to the ships. We made one trip up there, and then we came back to Leyte Gulf again, and then Japan surrendered.

At that time we were alongside of a Navy ammunition ship, and we were taking some of their cargo aboard our ship. And they did the same thing with the pyrotechnic flares and everything, and it was quite scary then because the hatches were open. Of course, nobody realized it, that we were still operating. But we got through that all right, and then we laid there for almost three months because we had a full load of ammunition and nobody needed any ammunition anymore! And finally they decided for us to come back home to San Francisco and discharge the ammunition at Port Chicago. So we was up there about six weeks discharging the ammunition.

And then the ship went around to Baltimore to take materiel and supplies out to—wherever. The company called me back again to take a motor ship out to run coast-wise.

And I was on that ship, a little, small diesel ship. It was good for the "steam schooner" trade. The only problem was, it couldn't carry enough cargo, so they turned that ship back in and took a Liberty ship. And everybody said a Liberty ship was too big to be a "steam schooner" to get in and out of a small port. But we had an old "steam schooner" skipper, and they got it in and out and everything. And I was on that ship—the *James Lick*—for 9 years.[16]

*After signing off the* James Lick, *his seventh Liberty Ship, Morgan went ashore as port engineer for Pacific Micronesian Line. Concurrently, he served as non-exclusive surveyor for the American Bureau of Shipping, and as correspondent for U.S. Salvage and Lloyd's Register. In 1962, he returned to sailing as chief engineer for Pacific Steam Navigation System, then later as first assistant and chief of six American President Lines (APL) vessels—bringing the total of U.S. Merchant Marine ships on which he served to 36. Retiring from the sea in 1968, Morgan continued working for APL, as senior port engineer, based in California with travel by plane to the U.S. east coast, Central America, Africa and the Orient. In 1976, he began independent consulting work as a marine surveyor and port engineer, with assignments including damage surveys for Bureau Veritas and Norske Veritas, reefer evaluation studies, vessel lay-up and transfer, and his first historic preservation project—reconstruction of the paddle wheel of the 1926* Delta Queen, *operating on the Mississippi and Ohio rivers. Next came mechanical restoration of the SS Jeremiah O'Brien (National Liberty Ship Memorial, San Francisco). Then, with the* Jeremiah *on line, Morgan and his black gang reactivated the 1907 steam tug* Hercules—*one of the National Park Service's fleet of historic vessels, in what is now S.F. Maritime National Historical Park. Morgan died at 83 in 1997 and* Hercules *reverted to inactive status in 1999, but that may change. Morgan's widow Joanie is aiming to bring the tug back to life for the second time—a goal now enthusiastically pursued by* Hercules' *current black gang.*

CHAPTER 15

# Dennis A. Roland: A Prisoner of the Japanese

*Dennis Aloysius Roland was born in New York in 1908 and lived initially on the lower west side of Manhattan in the Greenwich Village area.*[1] *He developed an interest in going to sea while watching ships move along the East River. In 1928, he shipped out for the first time as deck cadet in SS* Santa Louisa, *then shipped out regularly in the 1930s as OS, AB and bosun. At the time of the attack on Pearl Harbor he was in Calcutta, India, as third mate in MV* Excellency. *After returning to Boston, the ship was renamed* Sawokla, *and Roland shipped out in her again, in June 1942, as second mate.*[2] *In November, 11 days out of Colombo, bound for Cape Town, South Africa, with a cargo of jute, they encountered the German commerce raider* Michel.[3]

### "We're going over the side tonight, fellas!"

We were riding blacked out, and the Old Man had left orders on the bridge: "If you should spot a ship coming your way on a collision course, you turn on your running lights." So this is just what the junior third mate on watch did. He turned the running lights on, and the German raider couldn't understand it. Of course, he placed his shots right on the bridge.

At that time, as second mate, I had left the bridge and spent a few minutes up there while the other fellow got his eyes accustomed to the darkness. I was off watch then. This young Stanley, by the way, had been a maritime cadet, and this was his first trip on his license. I wasn't gonna go out on that ship at that time because I didn't particularly like the Old

Dennis Roland testifies at a congressional hearing held on Liberty ship *John W. Brown*, then a school ship in New York, in support of transfer of the ship from government to private control for development as Merchant Marine and Armed Guard museum, 1983 (photograph by Michael Gillen).

Man.[4] [But] he begged me to stay [since] I had made a couple of trips with him while he was cadet. We got along nicely although I was 10 years older than he. When he came to relieve me on the bridge—I had the four to eight watch—he came up and got his eyes accustomed to the darkness, and I told him, explained certain things to him, what he should do, and it was somewhere around maybe about 20 minutes after eight that I left him. I went below to see the chief mate. The chief mate had been suffering from an eye condition—I think it was glaucoma—ever since we left the Persian Gulf.[5] The doctors in the Persian Gulf, in Colombo and Calcutta couldn't help him, so now he had to be kept in total darkness. So each day I used to go down to see him, and I'd say, "This is what went on during the day."

The gunnery officer was a [lieutenant] j.g.—a helluva nice guy out of Westport, Connecticut—Lloyd Livingston George. And he was a rather tall fellow, and I was short: 5'3½".

At about that time we heard one bell strike, which could mean ship's time—8:30—or it could mean a ship sighted on the starboard side. I said to the mate, "Well, there's one bell. I'm tired, I think I'm gonna take a shower and hit the rack." And just as I was about to leave, Lt. George came in the room and said, "Rollie, did you hear that?"

I said, "Yeah, Lloyd, I think it's just 8:30, and I'm tired." I was generally up around three in the morning.

So I stepped out into the passageway where we had a dim light, and looked at my watch and saw that it was 8:35. And I said, "My god, my watch can't be off that much." I left George. He went up the inside passageway to go up to the bridge, and I had taken a couple of steps when suddenly the ship shook as if we had run aground. And the passageway was then filled with a lot of dust and haze.

I hardly took another step when there was another, and another, followed one right after the other. And I looked over at my room and we already had about six inches of water in it, and we had a port list. So I reached in and I saw—I wasn't married then, by the way—I saw my girl's picture smashed, laying down on the deck, and everything was a shambles. My nice clean bunk was a mess. And so I took my helmet and my going-over-the-side kit, and I came out of the room.[6] I was in a complete set of whites, with choker collar and everything else. And I was wearing a helmet.

So now, I left the starboard side and I crossed over to the port side—there's a passageway just forward. And I met some of the men. I [had] tried to get up to the bridge to see if I could help Stanley out, but everything was torn away. I got as far as one deck up, which was the Old Man's quarters, and I noticed a bunch of these tracer bullets—they looked like fireflies—zipping all over the place. I wasn't crawling or anything—it wasn't in me to crawl, I don't know why—[and] I thought to myself, "Look at all these fireflies and if I go in there I'm gonna get hit."

And everything was in a shambles so I decided to go down again, on the main deck, and went across, and that's when I met some of the lads. And they said, "What's going on?" In the meantime this German raider was still pounding the hell out of us. So I said, "Well, fellas, it looks like we're gonna go over the side tonight."

If I recall correctly we had a fairly rough sea with a—There was more than whitecaps. Visibility was fairly good, but there was no moon out. No moon out.

I said, "Let's get up on the boat deck and see what we can do." Well, my boat station was on the starboard side, but when we got there the ship had a terrific port list and the whole boat deck appeared to be ablaze. And I couldn't actually cross over to the starboard side. With a port list you couldn't very well launch your lifeboats on the starboard side because they'd be right alongside the ship. But on the port side the #2 and #4 boats were still frapped in and right behind—maybe a couple of feet away—huge flames: this fellow was still pounding us.

And I said to the fellas, "We'll get #4 over." But I took another look and saw that #4 was cut in half and swinging at the davits. The only one that seemed to be OK was the #2 boat. So I said to one of the fellas, "All right, you get down and start lowering away." We tripped the pelican hooks and the boat swung out. Now all we had to do was start lowering away. Well one of the fellas lowered away on one end, and I lowered away on the other end when the boat got hung up—it got hung up on the ship: the ship now was not only listing, but rolling in the sea. And we got hung up on the side of the ship that had these jagged holes in [it]. So we got down a ways, and I said to one of the fellas, "All right, we'll clamber down on the [rope] falls." So as we were going over the side, there was an ordinary seaman on my watch, and I said to [him], "Ivan, cut those lines!"

He said, "All right, Mr. Roland." And I wrapped my legs around the thwarts and held him by the legs while he cut the falls with his knife. And when he finally got through, we flopped into the water. My next order was, "Well, who's all here?" And he said, "The chief mate is here." And I said, "Well, how the hell did he get out?"

And I started checking heads, and Stanley Wilner was in the boat [which] I didn't know, with all the smoke and excitement and noise, and—there was seven of us there. So I said, "Well, all right, we're all here." And we were free now of the ship.

The ship—The screw was still turning, the screw was still moving since it was still moving and nobody didn't shut it down. And we passed closely to the screw, under the counter, and as we passed under the counter I could see tracer bullets coming our way. So I yelled for everybody to duck. You could see these tracers bullets headed right for you. So when we ducked underneath the waves and came up again there was no more shooting at us. But we looked around and our boat had now filled with water and was disappearing from underneath our feet. Now you say, "How could it be [because] you had air tanks?" But, yes, we had air tanks which were filled with kapok to prevent air escaping in case we did get [hit] but we were so riddled that the extra metal straps that they put on the air tanks had all been shot away.

So we broke out some oars, but between this fella shootin' and all the other excitement the boat was gone in a few seconds. So now there was seven of us with our life jackets on, clinging on to oars, floating around, and that was the end of everything. And we're riding up and down of these waves and we see this flotsam going by [and we're] trying to catch something, but we don't have anything but the two oars and we're hanging on to each other. And a couple of days before that we had caught some huge shark, so now we were afraid in a way that there would be sharks about.

But as we're floatin' around I've still got my set of whites on. I lost my helmet [but] I got my white shoes on and all, and somebody said, "Let's kick our shoes off." I think it might have been Stanley. I said, "No, Stanley, if we're gonna die, let's die with our shoes on. What the hell's the difference?" It's crazy things—there's no heroics, believe you me.

I said to Stanley, "Stanley, pinch me."

He said, "What for?"

I said, "Well, I want to know if this is a nightmare or not."

So I think somebody else said, "Well what do you want to get pinched for?"

And I said, "Well, it's as simple as that."

And we're floatin' around out there, and I'm lookin' up at the sky, and I see Sirius up there, I see the stars up there, and I'm figuring out what time it is in New York. And I thought, "Well, now, it's Sunday in New York, and pretty soon we'll be dead, and I wonder if they know about it. And I'll know if there's a heaven and a hell. But I can swear on any stack of Bibles—whatever you want—that I was not excited. Maybe I was just too stupid to be excited. I did find out later [that] I was banged up: I still carry shrapnel in my knees which causes me a little bit of discomfort; they could never get it out.

Now we're floatin' around in this heavy sea. We're up on top of the waves and down in the trough, and suddenly we spot an object. There was no moon out but you could see the line of demarcation between the sea and the sky. And off on the horizon we spot an object: first it's on one side, and [then] it's on another. It turned out to be the German raider on a zigzag course.

I don't recall how many hours we were in the water, but I will say maybe four hours or so. In my particular case—speaking for myself—I felt like someone had taken hot pepper and thrown it in my eyes. That they had gotten a wood rasp and ran it up and down the inside of my throat. And I was pretty uncomfortable, in other words. And then of course I had all these wounds. I had my hand ripped open, which I didn't realize at the time. But these were minor things compared to what others had.

One fella I recall—Ruiz—he had been sitting aft. He had been cut open: his belly was wide open [and] his guts were sticking out, and he said he was just waiting to die. And he was holding his guts in with his arms. But apparently he was picked up.[7]

At about the same time we spotted one of our Navy donut rafts. We managed to grab that. There was nobody in it so the seven of us got on to it. And I was hangin' on the outside, and [moved] the chief mate inside. And as the raider came alongside close to us I said to the fellas, "Let's all yell for help in unison." So we shouted for help in unison. But of course he didn't hear us because we were on his weather side. He maneuvered and placed us on his weather side so we drifted up against two Jacob's ladders that he had over there. Now these Jacob's ladders are going up and down—the ship is stopped, and they're going up and down—and the Germans were shouting for us to come up in a hurry. The ship was standing still and they were likely to be attacked.

So I started to get the fellas up, and, as I said, the Jacob's ladders were going up and down just like a fast elevator—15, 20 feet at a time. So I got everybody up except one fella, the fella in the raft. It was his first trip to sea, a wiper. So we were the last two there, and I said, "Now, Richie, when that ladder comes you grab that one." And I said, "Keep your eye on that ladder when it comes down the next time."

We still had our life jackets on. So we concentrated, and when I saw my ladder come down where I could grab it, I grabbed it and went up a couple of rungs. By that time I was really tired, you know, having swallowed all that water. My legs were bleeding, my hand was bleeding, but as I say, those things I didn't realize. And when we went up on the next swell, it came down and I hear Richie yelling: he's yelling he's got his foot caught in the mesh. And I'm thinking, "Oh, my god, you're an officer, and you've got to look after the men." So this one time I very reluctantly said, "All right," and I went down a couple of rungs, and I had my leg hooked in between the rungs. And when the raft came up again I let go and dropped in. And that's when Richie said, "I can't get out, Mr. Roland, because my foot's caught in the mesh." The bottom of the raft was a kind of mesh. So both he and I tugged, and in the meantime the ladders had made a couple more turns up and down. And finally I got his leg out, so we managed to free his leg. So I said, "Now Richie, get on that goddamned thing and hang on and climb up."

So when the ladder came down again I made sure he was on it first, then it came down a second time, you know, after I saw he was on the ladder, then I grabbed the ladder, and I said, "I'm not going back in that water anymore." As far as I knew, I was the last one up off the raft. So the next day they did find the first assistant engineer floating around on a mattress. He was lucky to be able to stay afloat on a mattress with that heavy sea running and all of the waves.

But in any case, when I got up on deck and reached the gun'le, the next thing I knew somebody reached over and pulled me aboard like a sack of potatoes and dropped me on the deck. And there I was, flat on my back in a set of whites looking up, and I see these Germans!

So they spoke English fairly well, and they hustled me down to sick bay and patched me up a little, took all of my clothes off and everything. And then they gave me a little bit of a towel, And then I had to go forward—this was aft—and I was given first aid. And I'm laying down on this cold deck when a couple of officers came down and started questioning me. Then they took me up to see the Old Man, Ruckteschell.[8] He was pleasant, nice, and he questioned me and all, and since I was navigating, he said, "Well, you went here, you went there...." And I said, "Well if you know so goddamned much what the hell we did, why bother me?" At that time, I wasn't being nasty, I was just tired and disgusted: I didn't give a damn, let's put it that way.

So now we're on the raider, and the raider's underway, and they put the officers in one compartment, and the unlicensed personnel, not including the gun crew, in another. So the [chief] mate was aboard and he was taken to sick bay to take care of his eyes. And Stanley Wilner—he had gotten married just before we left New York—he had a big chunk of meat the size of your fist taken out from the inside of his thigh—believe it or not—and his testicles were up about the size of a large grapefruit. They treated him, and now if you ever see him—if he ever shows you where he was hit, I think it might have been a .50-caliber bullet, whatever it was, it just took this piece of flesh right out—they filled it up where it's nice and smooth. And they also fixed the mate's eyes, which they couldn't do in Colombo, they couldn't do in the Persian Gulf, and couldn't do in Calcutta. We were about 10 weeks aboard, give or take, but before we got off the ship he could see; he was well.[9] You've gotta give the Germans credit for that.

So I'm the senior officer who's ambulatory, and I was made liaison officer. Later on they hit two other ships. They got the *Empire March*, a British ship coming home on its maiden voyage, and all her officers were killed.[10] So I was still liaison officer between the Germans and ourselves.

And then they got the Greek ship *Eugenia Levonis*.[11] They were all drunk on St. Nicholas Day. And they had some beautiful mahogany clinker boats which the Germans took aboard. And the clinker boats had whiskey aboard: Scotch whiskey. Those fellows were loaded! But the captain came aboard, he was about my size. And the Germans were methodical: they saluted [him] and told the captain, "You will have to be liaison officer in charge of all hands." And he pleaded that he was sick, and so forth, and so the German came to me and said would I mind continuing. What could I say?

Now to keep law and order—Don't forget when you've got a lot of people cooped up and not anything to do, I had to have a kangaroo court to keep law and order. And it was either that, or I told 'em, "Look, you're not gonna listen to me, I'll just turn you over to the Germans if I can't control you." I had no real authority except to keep people in line, and try to make 'em understand.

We were aboard on Christmas Day of '42, and the Germans gave us materials to make a Christmas tree. For example they gave us cans to make leaves [and] wire to put through. Well, we made a Christmas tree. They showed us how and then they sprayed it green. And for three days we had a celebration. It was good for us because whatever reefer box they opened up, this is what we ate. For example, at one point we were getting' nothin' but liverwurst; you got maybe an inch and a half of liverwurst or salami.

One time they gave us what they thought was a delicacy: lard, plain lard. And we couldn't eat it. So being liaison officer, every day, twice a day the German officer would come down, and salute, and I'd salute, and he'd say, "Any wishes?" And I would tell him what we needed: if some fella had a toothache, or if we were cold, or one thing or another. And he'd take care of all that sort of stuff. So I explained about the lard, and he was astonished. And he says, "Oh, that's a delicacy amongst the German."

"It may be so, but we're not accustomed to it."

So he changed our diet again.

And before we left the ship I requested a pencil and paper, and I wrote a letter of thanks to the captain and the crew for their treatment and so forth, and I passed it around—and as far as I knew everybody signed it—and turned it over to the captain. Of course, we knew we were getting off soon. And he said he regretted having to turn us over to the Japanese. Of course, although they were allies, apparently they didn't see eye to eye, you know.

About the third of February, since the ship could not get through the Atlantic blockade, the ship was ordered to Japan [via] Singapore, and I figured, oh, Jesus, I'd rather be in a hot climate than a cold climate. So we heard all the rumors, and they used to put out communiqués every day. So in any case when they learned that they couldn't get home, oh, they were pretty well upset, you know, they had the same problems as we had: "Gee, I hope my wife is safe, I hope my sister is safe." It's the same problem 'cause you know we were bombing the hell out of them.

So they were making us little packets of chocolate, and at Christmas they gave us a couple bottles of Beck's beer. Some chocolate balls and chocolate bars they got off some Dutch ship, whiskey—a bottle of whiskey, for so many people, you know—and they treated us pretty well. At times we got potatoes which we never got before because they didn't have sufficient fresh potatoes to feed their own crew. But we got a very skimpy diet. It was enough to keep us going, I guess, because my weight dropped like everybody else's—considerably.

But in any case when they learned they weren't going home and we had to go to Singapore they were pretty well upset. So the ship turned around and eventually we got to a place called Tanjung Priok in the Dutch East Indies. Well, I'd been out there many a time, and so one of the officers said, "Do you know where we are?" I said, "Yes, this is Tanjung Priok" 'cause I knew it. But the Japanese had given it a different name.[12]

And while we were there—we spent a couple of days—a couple more raiders came in. And later on, when they wouldn't accept us ashore in Tanjung Priok, the ship turned around and went up to Singapore, where we were released.

So when we were marched off the ship, and I was still in charge as the liaison officer, and I was introduced to a Japanese officer, and he said to me, "Ah, pretty soon you will all be going home—you'll be repatriated—and you'll get mail and packages." And I said, "That's a pretty nice thing to hear." [Laughing] We never *were* repatriated. And later on we were absorbed into the [prisoner of war] ranks of the British, Dutch, and Australian troops.

And about five days after they [chief mate and unlicensed personnel] left [for Japan] we became—about five of us Merchant Marine officers, and a couple from some other ship—made up into what the British call "H Force" to go and work on the Burma-Siam railroad—they called it the "railroad of death." And this is where I worked on the River Kwai Bridge.

SS *Sawokla*, inbound, 19 June 1942, about five months before her fateful encounter with the German commerce raider *Michel* in the Indian Ocean (Mariners' Museum, Newport News, Virginia).

*After being put ashore in Singapore with other prisoners held for more than two months on the German commerce raider Michel, Dennis Roland then became a prisoner of the Japanese for the next two and a half years until his release in September 1945. For much of that time he would be involved in forced labor on the infamous Burma-Siam "death railway" and what would become known as the River Kwai Bridge.*[13]

## A Prisoner of the Japanese

I was thrown in with a couple of other lads, and then we went up to work on the death railway. And we worked on that for a while.

We lived in huts similar to that [depicted in movie]: just made of bamboo slats, and we had about 20 inches of space. And the bamboo used to be about that thick and round except they would split it into four. And every so often there's a ridge—my god, that ridge would dig right into you if you tried to lay on that. But that's the way it worked.

We were given something like seven ounces of rice a day—and whatever you could scrounge. The Japanese had very little [due to] their lines of communication. I'm not making excuses for them, but let's look at the facts, and their treatment—they treated their soldiers pretty rough. I've seen a sergeant take the butt of his rifle and smash a corporal right in the face with it; you know, no joking around just really gave the butt of the rifle [and] opened up his face. And when I think of General [George] Patton, [who] had to make a public apology for slapping a soldier, it goes against my grain.

But up in the jungle at one time Stanley and I—it just goes to show you how different people were—Stanley and I were sittin' in this jungle path [for] what they called a *yazmae*—a rest—for a couple of seconds, and suddenly we're just squatting there in the dirt and looked up and there's a Japanese soldier, with his gun, bayonet and so forth, and he said to us—we didn't get up—*okayga* meaning "are you all right?" So without saying much more he reached inside his shirt and pulled out a salted fish. Now I don't know where he got it from—it might have been his rations— and he handed it to us. And we thanked him, saying, *arigato*—thank you— and he left. Now that was a deed of kindness.

So we had a little clearing in the jungle—maybe about the size of this room—and the Catholic priests, they would go ahead and say mass, during the time that we had a few moments. You would be attending mass, and who would be right alongside of you would be a Japanese soldier in full regalia. And I got to thinking, "Now who is God going to listen to: *him* or *me*?" See, these are the crazy thoughts that go through my head.

You know, the Japanese, if you had a ring on, for example, they wanted to buy it. They would never take anything. But if they pestered you, [you] might say in pidgin English, "My wife gave it to me as a present," and they wouldn't bother you anymore.

But this is another reason why—it's really my sense of humor—Stanley's sense of humor is really what kept us going. Because—I've had malaria pretty badly—I got it working on the River Kwai Bridge, climbing the one, like you saw in the movie.[14] There were two of them: there's a metal one too. And I used to go up there.

I never used to believe in hypnosis, until I learned the hard way. The Dutch were pretty good at hypnotizing people, and there were a lot of people with jungle ulcers. In other words, the—sores that would [go] right down to the bone. And the doctors—the medicos—they had nothing to work with, believe you me. It's like saying work on a car and you don't have a wrench or screwdriver. How are you gonna do it?

They would scrape right down to the bone and put maggots in there. The maggots would eat the dead flesh. Of course the pain was excruciating [but] you either go one way or the other. So they hypnotized, as simple as that. That's the only thing: they had crude instruments. The Japanese didn't have anything themselves.

I was with a group of three British officers, and we carried a Japanese soldier over some jungle path [to an aid station] about five miles away. He had a broken appendix, I think, and the poor devil, slippin' and slidin' in the mud, you know, and we dumped him a couple of times—not intentionally because we were falling down—but we learned later on that he died. But it wasn't done intentionally. By that time my weight must've been down to 80, 90 pounds. And when I finally was released I was down to five stone, which is 70 pounds, suffering with malaria and a few other things.

But I and a group of British officers, we were gonna steal a bomber. This was around July the fifth if I recall correctly—that date I recall correctly—'45. And I was arrested by the Kempi—the Japanese secret police—somebody turned me in.[15] And I was taken before some Japanese officer in the presence of some of the British officers who ran the camp. This was back in Shanghai, where we finally came to before we were released. So for two days I was grilled: they wanted to know who [else was involved].

Well, when I first came into the hut I had some things I wasn't supposed to have, but I learned in my travels on the *Steel Navigator*—going around the world—I used to go to the old world theaters in Bali and other places like that and I used to see some of their stage plays. The stage hands would come out in front of the actors, pick up whatever had to be done in the way of changing scenery, make noise, but to the Oriental mind they did not exist since they were not in the play: you obliterated them.

So now, when the Kempi came to arrest me and I had my kit with a lot of things which I wasn't supposed to have—for example, I had knives, and binoculars, and I had the *Asahi Shimbun*, which is actually an English-printed Japanese newspaper. And what I didn't want them to see I would place to one side, what I wanted them to see I would place right before them. Now it's quite obvious that all you had to do was reach over and you could touch that newspaper. But to the Oriental mind I didn't want them to see that, therefore they honor your wishes whatever it was: it didn't exist!

So now I'm up before this Japanese officer who's questioning me who my cohorts were. We were gonna steal this airplane—I knew where [it was]. I had learned, like in the Navy you had one primary job and about a hundred collateral duties. So I had the primary job: I was gonna be the navigator on the plane. We were gonna steal what you call a "Betsy" bomber—twin-engine job—and fly it to Borneo. We had flyers with us, and I was supposed to supply arms and things. Well, I knew where they were, I knew where I could get them.

So when the Japanese officer was questioning me—of course, the British also wanted to know who were the British officers that were involved—of course, they were sort of jeopardizing the camp in a sense. But I had one thought in mind: I can't tell them anything, because if I do, it's like once you tell them one thing and you finally come to the end and you can't tell them anything else. There's the old story about getting the olive out of the bottle: the first olive is hard to get, the rest all come easy until eventually there are no more olives but then somebody will say, "Well, you're holding back, you're not giving us all the information."

And I thought, rather than give them anything, I had to protect myself, protect the other people, and I professed innocence all along the way. So about the second day of this questioning I said to this Japanese officer, "I would like permission to say something." And he said, "All right."

And I leaned my [Army Air Corps] tattoo forward, and I said, "I know, perhaps we all look alike—the British and the Americans—[but] I am not British, I am an American." And I showed him my tattoo. He still thought I was a flyer [who had been] shot down, but I couldn't make him understand [the circumstances of] that. I let the imagination run wild, it didn't bother me none. So I said, "There's one thing I must say, that I regret that I have brought disgrace upon my fellow countrymen." And that goes big with those people. So, I wasn't kiddin' in a way, because here I am on [and] if it wasn't so close to the end of the show, as we say, I may not have been here today, or maybe been beaten up real badly, we don't know. So he glared at me through his glasses, and said to me, "You are an officer and a gentleman, and officers don't lie." And he got up and walked away.

Now, I went back into the camp—after two days—and a couple of days later a British officer sent his aide around and wants to talk with me. So out of respect for him I went over there, and he started questioning me again about who was in on the deal. And I wouldn't tell him, of course; I would be jeopardizing these other people. The British would bring them up on charges after the war is over. So after an hour or so there, and this fellow had become a bit arrogant.

The next day he called for me again, and I went again. This time—he had makeshift chairs, but he didn't ask me to sit, and I didn't volunteer to sit down out of respect for the rank and all—he outranked me. And I was talking, but finally he blurts out, and he says, "Well if you don't tell me" and he's shakin' his swagger stick at me—"if you don't tell me, I'm gonna turn you over to the Japanese."

Well this is when I turned loose four-letter words—and they weren't "love"—and was just—So in any case I told him off in no uncertain terms and said, "If you try and stop me from leaving here—I am not *your* prisoner—and when that meatball [red circle on Japanese flag] comes down from there it's gonna be [replaced by] the American flag, and it's gonna be American newspaper people, and I'm gonna tell them how you threatened my life. And you try and stop me from walking out of here." Boy, I'm tellin' ya, I could've ripped him apart.

When we came down from the jungle, the Japanese were gonna send us on a prison ship to Japan to work up there. But we were in such bad shape that they figured we'd probably die along the way. So they sent other people up who hadn't gone up to work on the railroad.

These fellas asked if I would be their officer representative. So I said yes—what else could I say? So one day they came to me and they said, "Mr. Roland, we understand that those people who didn't go 'up country'"—that's what the British termed working on the railroad—"they sent [notification] postcards home." And they said, "We'd like to send postcards home." So I said, "fine," and I went to the British commandant—the people who run the camp—and I said, "Look, I want to be taken to the Japanese commandant, and I want to get some postcards."

"Oh, we can't do that!" In other words, they didn't want to make waves. Well, after the third attempt, I said to them, "Look fellas, let's put it this way. We're Americans, you sent postcards home, I want you to take me up to see the Japanese commandant, but if you don't, I'm going up myself and you're not gonna stop me!"

So they brought me up there before the Japanese officer again, and he looked at me and smiled and said, "Ah, so." And [I said through] the interpreter, "We work with the IJA [Imperial Japanese Army], we built your railroad, we built your bridges, and all we're asking for is a postcard to send home like everybody else did." He said, "All right, you'll get postcards."

We had something like five days, and 24 words to put on it, so they issued pencils, [and] everybody is happy. And what should I put on it, what words weigh more—like on a telegram, to cut down expense? Well, I didn't know if my mother was alive or dead, and I didn't want to worry her. Before I left [the States] I said, "Don't say anything, I don't know when I'm coming back." I told Margaret, my wife—well, we weren't married—I said, "We can't get too serious because I'm going out to the war zone, and I don't know when I'll be back, we don't know." I said, "We'll see what happens."

But in any case, the 24 words. I got my original [post]card at home, and it was sent out by Radio Tokyo, something like—they got the message straight—something like 50 words, and it ended by saying, "Cheerio and God bless you from Tokyo." Now, after I came home, my wife, [she] had been making novenas [and] praying for me.[16] And I was still sick. I was down to about 70 pounds [and] came home to find out I'm legally dead, [the] government issued death certificates, paid insurance, and I had no legal home: my mother had died in a fire. And my head was as big as a pumpkin. And I decided, well, the devil didn't want me, and she wanted me, so we got married. And we're still fightin' to this day! But, I mean, we take care of each other.

*Roland was involved for many years after the war in efforts to seek recognition and veterans benefits for merchant seamen. This included his support of Project Liberty Ship which has successfully restored the SS* John W. Brown *as an operational memorial museum. Roland returned to Burma in 1976 as part of a multi-national reconciliation effort to honor those who had worked, as prisoners of war, on the Burma-Siam "Death Railway" and bridge. He died in New York, at 76, in 1984, and his ashes were scattered on the sea.*

CHAPTER 16

# William J. Shearer: "She was there, and all of a sudden it wasn't"

*William J. Shearer was born in 1919, and first went to sea in 1937 as ordinary seaman in SS* Conoyes. *A longtime resident of Cumberland, Maryland, he upgraded through unlicensed and licensed ratings and was acting chief mate in SS* Wacosta, *which joined Convoy PQ-18 to North Russia in September 1942. His ship was in station close to the ammunition-laden SS Mary Luckenbach when that ship was torpedoed.*[1]

The *Mary Luckenbach* was ahead of us in convoy. [Its] cargo was ammo. When she was hit the force of the blast broke windows in [our] wheelhouse.[2] The only thing I can say is, she was there, and all of a sudden it wasn't. It got hit, and when she got hit I was standing on the starboard side of the wing of the bridge. It knocked me down, and the other people that were there with me. She blew a hole in the ocean that to me was, you know, a *big* one, like it would take a long time for 'em to fill up that gap from the intense explosion. I remember just little flakes of paper coming down from the atmosphere afterwards. There was *nothing* [remaining].

And we just—I don't know, moments after that we got hit.[3] The sea was smooth, and the visibility was good. Torpedo bombers came in—it looked just like a swarm of bees—and they were very low: only approximately 100, 150 feet above the water. We all probably spotted them simultaneously, myself, the captain, gunnery officer, and deck cadet, who at that time was Tyson, Victor E. Tyson.[4] They were off on the starboard bow, roughly 35, 40 degrees—they were not four points.

And [we] only had two 30-caliber machine guns, right on the wing of the bridge, and an old World War I [deck] gun on the stern. It was maybe a 5" or something; it didn't elevate too high. And that was it. But when we left, why, we thought we were in pretty good shape.

Our [convoy position] number was 83, I believe. I think there were two columns to our right, to our starboard. And we were a little bit upset because the *Mary Luckenbach* was behind us, and they changed position with us—the commodore changed the positions. She was very erratic, and we really didn't like that. But that's what happened.[5]

We were all ready. I think my reaction and everybody else's was, "What's going to happen?" There was complete silence; there wasn't anything said, as I remember. We were just waitin' to see what was going to happen. We had small arms ammunition in #1 and #2 holds. In that type of ship in those days #3 hatch was midships. And I believe that there was a dive-bomber that dropped a bomb up in there, but the ammunition didn't explode. And I don't know why, and I guess nobody else knows.

We were hit on the starboard side—around #1 or two hatch—and she took a quick list to starboard. A lot of spraying came up on the bridge. And when we were abandoning ship all kinds of shells were being fired over the ship, going into the superstructure. They [other ships] were firing at the torpedo planes. We were getting hit in the midship house, in the bridge. And there was .50-calibers ripping the tarpaulin [covering] of number three hatch. But nobody got hit.

I launched #2 boat, which was on the port side. At that time the after boats—there was a break there after #3 hatch—they were on the boat deck aft. I don't remember how many men [but] I think there was about 18 or 19 men in my boat. And there was one man there, his name was Peterson; he was an able-bodied seaman. He had his arm between the lifeboat and the ship's hull, and I kept hollering to him, "Peterson, pull your arm in!" He didn't answer me.

And we drifted clear of the stern. He had a hold of one of the mess boys—a black boy—and he had blood coming

William J. Shearer, November 1942, photographer unknown (W.J. Shearer).

*Top:* Prewar photograph of SS *Wacosta*, Weber River, en route to Bremen, Germany, 17 March 1939 (W.J. Shearer). *Bottom:* Photograph by unknown merchant seaman of SS *Mary Luckenbach* at the moment of explosion in Convoy PQ-18 (War Shipping Administration).

out of his ears, and nose, and eyes. He—after we were picked up—recovered. But when I was hollering to him he just didn't answer me; he just looked at me with a blank expression.

We all made it. The only one that I remember that was hurt was this mess boy. And the captain for some reason or other, he was the last one, and he had to jump overboard. And they threw him a heaving line and pulled him aboard one of the rescue vessels. His name was Jensen.[6]

We were rescued, I would say, within a half hour. And then we were later transferred to the antiaircraft cruiser *Scylla*.[7] They were really great to us. And we transferred at about 15 knots, jumped from one deck to the other, and if you missed—you knew what [would] happen. If you missed—I wouldn't be here, and anybody else that missed wouldn't be here. That's what we did: we jumped. They banged these two vessels together, and we went from this rescue vessel, which was a minesweeper, over onto the quarterdeck of the *Scylla*.

The *Scylla* turned around and brought us back and we were put ashore at Scapa Flow.[8] Well, the town was named Thurso. And from there we went to Glasgow by train at nighttime. Cold. We were glad when we got there. And they put us up in the Beresford Hotel.

And we came back on the *Queen Mary*, [which], at that time, her bow had about 90 feet of damage. She [had] left England to come back to the States, but this cruiser was escorting the *Queen Mary* and went across her bow, and the *Queen Mary* hit her and sunk her.[9] Tore up about 90 feet of the bow. And she came back into Greenock [Scotland] there, and that's when we boarded her and came back. And we went into Boston 'cause they had—I believe at that time it was the only yard here that could handle her, the repairs.

And this is another thing I'll never understand: that nobody was lost on our ship.[10]

*Shearer served as a licensed Merchant Marine officer for the duration of the war, obtained his master's license, and continued to ship out well into the postwar period, retiring in 1970. He passed away in Cumberland, Maryland, at 72, in 1992.*

CHAPTER 17

# Henrik E. "Hank" Sievers: Cargo for Pearl and Nawiliwili

*Henrik E. "Hank" Sievers was born in Marin County, California, in 1911. He took to the saltwater at an early age, sailing on San Pedro Bay. He joined the U.S. Naval Reserve at the age of 17 and received training during summer cruises on World War I–vintage four-stack destroyers. He first shipped out in the Merchant Marine in SS* President Jefferson, *American Mail Line, out of Seattle, in 1930. Working his way up through unlicensed ratings to quartermaster, Sievers then earned a third mate's license in 1934, shipping with Dollar Steamship Lines, and then Standard Oil Company of California. He was chief mate in the tanker* W.S. Miller *when word was received of the Japanese attack on Pearl Harbor.*[1]

I think we were expecting war, 'cause you had Marine [Corps] guards in the engine room and on the bridge going through the Panama Canal at that time; it started in around '40.

And we ran from Aruba to Constable Hook, which is in New York—right across from Staten Island—[New] Jersey—with gasoline. And we'd pump it right across the dock into British tankers, and that eliminated the British having to go to the Caribbean for the aviation gas or what else they needed. So I think we were a little more than neutral at that time. And we were getting a 25 percent war bonus before December 7, 1941. And this kept up for some time.

Finally, we were sent from Aruba too [and] were supposed to make three trips to Santos, Brazil, and Rio [de Janeiro]. And we were taking kerosene from Aruba to Brazil, which was Lend Lease or some kind of a [President] Roosevelt donation to the Brazilian government. They had trouble destroying the coffee, which was to maintain the price. It was like killin' little pigs to keep up the price of pork; they were doing that, too, at that time.

But anyway, Brazil was an ally of ours and gave us bases when we needed them down there, for watching the South Atlantic, and so on, 'cause there was sinkings every day on the north coast of South America, and up the East Coast.

On December seventh we were in one of these kerosene loads across the equator southbound. After that trip we were supposed to go north of [Cape] Hatteras from Aruba, again on this British gasoline deal. But if we had, I wouldn't be here now.

The captain got a wire from the U.S. government, and there was a sealed envelope in the safe, and that told him to proceed to his destination, which was Santos [Brazil]. And then at Santos—that's near São Paulo, a big coffee port—and the kerosene as I said was to burn coffee with. I guess that ship carried 75,000 barrels, I don't remember now.

I had a "Pilot" shortwave radio I always carried with me, and I heard the broadcast on German radio about the next morning, and they named all the ships in Pearl Harbor that were sunk, which is news we didn't get until weeks later when we got to the United States.

[We] discharged in Santos, and instead of going north to Hatteras the ship was rerouted on the way home through the Canal again, and into Los Angeles, and we immediately loaded aviation gasoline—in about 12 hours—for Pearl Harbor. And [we] were the first [merchant] ship in Pearl after the event.

The ship didn't have any guns on it, no gun crew, but they had a convoy and they had some destroyers [for escorts]. [We] worked our way to Pearl, and we took part load to Pearl and the other part to Nawiliwili in Kauai.[2]

There were some [storage] tanks in Nawiliwili—up on the hill—that had been shelled by Japanese submarines. And these tanks had been repaired, and we brought the first gasoline into Nawiliwili around the first of the year. And between Pearl Harbor and Nawiliwili we

**Captain Henrik Sievers, San Francisco, May 1982 (photograph by Michael Gillen).**

Prewar photograph of tanker SS *W.S. Miller*, unarmed and with the American flag painted on the side for identification as noncombatant, 3 November 1941 (U.S. Coast Guard/Mariners' Museum, Newport News, Virginia).

had four destroyers—one on each bow—and those guys were trigger-happy with depth charges: every time they heard a porpoise or a whale they fired depth charges that cracked the toilet bowls and sinks and different things on the ship. And I gave up smoking permanently at that time, because of the gas.

And after that we came back from the Hawaiian trip, and back on the [West] Coast. And we had convoys on the coast. They didn't put guns on the [W.S.] Miller for about six months.

And I stayed with the Standard Oil tankers pretty much until 1943 [when] I went captain of a Liberty ship operated by the Alaska Transportation Company.[3]

*Captain Sievers served in command of five Liberty ships, and one Victory ship, from March 1943 until the end of the war. These were, with Alaska Transportation Company, the* Hall J. Kelley, Sacajawea *(a troopship operating in the Pacific),* Henry M. Stephens, *and, with Olympic Steamship Company, the* Yale Victory *and* Josiah Royce. *He continued to ship out as Ship Master, mostly with American President Lines, until 1974. He passed away in San Francisco, at 79, in 1990.*

CHAPTER 18

# Robert B. Smolen: "Captain, they're gonna machine-gun us!"

*Robert B. Smolen was born in New York in 1921, and was working as a machinist there at the time of the attack on Pearl Harbor. He entered the U.S. Merchant Marine Academy in Kings Point, New York, received some basic engineering instruction, and shipped out as engine cadet less than three months later in March 1942 in the Liberty ship* Daniel P. Morgan *for the North Russia run. The ship departed from Columbia, North Carolina, proceeded alone to New York, then in convoy to Halifax, Nova Scotia. From there the* Daniel Morgan *proceeded in another convoy to Reykjavik, Iceland, where it remained at anchor through May, finally departing for Russia in the ill-fated Convoy PQ-17 on 28 June. This voyage was his first experience at sea as a merchant seaman.*[1]

While we were [proceeding] in convoy—this was probably July second or third—we started getting airplane attacks—torpedo bombers, high level bombers, and dive bombers. We were at battle stations, [and] my station was up on the 3"/50 antiaircraft gun, on the bow, loading. Somebody handed it [shell] up, and as a loader I shoved it in the breech. And we had two fifties on the flying bridge, and a 4"/58 back aft.

We didn't do much sleeping for about five days, I can tell you that. We were cooking continuously, either under attack or getting ready for attack. Then they took all of the big [escort] ships away, supposedly to tangle with the German fleet that came out. This destroyer came around and told us all to scatter and proceed to our destination. So we scattered, and ended up sailing with the *Fairfield City*, an old freighter. About 35 dive-bombers started working us over and she got hit first.[2]

They'd come in waves and start to peel off. They made—I don't know how many direct hits on her, but they had to take to the lifeboats. The ship sank. Our captain thought about picking them up but they didn't want any part of us: they told us to go on. I don't think we'd have been able to pick them up anyway because we were under attack as well and, you know, you wanted to keep moving so that you didn't get hit.

We did shoot down a few planes. They'd come in low over the water and they weren't hard to pick up. Our gunnery officer claimed we shot down two or three.[3] I did see one get hit. I had been assisting on the forward gun and went aft to get coffee or something for the gun crew. I was amidships when I saw him go by, and our 3"/50 hit him.

The first thing that went on our ship was the steering: near misses from the bombs had knocked it out. Then we took a torpedo from a sub. I was midships when it hit just forward of #3 [cargo hatch]. We pretty much knew we were going to be sunk, and we were ready. In fact, we had all the gear in the lifeboats, and we got off in the boats pretty well.

We did lose a couple people, caught between the boat and the ship as we lowered the boat. They disappeared. They just—that was it. We may have lost one or two more in the ice-cold waters.[4] The water was about 29 degrees. I was lucky enough to get off in a boat.

We were in the boat when the ship went down. She went down stern first, and as she went under the forward gun went off. Then the sub came in alongside—a big, white sub with a red dragon painted on the conning tower.[5] One of the fellows in the lifeboat noticed one of the Germans had something in his hand, and he said, "Captain, they're gonna machine-gun us!" As it was, it turned out to be a camera, and everybody was greatly relieved. They were just taking pictures of us.

The skipper of the submarine was a young guy—maybe 28—with red hair and a beard. He wanted to know what the cargo was we had, and the Old Man just said something like "general cargo." The sub skipper just laughed; he knew what the cargo was. But he was very nice, and gave us a course to land.[6]

We had one motorboat, and we wound up with that pulling the other boats. And I guess we were in the water 10 or 12 hours. This was in the White Sea, now. Then a Russian tanker picked us up—the *Donbass*, I think it was—a big Russian tanker.[7] Then the German planes came out and started going after us on the tanker. But we made It into the Russian naval base at Molotovsk. We were taken off the tanker and put on a small boat that took us down river to Archangel.

Archangel was really just an outpost, and it was pretty crude living.

We were in the hospital, I guess, about two or three weeks. We slept on straw mattresses, I remember that. It was a real hard bunk. We'd get breakfast probably around 10 or 11 o'clock in the morning: it was mush, some kind of mush. And they gave us bread and whatever they had to eat. If we were lucky and didn't have an air raid, we'd eat. If we had an air raid, we didn't eat. That's the way it worked.

I lost about 40 pounds over three months. Let's see: we were hit on the 5th of July, and we didn't get out of there—I guess it was late in September. They didn't send any more convoys up there after ours for about three months. Actually, the next one they sent up was the one we met up near Bear Island. We were on our way back and we passed them.[8]

Anyway, about a week after we moved out of the hospital they moved us into the Intourist Hotel, which was a little bit better. There were, I believe, four of us in a room. The rooms weren't very big. And as I said, we had one meal a day that we were pretty sure of. Once in a while we'd get this deer meat. That was a delicacy: it was a treat.

We were lucky in the evening if we didn't get an air raid, but most nights we had one. You'd just find some place, under an arch, you know, somewhere low in a building. They didn't hit the hotel but they did hit the hospital the week after we got out of there.

They tried to entertain us. We used to have dances and things. And

**A merchant ship, probably from Convoy PQ-17, at the moment a torpedo detonates after being dropped from a German Heinkel torpedo-bomber off the North Cape (U.S. Coast Guard).**

then they even had classes where they taught you a little bit of Russian during the day. But it was pretty dull. They also had a pretty nice beach where we spent most of our time. As I said, it really was an outpost and there wasn't much to see; you could see it all in a day. It was pretty crude, and most of the houses were wooden. You know, nothing was really permanent. Once in a while we'd see a movie, an American movie. I think they showed it in an old schoolhouse, if I remember correctly. I remember seeing Jimmy Cagney in *The Oklahoma Kid* once. That was really a treat.

You weren't allowed out after certain hours because they were afraid of paratroopers. They had a curfew at night, and they were pretty strict about it. Christ, I can recall we were out one evening on the outskirts of town and there was an air raid, and we didn't get back in time. The secret police picked us up and took us down to the station and we had a time before we got out of there. They finally realized that we were survivors.

We had a naval attaché up there at the time, a commander.[9] That was where we got our news, but there was very little of it. They said they wouldn't even try to get us back until they felt it was safer. But we finally got word from the commander, and I think we had about a day's notice. I guess it was the end of September when we left on the *West Nilus*, an old West Coast ship. It was one of the ones that had made it through. They didn't have much to eat on that ship either. I think they had macaroni and cheese, and that was it. That's what we had for breakfast, lunch and dinner: macaroni and cheese.

We went into—not too far up from Glasgow [Scotland]. The town we wound up at was Hamilton. They had a big—really, a survivors camp—and they had these big, huge partitions up, where they had bunks. They gave us plenty of food, and they opened up the town for us; anything we wanted, we got. But it was great, and we were there for a couple of weeks. And then we came back on the *Queen Mary*, probably in October, to Boston.

*Smolen returned to the Merchant Marine Academy soon after this and shipped out again, as engine cadet in the SS* African Dawn, *a C-2 type cargo ship. After a lengthy voyage to Liverpool, England, back to New York, and then to South America and South Africa, he returned to the Merchant Marine Academy to finish his studies there, graduating in early 1944. He sailed on a series of ships for the duration of the war, as third, second, and acting first assistant engineer. Smolen spent several months in the Liberty ship* James Woodrow, *as third assistant, in support of the Normandy Invasion—first arriving on D-Day Plus Two—and subsequently shuttling troops to the beachhead from England. On V-E Day in May 1945 Smolen was at sea in yet another Liberty ship,* Francis Vigo, *as acting first assistant engineer. After the war, Smolen continued to ship out, and worked for a number of years on tanker ships out of New York. He eventually became a teacher and the principal administrator of the Maritime Trades High School in New York City, which for many years was located in the Liberty Ship* John W. Brown *(now a fully restored and operational museum ship with Project Liberty Ship in Baltimore). Smolen lived with his family in Massapequa, New York.*

CHAPTER 19

# John H. Tiencken: "I hated to see her lost"

*John H. Tiencken was born in Florida in 1911 and spent his boyhood in the Savannah, Georgia, area. He first shipped out in the Merchant Marine in the* Lake Treba *as a 15-year-old in 1926 and continued to sail off and on throughout the 1920s and 1930s in unlicensed deck ratings from various ports. A few weeks before the attack on Pearl Harbor he signed aboard the diesel-powered MS* Lake Osweya *in New York as able seaman for a trans–Atlantic voyage.*[1]

I would say around the latter part of November, what comes up at the Doghouse[2] but the *Lake Osweya*, a Ford ship going to Iceland. She's carrying Army cargo and Black Horse Ale for the British navy. She was a beautiful ship, just as neat as a pin, and the finest-feeding ship I was ever in—before or since.[3]

First they put us in a convoy. We joined the convoy in Sydney, Nova Scotia, and from the day we joined it we had trouble because it was a nine-knot convoy and the *Osweya* could not slow down to nine knots. She had a Sundoxford diesel in it, and if you slowed down too much that Sundoxford would stop, then they had to jack it over. They had a hell of a time.

So finally off the Grand Banks we got heavy weather, and the convoy heaved-to. That was the straw that broke the camel's back [for us]: the convoy heaved-to, but we couldn't. At the slowest we could run, we ran right on through the convoy. So we'd run through it and come back on the stern of it, and do the same thing all over again.

So the captain finally said, "To hell with this noise, we're not at war anyhow, and what am I doing taking a chance on our ship with all these damn coal-burners slowing down. And I can't run this slow. So I'm going to Iceland, to hell with the damn convoy."

So we bailed out, pulled out of the convoy and we did go on to Reykjavik, Iceland, and [were there] when war was declared. Sunday morning, on December the 7th the Japs hit Pearl. I got the message at 6 a.m. if I'm not badly mistaken. The mess boy came running back, and woke me up and said, "Son of a bitch, we're at war, the Japs have hit Pearl!"

Well, we were quick to do something about it. The Old Man had all hands out at 8:00 that morning. It was windier than hell—blowing a gale—but it was not raining and it was dry enough. So we started painting that son of a bitch gray, battleship gray; we painted her from the foretruck to the waterline—gray.

And we put up makeshift blackout curtains on the portholes and on the entrances—on the doors—and we prepared for war; we prepared to put her in wartime condition just the same as the British ships were. In other words, we had her blacked as much as possible with the materials we had to work with.

Now when we did get to the dock, and we did unload, then we got orders to join a convoy 300 miles off the coast of England; we were to go to a position there and wait on this convoy to come out. We were to cruise up and down over a 20-mile area. This we did, for three days after we arrived there. For three days we cruised up and down, but no convoy.

Finally, the Old Man said, "To hell with this, I'm going to the States. This is totally ridiculous! Me over here off the British coast, and I could've been damn near to New York by now if they'd let me go from Iceland." We could do 18 knots, so he rung her up and we went on the course: we set a course for New York.

Two or three days later I'd come up to take the wheel, and I had the first lookout, I believe. I walked out on the wing of the bridge and I saw some-

John Tiencken in his hotel room, New York, New York, 1986 (photograph by Michael Gillen).

thing dark right over on the beam. I couldn't make out what it was, so I asked the guy I was relieving [on the wheel], "What's that over there on the beam?"

He said, "It's a cloud."

There wasn't supposed to be nothing on the beam, so if it's a cloud, well, all right. But a couple of minutes later I spotted something ahead that looked like a blue light, a wakeboard light. So I walked out on the other wing—out on the port side—and there's another cloud over there. I said to the mate, "Do you see that dark object over there on the starboard side?"

He said, "Well, the second mate told me it was a cloud."

And I said, "That's what the lookout told me, but I think I just saw a blue wakeboard light up ahead. I just got a glimpse of it a little bit on the starboard bow." And then I said, "There's another cloud over there on the port side."

He walked over on the port side with me, and we look this over, and things just don't look right. After a while we saw lights and—Jesus Christ, there's ships all over the place! We'd run right up in the middle of the convoy! Well, I mean, all hell busted loose, and here comes a corvette. He got up alongside and turned his guns on us. So he's got the guns trained on us, and he's got a loudspeaking system, and he says, "Fall out of the convoy and back to the rear of it!" He told us what to do, and we did it.

We stopped the engines and let the convoy go by. Identification numbers? We gave it to him. Then we waited till daylight with the corvette laying alongside us, with his guns playing down on us and everything. We ain't got a gun, we ain't got a firecracker. The only thing that we've got aboard is a Lyle gun. And sure enough, come daylight, they boarded us.

"Well," they said, "you were supposed to turn off and join up with us off the English Channel."

"Well," the Old Man said, "I stayed there for three days and I cruised in the 20-mile area."

"Oh," he said. "Well, we had to change course," and this and that.

But anyway, now they sent word by Morse back to the commodore and tell him that we're OK, and we're American, and this and that. The commodore asked the captain if he wanted to join up [with the convoy], and the captain thanked him very much, but told him "no" [that] we had hopes of being home for New Year's, and this was a seven-knot convoy, and that he had an 18-knot ship and he couldn't run seven knots.

So, all right, we were allowed to pass, turned loose. They wished us

**The MS *Lake Osweya*, early war period, with typical box-type, quick-release life rafts visible on deck (Mariners' Museum, Newport News, Virginia).**

well, and we went on our way, run that damn thing back up to 18 point five or whatever she would do, and we come on. That night the convoy was hit, and hit bad. We head the SOSs, and we heard the messages, but were way the hell and gone in front of them.

Anyway, we come on in and come in lone duck. We went to Caven's Point. We had rocks on board for ballast, heavy rocks. They were building Caven's Point at that time, so we went over to dump the rocks there. And then shore leave was granted.

I was going to stay on the ship and sign on [for another voyage] but I was going with this girl up in Washington Heights. She had two children and worked for Naval Intelligence. She spoke Polish, Russian, German, French and she spoke English fluently. And she was a good-looking broad. Well, we spent several days together, but then the ship was gonna start loading, and in the morning I was gonna go down and sign on. But she said to me, "John, do me a favor: don't sign on that ship."

"Well," I said, "why not?"

"Well," she said, "I don't know. I'm very fond of you, and the kids are too, and I've got a premonition about this ship. I don't believe that ship's going to make it through this trip."

I said, "Ah, Helen, that thing is fast. She'll outrun a submarine any day, even with the sub on the surface."

But she kept on, and on, and on, and says, "Well, I'd like to have a few more days with you anyway."

So I said, "Well, all right, OK, I won't sign on."

I went down to the ship and said, "I'm signing off." So I paid off for the coast-wise run—got four days coming—and I signed off. The ship left New York without me, bound for Halifax, Nova Scotia, to join a convoy. But she was never heard from again. She was loaded with ammo, and somewhere between New York and Halifax she got hit. They never got an SOS [off] or nothing. They never picked up a life raft from her. She just disappeared, and that was all there was to it.[4]

I met some of the crew's wives later, and one of 'em's mother, and they just couldn't understand it. Nobody ever informed them of what had happened. The guys—the ship just vanished, and so did the crew.

Anyway, she was a very happy ship, and I certainly hated to see her lost.

*Tiencken worked on various ships—including the SS* Dixie Arrow, *SS* R. W. Gallagher, *and SS* Edward L. Shea—*before shipping out in the SS* Gateway City *in late April 1942 for North Russia. He would be with that ship for more than 10 months. Despite having his ship turned back from Convoy PQ 17—the ill-fated "July 4th convoy"—because of hull bottom growth that reduced its speed below convoy requirements, Tiencken finally got his wish to visit Russia when SS* Gateway City *departed for Murmansk in the first of the resumed northbound convoys—JW-51A—in mid–December 1942.*[5]

## Christmas in Murmansk

We got back to Loch Ewe, Scotland [from shipyard in Belfast] and were hung up there for three or four days. But eventually we were on our way to Russia.

Each one of the ships that remained behind gave us a three-whistle salute as we departed: they knew where we were going, and they saluted us. Everybody got out on deck and waved. They gave us a real send-off. The *Gateway City* was the first ship out. I was stationed on the 20 millimeter on the port wing.[6]

The Limeys had spent three days putting up a target for all the ships in the convoy to shoot at. We had these new guns that had been put on in Belfast, and we'd had plenty of practice with them. We knew how to use them, there was no bullshit about that. So we come on this target, and the English pilot told us, "all right, *you* can fire the forward gun."

We'd been given five rounds for the 3"/38 forward and five rounds for the 5"/50 aft. The first round from the forward gun took about half the target away. The second shell hit and damned near all the rest of it went. After the third shell there was no target left. Well, the pilot jumped straight up in the air and said, "Jesus, Yank, where the hell did you get that gun crew from? You weren't supposed to hit the target, you were supposed to shoot at it to see how close you could come to it! It took the British navy three days to put that target out there. Now the rest of the ships haven't got anything to shoot at, and neither has your five-incher aft!"

Well, the Armed Guard lieutenant said, "We train our gun crews to hit what they're shooting at; we don't train them to miss it. We've had plenty of practice, and we've been under attack. We know that if we don't hit that damn plane or submarine, why, it's too bad for us. What we shoot at we aim to hit. If you didn't want us to hit that target you shouldn't've put us on the range and told us to shoot at it."

We were the first to go out, and then we formed up in a convoy. We were supposed to have heavy fog and snow at that time of the year, which made for good cover. So [after earlier convoy losses] they waited until this time. This is what was determined from the weather reports and previous years and everything. On the other hand, instead of that, we got beautiful, clear weather: you could see every ship in the convoy, anytime of the 24 hours of darkness, practically just a little twilight, not much. But the northern lights just lit up [the sky], and they were beautiful. I wish I had a picture of them. But when they come on it was just as bright as day.[7]

So we didn't see a goddam thing: no airplanes, no battle craft of any description, nothing. And we went around [to] the river going up to Murmansk. We picked up the pilot at the mouth of the river: he was right there waitin' for us. And a Russian destroyer did meet us about a hundred miles before we got to the mouth of the river, and he escorted us the rest of the way—in other words, up to the pilot station. The pilot came on board and he brought two female interpreters with him. And he spoke English as well.

And so he informed us that there hadn't been a plane over Murmansk in the past six weeks. That they'd bombed out the dock area, and they'd bombed out the switchyard, which was right at the head of the dock where they switched the engines in order to bring the freight cars down to pick up the cargo off the dock and then they'd take it back and make it up in the yard. And they'd bombed that yard out. And as far as the Germans were concerned there wasn't a building in Murmansk that had not had a direct hit, the whole damn place.

But they didn't know it but the Russians had rebuilt the dock, under cover of darkness, and they hadn't even had an observation plane over in six weeks. And they had rebuilt the railroad yard so they were ready to put us into the dock. We could unload. And they took us right in: we got in Christmas Day, into Murmansk, and we docked right around noon.

And while we were having Christmas dinner, Franklin Roosevelt got on the air, we listened to the radio: we could receive but we couldn't send. And he said he was happy to inform the American people that the American Navy had just succeeded in putting a large convoy into Russia. Well, Archangel was closed up tight as a horse's ass in fly time. You couldn't put a ship in over there, so it had to be in Murmansk; it couldn't be nowhere else. And he didn't get off the air good when Winston Churchill got on and said that he was happy to inform the British people that the British navy had just succeeded in putting a large convoy into Russia. And 30 minutes later we had an air raid—30 minutes after they had gotten off of the air.

[The Germans] didn't send [high altitude] bombers over because they knew we all had ammunition—every one of us had ammunition aboard. And all they had to do was hit one ship with an incendiary bomb. They're magnesium and when they land they just bust like a firecracker, and they'll burn through steel plate in nothin' flat. So they sent Stuka [JU-87] dive-bombers over, and you can't hit those sons of bitches. The only way you can get one—and we did get one, either the *Gateway City* got her or the *Northern Sword*, one of the two—but the *Northern Sword* was on one side of the dock and the *Gateway City* was on the other.

And it happened that I was aft and on deck, and no air raid [alarm] went or anything else and this was a sneak attack. They'd take off of the frozen lakes in Finland, gain altitude, cut their engines off and then they would coast into Murmansk.

And I saw this kid [from the Armed Guard]. They had one man in each gun tub but one man could not cock that 20 millimeter 'cause you had a lanyard, old style. They come up later with a new one and one man could cock it. But you couldn't with the ones we had: it took two men. You put a lanyard over the barrel, and one man on each side, and pull down for all you were worth until she was cocked. *Then* you were ready to fire.[8]

And we had [ammunition] canisters. Later on they came up with [a belt-fed system] but then we had canisters, plenty of canisters on hand with the tension set on 'em and every third bullet was an incendiary to show it was—a tracer. But they were all incendiaries: every one of 'em had TNT in the nose of 'em.

So I bounced into the [gun] tub and helped—Chiz, I believe his name was. He come from Wilmington, Delaware, if I'm not badly mistaken. But anyway, I bounced in, helped him cock the gun, and then I stayed in the tub with him to replenish the canister when it run out.

And he turned loose with that goddamned 20 millimeter. And one across the dock on the *Northern Sword* fired and the carpenter fired that. Well, I'm standing right alongside of Chiz, and in case he gets hit I'm gonna take the gun. But he needed me to help him cock that gun; he couldn't do it by himself. And the other kid on the other side never fired his gun—there was one right across the deck [of *Gateway City*] on the other side—but he couldn't cock it by his self. And I couldn't leave [my] gun to go over and help him cock his.

So it was the only two guns. No air raid went off, no air siren. But one of us—either one or the other, either the *Gateway*'s bullets or the *Northern Sword*'s—hit that guy and it must have hit him in the bomb rack just as he come to the end of his run and he opened his bomb bay doors. And I know that our tracers were going right into that plane: I could see 'em and that Chiz was really hitting that son of a bitch. And the carpenter across the way was hittin' him too.

But all of a sudden, before his bombs come out of the bomb bay, he blew up. And he just *blew*—just one big, blinding flash just as he had opened his bomb bay doors. There was all kinds of fire up there, and he fell all over the harbor—pieces of him—and they picked it up out in the harbor and shit. He was just finished, completely.

Well, anyway, the first thing that they had to unload was those two planes [on top of cargo hatches] because they brought barges alongside and the heavy-lift crane. And they unloaded the two planes onto the barges and hauled them across the river. And we stayed there at least 30 or 35 days unloadin' and when we left there those two planes were still sittin' there on those barges right where they'd put them.

And the foodstuffs was in [cargo holds] four and five, and the ammo was in #3. And they went right to work on four and five. They took the foodstuffs, and it was nothin' to look down into the hold and see the longshoremen down there where they'd eaten raw flour: their face just coated with flour where they were eatin' it.

Another thing that they started [to do]: we'd dumped garbage and they would go in the mess rooms and take the garbage out of the pails, whatever we dumped in the pails. So we quit dumpin' garbage. Instead of that we got a gang of #10 cans and everything that was left over we'd put in the #10 cans and put it back in the steering engine room. They kept steam on the steering engine all the time to keep it from freezing.

This little Canadian corvette pulled alongside and he told us a story. He said that he'd just escorted a convoy across the Atlantic and didn't have time to get any grub or medical supplies or anything, and he had several wounded men on board and that he needed medical supplies and they didn't have a drop of tea and they didn't have no milk or nothin' else, and they didn't have time to get no stores. And they were totally out, and could we spare 'em anything.

Well, we had medical supplies: we could give him all the medical supplies he wanted. So, we did, and we had tea—plenty of it, because nobody drank tea 'cause everybody wanted coffee—and we got all the tea that we had when we left the States. So we give him tea, and we give him milk, and we give him whatever we could, whatever we could spare.

And of course it's understood that we were gonna order stores from the Russians, and the Russians had told us that they're gonna give us stores, and the steward made a big list of stores. But anyway we were promised by the Russians while we were there that all of us who made that trip up there was gonna get a month's pay as a bonus. And they kept their word. That's the only time I knew 'em to keep their word. We didn't expect to get it.

So the next thing that happened while we're alongside the dock is this plane divin' down right straight—there'd been a fight up top, we'd been watchin' it. Well this dogfight, there wasn't much of a fight to it. This Stuka was up there and, well, we can see two planes tangled. Well, the first thing—one of 'em peels off and he comes straight down. Everybody is trigger-happy—there ain't a son of a bitchin' one of us that ain't trigger-happy—and if a plane is comin' close to the ship within the range of our guns we're gonna shoot.

So sure enough this plane did come right straight down and he's comin' right *down*. We can't tell whether he's a Stuka or what the fuck he is—we don't know. So we opened up on him. A shore battery or two opened up, and we can't identify the son of a bitch and we don't know that he's a Russian. And every damn ship in the harbor opened up on him, and we shot him down. He was a Russian.

So, the Intourist come down and told us what we'd done: that we'd shot down one of their best pilots and blah, blah, blah, and this and that and the other, and now this has got to be corrected. So now they put two lieutenants to live right onboard the ship and stay there, and they give 'em one of our 30-caliber Lewis guns, and they're up there on the [flying] bridge. So the order is that unless they fire the 30-caliber Lewis we're not to fire. They're gonna identify the plane.

So they're always dancin' and jumpin' up and down, to keep warm, you know, and wavin' the machine gun. So one day I'm standin' right by #10 tub, and of course there's one Armed Guard in each—#10, all the time, and we got somebody right close to the 5"/38 and 3"/50. There's always somebody right around the guns. And so the Russians are jumpin' up and down and then—it dawned on me later but I didn't realize it then—they're hollerin' "Germanski, Germanski!" But they didn't fire the fuckin' 30-caliber. They're just wavin' and jumpin' up and down the same as they always doin'.

And I was on a gun, I was right under the bottom. I could've crawled into #10 turret and fired, or I could've gone into the big gun, either one. I was right between 'em. But they don't fire the 30-caliber, so the fuckin' Stuka comes down and the bombs missed us by about 50 feet; he dropped a stick of them, right out on the fuckin' dock [and] killed a dozen or two Russians.

So now the interpreters come down—the Russians can't speak a word of English—the lieutenants—so we don't know what the hell the score is; all we know is that they didn't fire that 30-caliber and we got orders not to fire until they fire the 30, and they didn't fire it. Now the interpreters—there's always a couple of interpreters aboard, females—so they talk to the Russians, and then they call us all together and said, well, the reason they didn't fire was because they didn't know how to operate the 30-caliber machine gun. It didn't fire when they pulled the trigger!

Well, they didn't cock it. You've got a knob on the side of it and you've got to pull that back and cock it, and that puts one [round] in the barrel and you can fire it. But they didn't have the sense to pull that knob back [and] they didn't tell us that they didn't know it. If they'd've told us, we would've shown 'em how to operate the fuckin' gun. But the reason they didn't fire it was because they didn't know how.

We took the gun right there when they told us the gun was no good, it wouldn't shoot, and I was standin' right there when she told us. I just reached over and he handed me one of 'em and I pulled the knob back, aimed up in the air and fired it 10 times. There was nothin' wrong with the gun.

But then the interpreter said, "Well, but you done somethin'—you pulled somethin' back!"

I said, "Yes, I cocked it. I put a shell in the barrel and cocked it. There was no shell in the barrel. Before, when he pulled the trigger, and the trigger didn't pull [was] because it hadn't been cocked."

"Well, they didn't *know* that," she said. "These fellas have never handled one of these guns before. Why didn't you guys show 'em?"

And the Armed Guard lieutenant spoke up and said, "Well why the hell didn't they tell me that they didn't know how to fire these? I'd've shown them."

Then the next thing that happened was there was a helluva gale of wind. And this little old Limey ship—little bit of a damn thing, which had discharged and with no ballast in it, and its wheel [propeller] half out of the water—he was about 3,500 tons, and he was ahead of us and he discharged and they wanted the dock [space] to put another ship in. They got more ships loaded that come up with us that they haven't got dockage for, you see: the side I was on took three ships, and the other side took three. And they had a little Russian coaster on the other side that they'd sandwiched in between two American ships. Later on one of the Stukas come over and he dropped his bombs right down his smoke stack, and he sank right alongside the dock.

But anyway, this pilot takes this ship away from the dock, and it's evident—quite evident—the ship's got no ballast in her, and the wind is blowin' a gale and it's plain as the nose on your face that this is damn stupid, that he cannot maneuver that ship: taking her away from the dock with no tugs. But the pilot took her away from the dock, and what the hell happened I don't know, but he lost control of her. Anyway, she wouldn't answer the wheel or somethin' or she couldn't get enough power to get steerageway—the wheel was $\frac{2}{3}$ out of the water—she had no ballast in her. And she blew right across the bay and cleaned out a Russian minefield. She must've hit two mines 'cause there were two explosions. And they put the lifeboats down and they all come back.

As soon as they got there they had a firing squad waitin' on the dock. And as soon as the pilot put his foot on the dock the firing squad took him—he walked right along with them: he knew what was comin'—and they took him right back across the dock and shot him.

And I said to one of the interpreters, "What in the hell did they shoot that man for, would you tell me?"

And she says, "Why he destroyed two of our mines, and he lost a ship."

And I said, "Well, for Christ All Mighty's sake, the man couldn't possibly do anything with that ship. Anybody with common sense would know that, that knows anything about a ship at all."

She says, "Well, he's a pilot, and he is supposed to know how to handle a ship, and he didn't do his job." So she said, "He automatically convicted his self. The best thing to do is not give him another ship: he might do the same thing over again." And she said, "He might have done that on purpose."

I said, "But, damn, the man didn't do it on purpose. It was evident that he was doin' everything he could. We was all standin' there watchin' and he was doin' everything he could to get control of that ship when she left this dock."

"Well, that's the way we do it, and that's all there is to that."

We ordered stores, and the steward made a helluva list. And we [had] carried all this stuff up there so now we figured we're gonna get some of it back. Now we need sugar, and we need flour, and we need this and that. And we carried tons of canned hams up there. We need some, now we're runnin' short of stores. So the steward sent the list ashore. They went over the list, and what did they send back?

They sent us down two bags of potatoes, one sack of flour, I would say about 300 pounds of salt cod fish, and some chocolate. He'd ordered coffee, and he's ordered this and he ordered that. Well, anyway, when they brought the stores aboard the steward says, "Well, well, well, but that's all we can get. We're goin' to England and we'll get stores there. We'll be in England in 10 days, and this is enough to last us 10 days."

And that's all we got, nothin' else. We didn't get one of those cans of hams back, not one bag of flour. No sugar. But the Steward said we were pretty well set on flour. But we did need sugar, and he says, "I could kick my ass for not takin' it out of the cargo before we docked, but I thought they'd give it to us as much as [we've been] bringin' it to them."

But, no, he didn't get it. And on the way back to Loch Ewe [Scotland] we were even eatin' [stored supplies] out of the life boats: we were eatin' the lifeboat chow before we got to Loch Ewe. So, again, he makes a big stores list in Loch Ewe when we got there. Now we're gonna join a convoy in Loch Ewe comin' on to the United States. So he sends a big stores list ashore, and the same thing happens.

We set up until 10 o'clock. [The steward] promised he's gonna cook stuff, and he's got his stove fired. "Soon as I get my stores I'm gonna make all of you guys the biggest damn steak" and this and that and the other, "and I'm gonna do this and that and the other."

So the drifter comes alongside—we got a boom raised and we're ready to take the stores. We got a cargo net out, and the whole damn deck department is standin' by, and we're gonna get a couple tons of stores. He's ordered fruit—and he showed us the copy of his requisition—and he's ordered hams, and he's ordered this and he's ordered that, and he's ordered the other. So we figured it's gonna take us half the night to take the stores [in]. Drifter comes alongside at about 8:30 or 9:00, and we're sailin' the next mornin' at six.

We throwed 'em down a sling, and we got stores back and that sling wasn't even half full. "Ok," they said, "that's it, take it up!" We brought it up on deck, and the steward is sittin' there. They sent us one fuckin' goat, two lambs, and a half a side of beef [laughs], about five pounds of coffee, and about 50 pounds of tea, [of which] we had two or 300 pounds already—we didn't order no tea—and some powdered milk. It was stuff we'd given to them, and they'd given it back to us [laughs]!

So the steward said, "Well, well, well, I'll tell ya what. I promised you guys a steak tonight, and that's just about gonna be it. And when I give each one of ya a steak, there won't be no more till we get to New York."

So, sure enough, he went in—the cooks went in the galley—and they baked fresh bread, and we had a steak, and they had enough potatoes to make French fries, and done the best they could do. They brought it out, and we got it at about 11 o'clock at night. We got a meal.

So the steward says, "Well, from here on out it's gonna be powdered eggs, and it's gonna be—I'm gonna have coffee once a day, for a while." But he said, "I doubt like hell if we can have coffee even in the morning the whole way to the States." He said, "I'm sorrier than hell, but that's the way it is."

So that's the way it was. And we come back eatin' out of the lifeboats. So when the tug come alongside of us [in New York] we hadn't had no coffee for three or four days.

Now [on the way back] we was makin' water [not properly ballasted because the Russians] give us some kind of shit they called "appetite" for ballast: we wanted 1,500 tons and they give us 500. It was somethin' like dirt, except for one thing: when it got wet it just got as hard as cement. So they give us that for ballast.

And we come on. They put us in a slow convoy, and we limped into New York, and we went right to the shipyard—to Erie Basin.[9]

And when we tied up—I don't know how it was arranged, whether they wired in or what—but they give every one of us $300. Captain Perkins was aboard, and the paymaster, and they didn't say bullshit except one thing: before any one of us went ashore they had the Navy security on board, and they had these two naval officers. And he called each one of us in separately and they told us what would happen to us if we even mentioned anything about that Murmansk run: "Don't breathe a *word*, don't tell anybody where you've *been*, don't mention Murmansk, don't talk about the Navy, don't do this, don't do that, don't do the other—Just forget about it, forget the whole damn mess. Don't talk about the *Washington*, the *Wichita*, *Tuscaloosa*, nothin'. Don't mention a damn thing. If you do, it's gonna be hell [and] you'll pay for it."

*Tiencken continued to serve in the Merchant Marine for the duration of the war in such ships as* Jean *and* George W. Woodward. *He generally shipped out as an able seaman, but also as acting third mate and acting second mate as need and circumstances arose. After the war, Tiencken continued to ship out in unlicensed deck ratings into the early 1970s. This included multiple voyages to Vietnam in logistical support of the war there. He settled in New York City, and passed away there, at 76, in 1987.*

CHAPTER 20

# Donald E. Zubrod: 42 Days in a Lifeboat

*Donald E. Zubrod was born in Brooklyn, New York, in April 1924. He was working as a bill of lading clerk for Waterman Steamship Corporation in New York City at the time of the Japanese attack on Pearl Harbor.[1] He joined the Merchant Marine the following summer and in August 1942—at the age of 18—went aboard his first ship, the Liberty ship* Roger B. Taney, *in Baltimore as purser.[2] Later, on bond-selling drives during the war, he was billed as the youngest purser in the U.S. Merchant Marine.*

We took the long voyage out to Suez by way of the Panama Canal, Cape Horn, Cape Town, and on up and arrived there close to Christmastime of '42. We sailed alone all the way. Coming back we formed a convoy in Saldana Bay, north of Cape Town, and for the first 36 or 48 hours about 10 ships were escorted mainly in a direction northward along the African coast. And then the convoy was dispersed to run—all these ships were in ballast—toward the South American coast.

We were supposed to assume parallel lines which were on the latitudes of certain cities. I recall the latitude of our city was Vitoria, Brazil. To attain that, we had to steam actually south for a few hours, and then just at dusk that night—the night of the seventh of February—we turned directly east. It was about 9:30 that night that a torpedo went directly across our bow. It was sighted by one of the gun crew on watch.

It was a very dark, windy, stormy night. Everyone was pretty well convinced that it actually was a torpedo, and we went into a full alert with zigzag courses, and opened up the engines as wide as we could. Later on, some said they could actually smell diesel fumes and heard the sound of diesel engines—a sub operating on the surface. But you couldn't see anything: it was a pitch black night.

It was about an hour after the initial torpedo [sighting] that we took one in the starboard side right in the engine room, right where the boilers were, I suppose. I was standing in the wheelhouse—I was actually the communications man between the gun crew and the bridge—and it sounded like the main engine went right up the fiddley behind me. I felt the entire ship lift right out of the water and then settle back down. It just lifted me right up, and when the ship came back down I think I fell down on all fours for a moment. I remember the big AB on the wheel just took off right out of there. There was an incredible noise and roar of steam escaping.

My assignment in the event of abandoning ship was to go into the captain's quarters and take the steel box containing the code books and throw it overboard, which I proceeded to do. And when I got out on the starboard wing of the bridge to drop it, I saw that the starboard lifeboats were gone, disappeared. The practice in those days was to carry them [swung out] over the side, and the blast had just taken them away. The davits were plastered back against the house. And the water was boiling, actually boiling with fire. I smelled cordite fumes from the torpedo.

Then I went to the port side. The emergency lanterns had been turned on, the lifeboats were already out, and there were probably a half dozen men sitting in each boat with lifejackets on, just sitting there. So the steward came along at that point and I took the line on the end of the davit and he took the other, and we proceeded to lower one lifeboat into the water. At that point the captain came along and asked me to go back into his stateroom for his briefcase, which had documents in it. This I did, and by the time I came back out the two lifeboats were away.

So I had to go over the side in the water and swim for it. I went down the knotted rope and jumped—maybe the last 8 or 10 feet. The ship wasn't settling, but she was dead in the water. I actually had to swim about 50 yards away from the ship. And it seemed as though just as I was pulled into the boat—the water was oily—another torpedo went right under us and there was a blast. That apparently sank her. Everyone was off the ship by then, except the three men on watch in the engine room who were just—exterminated. Nobody even bothered to look for them: no point in it.[3]

I would say that my feeling at the time was more numbness than anything else. And it was a very long night. The water was very rough, and

*Top:* Donald Zubrod, in the uniform of purser, USMM, during a war bond tour in the Midwest. The service ribbon, top row, is a Merchant Marine Combat Bar (John W. Zubrod). *Bottom:* The Liberty ship *Roger B. Taney* (Mariners' Museum, Newport News, Virginia).

when dawn came we were able to spot the other lifeboat which had gotten away, and one life raft with Navy gun crew on it. So we divided the men up into the two boats and it turned out we wound up with 26 men, and the other wound up with 28.

The other boat reported that the submarine had surfaced, that its captain wore a white uniform with shorts and epaulettes, had a beard and spoke fluent English.[4] He knew the name of the ship and even the destination. The destination was actually Port of Spain but he knew the course was on a parallel with Vitoria. So there may have been a security leak, out of Cape Town.

I was later told that out of the eight or nine ships involved, only one made it to her destination. I seem to recall a preponderance of Liberty ships, but there may have been some non–Americans in the group.[5]

So we had a dawn consultation about what to do and it was agreed by the senior officers that there was no point in making for Africa. We were about 600 miles off the African coast but the winds were against us, and when we got there we'd find nothing but headhunters anyway. So we decided to make for the Brazilian coast in hopes that we would either be picked up on the way by shipping traffic or make that little Trinidade Island that's about 1,500 miles off the coast of Brazil.[6] And we would try to stay together. Well, we became separated during the first night.[7] We sailed very briskly that first day, with the wind behind us. And we sailed very briskly for days on end: we were logging six, seven, eight knots over the first four or five days.

We took whatever was in the boats. Bear in mind this was in the early days of the war. Survival techniques had not been developed; we didn't even have fishing gear. The food was limited to malted milk tablets, baker's chocolate, something that Admiral Bird had developed up in the Arctic called pemmican—which was horrible tasting—and biscuits. And we didn't have much of that. Our water was very limited—relatively limited—if we were to go for a very long time. After the first week or so, when nothing happened, we actually limited ourselves to between four and six ounces, except on occasions when we got some rainfall and collected it in the sail when we would drink as much as we could handle at that time.

We also took an inventory of lifeboat equipment. There was a Very pistol, kerosene lantern, bailing bucket and blankets. No fishing tackle. The lifeboat was only 22 feet long, so there were very crowded conditions. We did see a ship on the second day, and it passed at a distance in heavy seas and didn't see our flares.

My impressions of the first two weeks: we were cutting notches in our lifebelt emergency lanterns. We had a steady wind and there was a lot of rain. There was cheerfulness because we were moving; we thought we'd make [it to] something within two weeks. The captain did maintain a log. And there was a lot of storytelling. It was very cold at night, and there were not enough blankets. It was hot during the day. There was some thirst, but not much hunger [pains] after the first few days.

And my impressions of the second two weeks: calmer weather. We had a sudden storm. I remember it was violent and we thought we'd capsize. There was incessant talk of food: people talking about fried eggs on top of steaks. Spirits were still fairly good but the food by this time was running fairly low. The pemmican and chocolate were gone. Beautiful sunsets and sunrises.

By the 35th day the spirits were very low. Some of the people were getting delirious. I even heard some music, and didn't feel any pain. And there was a lot of praying going on, a kind of universal prayer. And it was on the 35th day that we had the incident of the dolphin.

The chief petty officer with the Navy gun crew was a man called Sam Lopresti, who won the Vezina Trophy, I think in 1940 or '41 as the goal tender for the Chicago Blackhawks. He was a professional hockey player, a very strong man.[8] He had lashed his Navy sheath knife onto a boathook, but never had a chance to use it. This was right after noon on that day and everyone had dozed off. I was sitting directly athwart ships from him. The water was quite calm.

Suddenly, I saw him quietly reach over for that boathook with the knife on it. And he got up on his knees and in one motion he came down and brought about a 40 pound dolphin into the boat. He got him right, apparently, in the head and stunned him. By the time the dolphin recovered it took three or four men to sit on him and hold him down, because he really thrashed around. That was the only fish we caught during all that time.

We ate that dolphin: we cooked it, we drank the blood from it, those of us who wanted to drink it. I did. And we cut the fish into steaks, put kerosene into the bailing bucket with rags, cleaned out a flare container, put seawater in it, and actually boiled those steaks. Everyone got a share of it. And we hung the skeleton up to dry on the mast and ate the bones and the marrow for days after that.

I think at that point if something like that hadn't happened a lot of us just would have been dying away, because we'd all eroded mentally and physically. I was down to probably—well, they measured me when we got in not long after that and I was down to something like 85 pounds. Extreme malnutrition. So that picked up our spirits a little bit.

And we went on and on. It was the night of the 40th day. We didn't realize that we had passed south of Cape Frio, and whoever was on lookout that night saw the loom of the lights of Rio de Janeiro to the north. You can picture the loom: you are in total darkness and you see on the horizon a kind of a whiteness. And we assumed that must be the lights of Rio, and we turned north and sailed north all the next day.

I might mention that on the 41st night we were fired upon by the Brazilian navy. A destroyer or destroyer escort came along and started shooting at us. We saw the loom of a blacked-out ship and we sent up Very signals, and they fired on us. We could hear the shells whistling right over our heads. We assumed it was the Brazilian navy; they were a little trigger-happy. There had been some sinkings right outside of Rio with heavy loss of life in the preceding months.[9]

And on the morning of the 42nd day we sighted land.

There was no wind, so we rowed all day, in 10-minute shifts, until we were within no more than a half-mile from shore. It was a very mountainous and rocky shoreline. We saw smoke coming out north of us, and it was actually a ship leaving Rio headed south. And as he came towards us he saw us and signaled for us to come out to him. So we had to row back. And that's when we were picked up by a Lloyd-Brasilero cargo-passenger ship which was on its way to Santos and continued on to Santos. I don't recall the name of that ship.[10] I do remember how we were treated. The men broke down, openly, for the first time.

But all but two were able to climb the ladder. We were all assisted to hot showers and clean clothes, and then we all sat down to eat a meal. But no one ate—touched the food—until the last man was seated. The captain said a prayer of thanks, which I thought rather unusual and very touching.

We were brought into Santos the next morning, and the Navy came down and took us off to a local hospital, where most of us spent a month or so, and then we were sent back to the States.

We had some elderly people in there. The second and third mates were in their sixties. To the best of my knowledge everyone survived from that boat, on the scene [anyway]. I was a young boy but I wound up with acute catero-jaundice [sic], and wound up in the Marine Hospital in Staten Island for about six weeks when I got back.

It wasn't until many years later that I read Rachel Carson's *The Sea Around Us*. I don't think I would have understood what she was talking about if I hadn't eyeballed the ocean for six weeks at a foot off the surface. It's an entirely different proposition then and you get a real different feeling and view of everything. The ocean is very much alive all the time: the fish that you see there and things that are floating on it. The moods of the sea change so quickly. We went through a period there where for two or three days the ocean was as flat as the glass on this table here, not a ripple or even a swell. And when that thing broke, it broke into a violent storm where I saw at *one* time five water spouts, one of which passed within 25 yards of us. They were shooting a gun into it. Someone had said if you penetrate the spout that it would collapse. We thought it was going to overtake us; it probably would have destroyed us if it did.

Then there was the shark. There was a difference of opinion as to whether it was the same one all the way, but we had a shark with us from about the third day until the last day. For that reason no one was ever able to go over the side, where we could have helped the hydration problem with some baths. It was either a single shark or one after another relieving each other. But the shark was always there: you could always see its fin, two or three times a day, circling the boat. It was quite large, probably at least 10 or 12 feet. Sometimes he'd come right up alongside the boat, [so] we could measure his size pretty well.

There were a lot of dreams and fantasies. There was a lot of talk about food. Some of it was about women—exploits—but it was mainly about food. You know, in this restaurant here we were served this, and did you ever try this or that?

I want to say something about these fishermen. I don't think we could have done what we did—we took a little 22-foot boat and sailed it—I think on a maximum course we went close to 3,000 miles. But the way we went all over the ocean, for want of navigational instruments, we might have actually done closer to 4,000 in that period of time. We had some Gulf fishermen: fellows that used to work these little fishing boats out of U.S. Gulf ports. We had about three or four of them in the boat, and they ran the show. They knew how to handle sails and how to handle a boat in rough weather, how to steer it and get the best out of it. Without them—without someone with small-boat experience—I think we would have been kind of lost.

I had never considered myself a religious person before, or while it was going on. I made a lot of trade-offs, as people do in that situation. I guess after it was all over I pretty much forgot about the religious aspect, but then as time went by I became more involved in religion. I've spoken at religious conferences about this experience, and the religious impact at the time. As a matter of fact, I actually had a vision—a vision of a white angel—somewhere along about the 37th or 38th day. It could have been a hallucination, I don't know, [but] when I think back, I think perhaps it wasn't.

It seemed as though—suddenly I was alone on the boat. It was at night and I had been dozing. And I saw this white light come towards me; it had more or less the shape of an angel. And I heard beautiful, beautiful music, like organs playing and music swelling up. It seems like it lasted for quite a while, and then it just faded away. I don't think I was dreaming.

One other thing that I think I must mention. It didn't happen until that incident down in Chile when that plane with the soccer players crashed, and a book was written about it called *Alive!* There's nothing in any of my notes here, and it wasn't until I read that book—and it transfixed me—that it opened up a recess in my mind which I had totally blanked out, that we had talked openly about cannibalism.[11]

It was towards the end when it started to look pretty hopeless. You know, 40 days had gone by, and nothing's happening. By then no watches were running so we couldn't even come anywhere close on [figuring] what progress we were making. With adverse currents maybe we were being carried back across the ocean. Who knew? And it was discussed. Some said, "I could never do it," and some said, "I could." And, you know, I thought about it. If it came to survival and life I unquestionably would become a cannibal. I couldn't see myself killing for it, but the time was not very far away when one or more of them would go under.

I feel for those people who were in that Chilean incident. I *know* how they felt, and why they did it. It's a question of—you're not hungry any longer. After three or four days of that your stomach squeezes into a little ball and you don't get a single hunger pain; it just doesn't exist. There is a craving, mentally. It is the mental aspect and phase of knowing that if you didn't get nourishment you would die—that your days were numbered. You'd gone 42 days without really any food at all, and none in sight. How much longer could you endure without food? Not much.

Some of them, they didn't even want to hear it discussed in their presence. It was not an obsessive sort of thing, but the subject did come up in conversation and a few people expressed their feelings on it. I privately made up my mind what I would do: I didn't feel I'd have sufficient revulsion not to do it.

*After his period of recuperation ashore, Zubrod became involved for a period of time in war bond-drive touring to the Midwest and other areas. In pre-drive publicity he was billed as the "youngest purser in the Merchant Marine" at that time. He did eventually return to sea during the war, and for the duration. Zubrod had a long career in the maritime industry following the war, which included executive positions with Admanthos Shipping Agency. He also served as president of the Society of Maritime Arbitrators. Zubrod passed away in Georgia, at 83, in 2007.*

# Appendix A: Glossary

**Abaft**   Behind, toward the stern, relative to something aboard ship.

**Abeam**   On the side of the ship or at right angle to it.

**Able Seaman (AB)**   Unlicensed rating in deck department, ranks above ordinary seaman.

**Aft**   Towards, near, at the stern of a ship.

**Astern**   In back, rear of a ship; relative to motion, going backwards.

**Athwartships**   Across the breadth of a ship (the opposite to "fore and aft").

**Ballast**   Various materials—such as stone, water, or iron—used to properly trim ship and compensate after cargo has been removed.

**Batten**   Strips of steel or wood, usually tapered, used to secure canvas covering over hatch boards; to secure by using battens as in "batten down the hatches."

**Beach, on the**   General reference to being ashore, off ship.

**Beam**   An imagined line extending out from the center of the ship, on either side; width of a ship at greatest point.

**Belay**   To secure by winding rope or line around cleat, often using series of half hitches; order to stop doing something, as in "belay that!"

**Bilge**   Lowest portion of a ship inside the hull and where bilge water would accumulate.

**Binnacle**   Stand for housing compass, placed near ship's steering wheel for viewing by helmsman.

**Bosun (boatswain)**   Unlicensed rating, in charge of deck crew and activities, maintenance, securing for sea, etc., as a foreman.

**Bow**   The front or forward end of a ship or boat.

**Bridge**   Elevated, enclosed point on ship from which ship is conned, commands are given, navigation is conducted, and ship is steered.

**Bulkhead**   A partition dividing a ship into compartments; seaman's reference to any wall.

**Bumboat**  Small craft powered by sail, engine or otherwise, used by locals to carry goods for sale to, or trade with, ship's crew while in port, trade sometimes of an illicit nature.

**Bunkers**  Fuel oil.

**Chief Engineer**  Senior licensed officer in engine department; others would include first, second and third assistant engineers.

**Chief Mate**  Senior licensed officer in deck department, reporting to the master (captain); other licensed officers in department include second and third mates (see chart following).

**Commodore**  Naval officer in command of a group of ships.

**Corvette**  A British, Canadian, United Kingdom convoy escort and anti-submarine warfare vessel.

**Crow's Nest**  Position at highest vantage point of a ship for lookout purposes; on a Liberty ship an enclosed, cylindrically shaped compartment with viewing port, located at top of foremast.

**Davit**  Supports for, and used for, lowering/raising a lifeboat.

**Deadweight tons**  Carrying capacity of ship in tons of 2,240 pounds.

**Dog-watch**  One of two, two-hour watches (work shifts), from 4–6 p.m. and 6–8 p.m.

**Draft**  Depth of vessel below waterline, measured vertically.

**Fireman**  Unlicensed engine room rating, sometimes combined with watertender designation and function; other unlicensed ratings in department include oiler, wiper.

**Flying Bridge**  Platform constructed above pilothouse containing duplicate set of navigation equipment, wheel, binnacle, signaling device to engine room, etc., to provide better visibility while underway.

**Fo'c'sle**  From forecastle, a forward area which typically contained crew quarters, in common usage, any area aboard ship for crew accommodations.

**Fo'c'slehead**  Raised deck in the front (bow) area of a ship.

**Fog Buoy**  Also known as position buoy, towed astern while in convoy and ship not visible otherwise to enable those in ship behind to maintain position or station relative to ship ahead.

**Galley**  Nautical term for ship's or boat's kitchen.

**Gross Tons**  Entire internal cubic capacity in tons of 100 cubic feet to the ton.

**Gunwale**  Upper edge of ship's or boat's open side, pronounced "gun'le."

**Hatch**  Opening on ship's deck through which cargo is loaded and unloaded.

**Head**  Bathroom or toilet facility on ship.

**Heave-to**  Stop or slow a ship enough to contend with weather and or sea conditions, sometimes involves use of anchor if water is shallow enough.

**Hold**  Portions of ship in which cargo is stored.

**Jury**  Temporary repair; for example to a ship's rudder, which is then deemed "jury-rigged."

**Knot**  Measurement used for speed of a ship or boat; a knot is measured as one nautical mile (6,087.27 feet) per hour.

**Lee**  Down-wind side, opposite the weather side; in shelter of down-wind side.

**Leeward**  Downwind, away from the wind.

**Limey**  General reference for British sailor or seaman.

**List**  Slant of ship or vessel from upright position caused by shifting of cargo, uneven intake of seawater, etc.

**Longshoreman**  Person who generally loads and unloads a ship; stevedore.

**Lyle Gun**  Used for rescue and transfer of items from ship to ship or ship to shore, by firing a line that can then be secured at another point.

**Mate**  Navigation officer (third, second and chief).

**Mess (room)**  Dining area on ship; officer and crew mess.

**Monkey's fist**  Weighted knot-work in shape of ball placed at end of heaving line.

**Oerlikon**  Light, rapid-firing cannon firing variety of shell.

**Old Man**  Reference to the ship's commanding officer (master/captain).

**Overhead**  Ceiling.

**Paravane**  Mechanism installed on ships to prevent damage from mine explosions.

**Plimsol Line**  A marked load line on hull of ship to indicate safe point to which it can be loaded.

**Poop Deck**  Raised deck at the back end (stern) of a ship.

**Port**  The left side of a ship, looking forward.

**Pumpman**  Unlicensed rating on tankers, training to load, discharge or otherwise transfer liquid cargo.

**Purser**  Staff officer, administrative, reports directly to master; involved with record keeping, ship's funds, disbursements, inventory, reporting, preparation of legal forms, etc.

**Quarter**  Indicates a position relative to, and aft of, the ship's center line (beam), and forward of the ship's stern. Thus, if it is reported that an object or vessel has been sighted "off the port quarter" it would be on a line looking to the left of the after portion of the ship.

**Rigging**  Ropes, lines, chains, cable used to support masts, booms and working gear and parts on ship's deck.

**Scuppers**   Drains or openings to carry seawater off a ship's deck.

**Scuttlebutt**   Traditionally a drinking fountain or water container on deck; gathering place on deck; term for seamen's gossip.

**Slop Chest**   Compartment on ship from which seamen could periodically purchase articles of clothing, toiletries, etc.

**Sougey (soogee)**   Cleaning decks or painted bulkheads often with a long-handled brush and strong cleaning solvent.

**Splice**   Joining two lines (ropes) or cables by separating strands at ends and then combining by interweaving and tucking.

**Starboard**   The right side of a ship while looking forward, opposite of port.

**Starshell**   Fired from gun, releases flare suspended from parachute for nighttime illumination.

**Stem**   Frame at ship's bow that joins its two sides; connected to keel at lowest end.

**Stern**   Rearmost part of a ship or boat.

**Steward, Chief**   In charge of steward's department aboard ship; others in department include cooks (first and second), cook and baker, galley utility, messmen.

**Stores**   Generally, foodstuff supplies for galley.

**Tackle**   Combination of blocks and line (rope) used for raising and lowering heavy objects.

**Topside**   On or above the weather-deck; portion above the waterline, as in "I'm going topside."

**Very Pistol**   A pistol used for firing colored signal flares, named after Edward Wilson Very (1847–1910), an American naval officer.

**Watch**   A work shift, generally four hours on, four hours off while at sea. They are as follows: the 12 to 4 watch, 4 to 8 watch, and 8 to 12 watch. In the deck department, for example, a seaman would typically stand a third of a watch on the wheel, a third on standby, and another third on lookout duty.

**Watch Partner**   Crew member who shares duties with others on a specific watch.

**Winch**   Machine fitted with double horizontal drum, steam-powered or otherwise, used for pulling or hoisting, generally for handling cargo, raising (topping) cargo booms.

**Windlass**   Apparatus used for raising or lowering anchors.

**Wing of bridge**   Outside extension of the navigation bridge, on both port and starboard side, used for conning, lookout watch, navigation, and issuing commands.

# Appendix B: The Crew of a Typical Liberty (Dry Cargo) Ship During World War II

**Master**
(Officer in Command of Vessel)

## Departments

| Deck | Radio | Purser | Steward | Engine |
|---|---|---|---|---|
| Chief Officer | Radio Operator | Purser | Chief Steward | Chief Engineer |
| Deck Cadet | | | 1st Cook | Engine Cadet |
| 2nd Officer (Mate) | | | 2nd Cook & Baker | 1st Assistant Engineer |
| 3rd Officer (Mate) | | | Galley Utilityman | 2nd Assistant Engineer |
| (Jr. 3rd and 4th Mate added sometimes) | | | Messman (4) | 3rd Assistant Engineer |
| Boatswain (Bosun) | | | | (Jr. 3rd and 4th Engineer added sometimes) |
| Carpenter | | | | Watertender |
| Able-Bodied Seaman (6) | | | | Fireman (3) |
| Ordinary Seaman (3) | | | | Oiler (3) |
| Other Ratings commonly added: Deck Maintenance, Electrician | | | | Wiper (3) |

*Note:* Merchant Marine personnel only. On a typical Liberty ship the merchant crew usually numbered between 40 and 42 seamen. This does not include naval Armed Guard personnel who, on a similar type ship, would number from as few as eight to as many as two dozen sailors.

# Chapter Notes

## Preface

1. According to the U.S. Maritime Commission, which ordered construction of the vast majority of American-built merchant ships during this period, some 2,708 Liberty ships were delivered overall. This compares with 705 tankers, and 404 "Victory"-type cargo ships delivered during the same period. Frederic C. Lane, et al., *Ships for Victory: A History of Shipbuilding Under the U.S. Maritime Commission in World War II* (Baltimore: The Johns Hopkins Press, 1951), 4.

2. Project Liberty ship (PLS) was begun by Frank Duffy, a former merchant seaman turned stationary engineer in late 1977. Under PLS sponsorship an informational and organizational "seminar" was held at the Seamen's Church Institute in New York City the following year to more fully launch the effort to preserve the SS *John W. Brown*. Since the ship was still under U.S. Government control, a Congressional hearing was held in New York City on 11 March 1983, aboard the ship, to consider a bill, H.R. 1556, and to determine if a viable private initiative was available for transfer of the ship to private control for the purpose of preservation. After a lengthy and competitive process, Project Liberty ship was subsequently selected for that purpose.

3. After the *John W. Brown* was removed from New York to the National Defense Reserve Fleet, James River, VA, in July 1983 for storage, efforts continued to raise awareness and funds for eventually finding a permanent home for the ship. After a meeting was called in Baltimore to discuss this possibility with interested parties, a Baltimore-based effort of Project Liberty ship got underway. A nomination application for listing the ship with the National Register of Historic Places was prepared and submitted, and she was listed as of 1 March 1985. The ship was finally towed to Pier 1, Baltimore, on 13 August 1988, and then rededicated as a memorial-museum on 5 September of that year. On 24 August 1991, the *John W. Brown*, steaming under her own power for the first time since late 1946, completed trials on Chesapeake Bay. For more information about Project Liberty ship, go to: www.ssjohnwbrown.org.

4. Merchant ship losses were greater in 1941 and 1942 than the numbers of ships produced. The situation changed dramatically in 1943 for the better. Lane, *Ships for Victory*, 3; Samuel Eliot Morison, *History of United States Naval Operations in World War II*, Vol. 1, *The Battle of the Atlantic September 1939–May 1943* (Boston: Little, Brown and Co., 1947), 403–404.

5. The number of American merchant ships and seamen lost during World War II is difficult to pin down precisely. However, according to a War Shipping Administration report published in 1946, 733 American merchant vessels of at least 1,000 gross tons were either sunk in direct attack or lost to other war-related circumstances. As a result, more than 6,300 American merchant seamen were either killed outright or went missing. Samuel Eliot Morison, *History of*

*U.S. Naval Operations in World War II*, Vol. I, *The Battle of the Atlantic September 1939- May 1943* (Boston: Little, Brown and Co., 1947), 410.

6. The casualty rate comparison is in Joan McEvoy, esq. *Request for a Determination*, vol. 1, p. 34. This states that of the American Merchant Marine personnel registered with the U.S. Maritime Service during the war, an overall death rate of 2.8 percent was experienced during the period, compared to the 2.9 percent rate of the U.S. Marine Corps.

## Chapter 1

1. Interview conducted 14 May 1982 at Bailey's home on Telegraph Hill, San Francisco, CA.
2. Bailey refers here to the North Russia convoy routes which caused severe cases of frostbite among many seamen. For more on this see Chapters 2, 9, 13, 16, 18 and 19.
3. Bailey had been arrested in 1935 as a participant in the so-called "Bremen Incident" in New York City when a group of protesters went aboard the German passenger liner *Bremen*, tore down the swastika flag from the stern flagstaff, and threw it into the Hudson River. As one of the "Bremen Six," charges were eventually dismissed. For further details see Bill Bailey, *The Kid from Hoboken: An Autobiography* (San Francisco: BB Productions. 1993).
4. "All them other places" included various locations in the Pacific and South America as Third Assistant Engineer in the SS *John Paul Jones*; to Eniwetok, the Mariana Islands, New Hebrides, and Australia in the SS *Cape Grieg*; the Aleutians in Alaska as First Assistant Engineer in the SS *Samuel Gompers*; and to The Philippines for the invasion of Subic Bay as First Assistant in the SS *George Powell*.

## Chapter 2

1. Interview conducted 21 April 1978 at South Street Seaport, New York, NY.
2. As a C-1 at 417 feet 9 inches overall, the SS *Idaho* was the smaller of the standard C-type cargo ship types built after 1939. Five were delivered in 1940, and another 29 in 1941, and were powered by either steam turbine or diesel, and with a service speed around 14 knots. Lane, et al., *Ships for Victory*, 28–29.
3. The capital and largest city of Mozambique, Lourenco Marques was renamed Maputo after independence.
4. The Battleship HMS *Prince of Wales* and Battlecruiser *Repulse* arrived in Singapore in early December 1941 and were sunk by Japanese land- and sea-based aircraft on 10 December 1941.
5. The 410-foot SS *Lihue* was built in Seattle in 1919, and was operated by Matson Navigation Co. She was under the command of Capt. W. C. Leithead.
6. Ensign Peter Wendt, 25, attended the University of Wisconsin.
7. Accounts of this action, both stating that the submarine had been sunk by the *Lihue*'s gun crew "by the light of the U-boat skipper's flares," were subsequently printed in *Life* Magazine (May 1942), and *The New York Times* (March 20, 1942, p. 1). Photographs of crew abandoning ship, and later from launched lifeboat, were taken by Ensign Wendt and provided by his father, William H. Wendt. However, the report of the submarine having been sunk were more a function of need for good news early in the war, than reality; the submarine that attacked SS *Lihue*—*U-161* (Achilles)—was not actually sunk until September 22, 1943, when it was bombed off Bahia, Brazil with no survivors. Capt. Arthur R. Moore, *A Careless Word...A Needless Sinking: A History of the Tremendous Losses in Ships and Men Suffered by the U.S. Merchant Marine in World War II* (Kings Point, NY: American Merchant Marine Museum, 1983), 173.
8. The 410-foot, 5,444 gross ton SS *Kentucky* was built in Los Angeles, CA, in 1921, and home ported in San Francisco.
9. See chapters 14–16.
10. Interview containing this recollection was conducted and recorded on 12 December 1981. The SS *Isaac Coles* was built at the California Shipbuilding Corporation, Los Angeles in June 1942, and scrapped at Mobile, Alabama in 1967.
11. As an unlicensed merchant mariner, and despite what he had already been

through during the war, Bethell's snub by an ignorant Red Cross worker in Sicily— who would not even serve him *water*—was not that unusual. He would have fared better, no doubt, if he had gone ashore in the uniform of a Merchant Marine officer instead of the dungarees more typical of his rating. Despite the close—indeed, codependent—working relationship between the Merchant Marine and military services in wartime, and the relatively high casualty rate of merchant mariners in proportion to their overall numbers (see Preface, notes 2 and 3), they were still technically civilian and, as such, were denied services generally reserved for those in the military branches. The promise made by President Roosevelt for the postwar period, on behalf of a grateful nation, to recognize and reward the wartime service and sacrifice made by the Merchant Marine by providing basic, government-sponsored veterans benefits, died along with him some months before the war ended. Merchant Marine veterans were awarded and entitled to wear service ribbons and medals for area and combat service, heroism, wounds received and time spent in prisoner of war camps, but official recognition for purposes of entitlement to veterans' benefits would not come for another 43 years, after a long application and appeals process.

## Chapter 3

1. Interview conducted and recorded in Brooklyn, NY, on 16 April 1982

2. Launched at Newport News Shipbuilding and Dry Dock Co., VA, in 1921, SS *Beacon* had an overall length of 515 feet 6 inches. Her sister ship *H. H. Rogers* was torpedoed while in convoy on 21 February 1943. At that time she was under Panamanian registry.

3. The tanker SS *Typhoon*, with length of 400 feet, was launched as SS *William F. Hearin* at Newport News Shipbuilding and Dry Dock Co. in 1911, renamed SS *Colorado* and then *Typhoon*. She was acquired by the U.S. Navy under bareboat charter from War Shipping Administration on 19 October 1943, eventually commissioned as USS *Villalabos* (LX-145). Decommissioned in February 1946, she was returned to private commercial service.

4. This would have been on the evening of 16 February 1942 when the refinery and nearby ships at Aruba, Netherlands West Indies, were attacked by the German submarine *U-156* (Werner Hartenstein). There was little damage to the refinery itself, but several tankers were either sunk or damaged, including the American SS *Arkansas*, a tanker built at Bath, Maine in 1919, which was damaged while moored portside to the dock in Aruba. Aruba had become a British protectorate in 1940 after the Netherlands were occupied by Germany. The United States took over this responsibility, initially landing a force of 1,000 troops, on 16 January 1942, one month before Bradley's arrival there. Morison, Vol. I, 145; Moore, 340.

5. According to a history of the Esso fleet during the war, *Esso Manhattan* had completed six voyages without mishap to Texas, Curacao, Freetown, West Africa, Puerto Rico and Aruba before the ill-fated intended voyage from Constable Hook, NJ, to Curacao. It was initially believed, since the ship had not cleared "the protecting minefields," that the explosion causing her to split amidships was from a mine. However, some later reports noting multiple incidents of failure without exterior cause (weather, sea condition or war-related), concluded structural flaws had caused a number of ships—including *Esso Manhattan*—to suffer serious internal failure resulting in loss or damage that required major repair. For an early report suggesting mine damage see Standard Oil Company (New Jersey), *Ships of the Esso Fleet in World War II* (1946), 433–440. For a later history that places emphasis on the structural flaw argument see L. A. Sawyer and W. H. Mitchell, *Victory Ships and Tankers: The History of the 'Victory' Type Cargo Ships and of the Tankers Built in the United States of America During World War II* (Cambridge, MD: Cornell Maritime Press, Inc., 1974), 98–99, 153.

6. The *Esso Manhattan* was repaired by Todd Shipyards Corp. at Erie Basin, Brooklyn, NY, and returned to service 73 days after her mishap, on 11 June 1943.

7. This was the *USCGC Kimball*, which landed survivors at Pier 6, Tompkinsville, Staten Island, NY.

8. Built by Bethlehem-Sparrows Point Shipyard, Inc. at Sparrows Point, MD, for Sun Oil Co. of New Jersey, *Esso Harrisburg* was essentially a T-3 design, and had an overall length of 501 feet 7¾ inches.

9. The SS *Cherry Valley* was torpedoed by *U-66* on 22 July 1943 while en route from New York to Aruba in ballast. She remained operational, with starboard side ripped open, and managed to arrive at Puerto Rico two days later. She was repaired and returned to service. Sawyer and Mitchell, 152; Moore, 347.

10. The tanker *Esso Pittsburg* was built at Sun Shipbuilding Co., Chester, PA, in February 1943.

11. *Esso Harrisburg* was first hit by a torpedo from *U-516* (Tillesen) at 1930 hrs. EWT, and soon after by two more, on 6 July 1943 about 200 miles northwest of Aruba. The *U-516* survived the war to surrender in May 1945. For a lengthy description see *Ships of the Esso Fleet*, 506–510, and also Moore, 92.

12. Merchant seamen lost were: Capt. Ernest C. Kelson, Master; Randolph E. MacDonald, Bosun; Robert C. Henter, AB; Eugene S. Stachowiak, AB. Four members of the Navy Armed Guard were also lost.

13. Willis M. Hayden, Jr.

14. Lifeboat #1 with Second Mate Hayden in command was rescued by the Dutch *Queen Wilhemina* on 9 July, a day after survivors in lifeboat #3 were rescued by that ship. Survivors in lifeboat #4 and a raft were rescued by USS *SC-1299*, a minesweeper. Survivors in lifeboat #1 under command of Chief Mate sailed to the coast of Columbia near Santa Marta where it arrived on 10 July. Moore, 92.

## Chapter 4

1. The Liberty ship SS *Wade Hampton*, operated by Mississippi Shipping Co., was built at Delta Shipbuilding Co., New Orleans, in December 1942.

2. The SS *Wade Hampton* was in Convoy HX-227 en route from New York to Russia.

3. The SS *Wade Hampton* was torpedoed by the German submarine *U-405* (Hopmann) which was sunk in mid-Atlantic by USS *Borie* (DD-215) on 1 November 1943. There were no survivors.

4. Five members of the U.S. Navy Armed Guard crew were lost.

5. The British destroyer HMS *Beverly*.

6. Bosun John Sandova was one of three merchant seamen lost on the SS *Wade Hampton*. The others were Deck Cadet George C. Miller, Jr., and Ordinary Seaman John W. Wayson.

## Chapter 5

1. Interview conducted and recorded from New York by phone with Racine, WI, on 18 April 1987.

2. The C-1 was a new standard cargo ship type with an overall length of 417 feet 9 inches, DWT of 9,075, and rated top speed of 14 knots. The first five C-1s were delivered in 1940, and another 29—including *MS American Leader*, built in San Francisco—in 1941. These ships were partly powered by turbines, and some by diesel engines. Lane, et al., *Ships for Victory*, 28–29.

3. While it is believed by some that the U.S. Navy was somewhat late to initiate convoying for American shipping, the British, in the war since 1939, had begun convoying long before 1941.

4. The Brooklyn-class light cruiser USS *Boise* was launched at Newport News Shipbuilding and Drydock Co. in December 1936, and commissioned on 12 August 1938. She had operated between San Pedro, CA, and Hawaii, and did escort a small convoy to Manila in early December 1941, but arriving according to official accounts on 4 December. On 8 December she was off Cebu Island and then joined Task Force (TF 5) with USS *Houston* and USS *Langley* in the East Indies. Morison, vol. 3, 193.

5. There appears to be some discrepancy between official records regarding the timing of arrival of convoy escort—USS *Boise*—and Gorski's memory of his ship's arrival in Manila.

6. According to one account, Adm. Thomas H. Hart, Commander in Chief U.S. Asiatic Fleet, then in Manila, held a meeting with available merchant ship captains on 11 December 1941 and "urged them to depart

to the southward although he had no escort to offer them." Morison, vol. 3, 195.

7. In the end, according to Morison's history, 29 submarines—then the largest single submarine force in the U.S. Navy—were left as remaining naval defense of the Philippine Islands. Escorting merchant ships through mine fields might not have been a high priority option at that point. Morison, Vol. 3, 193.

8. Under normal circumstances, because of labor union contractual agreement restrictions, this might have been difficult to achieve otherwise. But these were obviously not normal circumstances.

9. Later in this interview Gorski will recall that the failure of some crew members to report before time of sailing might have occurred as *American Leader* was leaving Australia, not Manila.

10. Located some 750 miles northeast of Australia, New Caledonia was claimed by France in 1853, developed as a penal colony and mined for its nickel and ores. It backed Free French forces early in World War II, became an important allied base, and its capital, Noumea, served as headquarters for the U.S. Navy and Army in the area.

11. Gorski was being transferred in the Japanese transport *Junyo Maru* to another camp in Sumatra when it was torpedoed by HMS *Tradewind* on 18 September 1944. This resulted in the loss of more than 5,600 prisoners—including four of the eight survivors from *American Leader* on board—and Japanese "Ramushas" (slave laborers). Only 680, including Gorski, survived this incident. For more about the *American leader* see Moore, vol. 16, 486; August Karl Muggenthaler, *German Raiders of World War II* (Englewood Cliffs, NJ: Prentice Hall, 1977).

Hawaiian island of O'ahu some 12 miles northeast of Honolulu, was actually attacked some nine minutes before the attack on Pearl Harbor commenced. By 1941 there was a U.S. Army artillery unit stationed there.

4. As a result of the attack on Pearl Harbor eight battleships were damaged or destroyed (four were sunk, two subsequently raised and returned to service), three cruisers and three destroyers were either sunk or damaged; 2,402 were killed, 1,282 were wounded.

5. Originally named the *West Faralon*, the ship was built in 1921 in Los Angeles, CA. Operated by the American-Hawaiian Steamship Co. based in New York, the SS *Honolulan* was then under the command of Capt. Charles M. Bamforth.

6. Ship losses to submarine activity in the Caribbean Sea Frontier West and Bermuda Area in February, March and April 1942 averaged some 29 ships a month. That figure rose dramatically to an average of 42 ships lost in May and June 1942 in those areas. This does not include some 41 ships lost in the Gulf (of Mexico) Sea Frontier in May, and another 21 in June. Morison, Vol. 1, 135–148, 413–414.

7. The SS *Honolulan* was first torpedoed in the area of #5 cargo hold, starboard side, by the German submarine *U-582* (Schulte) at 1814 GCT on 22 July 1942 some 400 miles south of Cape Verde Islands. The Master ordered the ship abandoned at that point, and 36 crewmembers got away in three boats. About 15 minutes later a second torpedo hit near hold #3, and the ship sank quickly. The Master, Chief Mate, and Radio Operator jumped overboard and were picked up, as was another crewmember who had been blown overboard. None of the crew of 40 were listed as casualties.

8. See Moore, 129–130.

## Chapter 6

1. Interview conducted and recorded in Brooklyn, NY, in 1982.

2. Built at Maryland Steel Co., Sparrows Point, in 1912, the 416-foot SS *Dakotan* was operated by the American-Hawaiian Steamship Company.

3. The Naval Air Station Kaneohe Bay (now a Marine Corps base), situated on the

## Chapter 7

1. Interview with Paul Jarvis conducted and recorded in New York City, 28 August 1981.

2. The SS *Richard Henderson* was bound ultimately for Bandur Shahpur, Iran.

3. The SS *Richard Henderson* was in Convoy UGS-14.

4. Jarvis must be thinking of *Only Yesterday*, by Frederick Lewis Allen, published in 1931. This was a history of the 1920s. Allen (1890–1954) became editor in chief of *Harper's Magazine* in 1941.

5. Tethered to merchant ships with cable, barrage balloons were commonly used to deter low-flying aircraft from approaching too close. Many were also used, for example, during the D-Day invasion of 1944.

6. The SS *John Bell*, carrying general military cargo and aviation gas, was torpedoed off La Calle, Algeria, by *U-410* (Fanski) at 1915 GLT on 26 August 1943. Moore, 152.

7. The SS *Richard Henderson*, carrying mostly ammunition, was torpedoed about five minutes after SS *John Bell*—at 1920 GCT—by the same submarine (*U-410*) and was reported to finally sink, by the stern, at 0200 GCT on 27 August 1943. There were no casualties reported. Moore, 235.

8. This would have been the South African HMSAS *Southern Maid*, a 344-ton whaler converted for anti-submarine duty in the Mediterranean during the war.

9. Three life boats landed at La Calle, Algeria, on the morning of 27 August 1943. Survivors from the other three boats were taken aboard escort vessels and landed at Bizerte on 27 August 1943. Moore, 235.

10. The War Shipping Administration (W.S.A.) was established by Executive Order #9054 on 7 February 1942 to purchase, operate and train crews for ships constructed during World War II. Under the leadership of Adm. Emory S. Land, who had and continued to head the Maritime Commission, the W.S.A. became, in Land's words, "the Government's ship operating agency and the Maritime Commission its shipbuilding agency." It was responsible for operations of and training for more than 3,500 merchant cargo ships and tankers that became the U.S. merchant fleet during the war, and continued until 1 September 1946 when its functions were returned fully to the Maritime Commission. It did not seem particularly involved in initial response to landed ship survivors. Land. *Ships for Victory*, 161–62.

11. The Liberty ship SS *John Sergeant* was launched at Bethlehem-Fairfield Shipyard in Baltimore, MD, in September 1942, and scrapped at Portsmouth, VA, in 1972.

12. The battle for Okinawa took place between 1 April and 2 July 1945. Though hostilities were officially declared over at that point, attacks by kamikaze and conventional Japanese aircraft continued well into August.

13. A number of merchant Liberty- and Victory-type ships were either lost or damaged—mostly to Kamikaze attack—in the Okinawan campaign. These included: *Brown Victory* (damaged), *Canada Victory* (sunk), *Hobbs Victory* (sunk), *Josiah Snelling* (damaged), *Logan Victory* (sunk), and *Mary A. Livermore* (damaged).

14. It is more likely that USS *Pennsylvania* was not hit directly by a typical Kamikaze aircraft, but by an aircraft-launched torpedo. This did occur in Buckner Bay—named for an American general killed during the fighting on Okinawa—on 12 August 1945, well after general land-based hostilities had ceased.

15. This was Nakagusuku Wan (Bay), nick-named Buckner Bay in honor of Lt. Gen. Simon Bolivar Buckner, who was killed during the fighting on Okinawa. At least one American merchant ship—SS *Josiah Snelling*—was hit by kamikaze aircraft in that bay.

16. This was Typhoon Louise, which hit Okinawa on 9 October 1945, causing serious damage to American installations in the Buckner Bay area, and grounded some 15 merchant ships, some of which were not recoverable. Three Navy destroyers were grounded beyond salvage. It was estimated that some 80 percent of buildings in the bay area were completely destroyed by the 90 mile an hour winds of the typhoon. In Okinawa, some 36 people were reported killed, and another 47 missing.

## Chapter 8

1. Interview conducted and recorded in New York, NY, on 28 September 1982.

2. The 410-foot and 5,492 gross ton SS *West Notus*, operated by McCormick Steamship Co., was built in Los Angeles in 1920, and was homeported in San Francisco.

3. The SS *West Notus* was attacked by

U-404 at 0615 EWT on 1 June 1942 about 300 miles east of Cape Hatteras, NC. It was reported that some 50 rounds were fired at, of which about 20 struck the ship.

4. Four seamen were killed during the attack on *West Notus:* Hans Gerner, Master; Wilfred Clarkson, Radio Operator; Harry Morris, Third Mate; and Victor Wellcom, Third Engineer.

5. The German submarine *U-404*, then under command of Von Bulow, was later bombed and sunk with no survivors in the Bay of Biscay. Moore, 301.

6. The Swiss SS *Saentis* picked up 18 survivors, including Johanson, on 4 June, and delivered them the next day in New York. Eighteen survivors in the other lifeboat were picked up by the Greek SS *Constantinos H.* on 3 June 1942 and landed in Bermuda on 5 June 1942.

## Chapter 9

1. Interview with Ruel Lawrence conducted and recorded in Brooklyn, NY, 14 September 1979.

2. Alcoa is well known for its association with aluminum production, for which bauxite is a key raw material.

3. The SS *Arizpa* was a 400-foot, 5,437 GT cargo ship built by Merchant Shipbuilding Corp. in Bristol, PA, in 1920. Lawrence signed on this ship as Wiper for his introduction to work in the engine department "black gang."

4. Report filed by ship's Naval Armed Guard officer stated the cargo consisted of 8,200 tons of bulk nitrates.

5. In a report completed by Lt. (jg) Robert Chitrin, USNR, SS *Arizpa's* Naval Armed Guard officer on 23 February 1942, the following was said about the incident with the whale:

"Thursday, Feb. 19, at 1:03 p.m. an object was sighted on our starboard beam. Our course was 148 degrees true, our position 11 degrees, 52 minutes South Latitude, 79 degrees, 05 minutes West Longitude. The General Alarm was sounded and the ship was brought about so as to put the object astern and then on our port quarter. The 4-inch gun opened fire at 4,000 yards and expended 11 rounds, of which 2 were direct hits and the others near hits. Out two port 50 caliber machine guns opened fire at close range and expended 175 rounds each. The 30 caliber Lewis Gun operated by ships officers also opened fire at close range and scored many hits out of the 47 rounds expended. Close investigation showed the object to be a whale floating on the surface, on its side and one fin in the air. It was approximately 70 feet long, and was well scared by our fire. When the whale was first seen, it was in the sun, and the light shining on it gave it the appearance of a submarine three quarters submerged. The fin projecting in the air resembled a periscope, and there was no doubt in the minds of any of the ships personnel, or my own, that we had come upon a submarine." A note hand-written in a margin of this report, presumably by someone at Naval headquarters, commented: "should leave whaling for the Horshammer expidition [sic]."

6. According to a report subsequently filed by Lt. Chitrin on 18 March 1942, the SS *Arizpa* departed Tocopilla, Chile, on 26 February for the return voyage, transitted the Panama Canal on 9 March, and arrived in Wilmington, NC, on 18 March 1942. So Lawrence would have made his way back to Mobile, AL, from there, and then shipped out again, for Russia, a few weeks later.

7. Convoy PQ-17 left Hvalfjordur, Iceland on 27 June 1942 with 33 merchant ships, 22 of which were American. The first attack by German dive-bombers occurred on 2 July 1942, but caused little damage. Weather precluded air attack on 3 July, and then "all hell broke loose" on 4 July. By the time attacks by bombers and submarines ended some days later, two-thirds of the American ships had been lost. Morison, vol. 1, 181–191.

8. As it was explained or rationalized afterwards, reports that the Battleship *Von Tirpitz* and its group had set sail from Norway in the direction of this convoy as part of operation "Rosselsprung" ("Knight's Gambit") to destroy PQ-17 required the convoy escort to depart, thus diverting the German force away from the convoy. However, the Germans, overly protective of *Von Tirpitz* it seems in aftermath of loss of other capital ships caused it to be pulled back and

no longer a threat. In the end, the terribly costly decision to remove the escort and scatter the convoy was, according to one history, "based on an overestimate of the enemy's intentions." Morison, I, 185.

9. Captain Soren Mortensen. The order to disperse came at 1900 hrs. on 4 July 1942.

10. This did occur two days later when the SS *Pan Atlantic*, steaming alone and unescorted, was attacked at 1615 GCT on 6 July 1942.

11. One account describes a bomb hitting the forward well-deck and "blowing apart the entire forward section of the ship and toppling the foremast onto the pilot house" and causing the ship to sink within three minutes. Moore, 212.

12. Marshall E. Emanuel, Messman, was one of the 18 merchant seamen lost in the attack on SS *Pan Atlantic*.

13. Most other accounts make no mention of a torpedo hit on SS *Pan Atlantic*, but, then again, most other accounts were not written by someone who was there.

14. Of the Merchant Marine compliment of 36 seamen, 18 were lost. Of 11 in the U.S. Navy Armed Guard detail, seven were lost.

15. This is considerably longer—by six days—than what is indicated by the historical record. According to most accounts, survivors of SS *Pan Atlantic* were picked up by HMS *Lotus* at 0800 on 9 July 1942. But whereas some records state that these survivors were taken directly to Archangel by *Lotus*, Lawrence recalls that they were delivered to Murmansk, where they were then transferred to a destroyer for transit to Archangel. See, for example, Moore, 212.

16. This would have been one of the newer 20 mm Oerlikon rapid-fire cannons that the U.S. Navy had begun to install on its own and merchant ships in 1942. However, they arrived too late to help ships in Convoy PQ-17 when they might have made a huge difference in its outcome.

17. Of course, not everyone would have agreed with Lawrence's assessment of the Russians, nor his experience in Russia at that time. See, for example, Jack McCusker's recollections in chapter 13, above.

18. The SS *Bellingham*, Capt. Soren Mortensen, was a 410-foot, 4,435 gross ton freighter built in Los Angeles, CA, in 1920.

19. The ship was torpedoed in area of #4 hold, starboard side, by *U-435* (Strelow) at about 0615 GCT on 22 September 1942 some 45 miles west of Jan Mayen Islands. Moore, 29.

20. There were no casualties reported.

21. Survivors were picked up by HMS *Rathlin* and transferred to vicinity of Glasgow, Scotland.

22. This is inland, between Glasgow and Greenock, Scotland.

## Chapter 10

1. Interview conducted and recorded on 20 September 1985.

2. The 351-foot, 5,649 gross ton passenger ship SS *Chatham* was built in Newport News, VA, in 1926.

3. John Le Cato signed off SS *Chatham* on 30 January 1942 to attend the U.S. Maritime Service Training School, Ft. Trumball, NY, where he upgraded to Third Mate. The SS *Chatham* (Capt. Edward Anderson) with 428 passengers on board was torpedoed and sunk while in convoy (SG-6) between Sydney, Nova Scotia and Greenland on 27 August 1942. Seven seamen and seven passengers were lost.

4. The SS *Norluna* was under the command of Capt. Robert L. Casey, and was operated by the Merchant and Miners Transportation Co. She was built in a shipyard along the Great Lakes as part of a contracted 346 ships (of which 331 were delivered) intended for use during World War I. The so-called "Lakers" were generally 251 × 43 feet and 3,500–4,000 DWT (deadweight tonnage), and were produced in greater numbers than any other standard ship type during that period. The Rev. Edward J. Dowling. *The Lakers of World War I*. Detroit: University of Detroit Press.

5. This would have been German submarine *U-705* (Horn) which was later bombed and sunk west of Brest on September 3, 1942. There were no survivors.

6. Twelve of 34 merchant seamen were lost as a result of the attack on the *Balladier*, which was reported to have sunk just seven minutes after having been torpedoed.

7. The name of the Master of SS *Balladier* has not been determined.

8. Capt. Sir John Franklin was an Artic explorer who, after setting out in 1845 for another expedition, was lost with all 128 members of the party whose two ships had become icebound in Victoria Strait near King William Island. Various rescue parties—all ultimately unsuccessful—began setting out from 1848. The charts referenced here, if used at that time, would have been at least 90 years old.

9. Port Churchill is located on the western shore of Hudson Bay, in the Canadian province of Manitoba.

10. The *Bear* had a long career, starting as a sealer in 1874. She was used by Adm. Richard E. Byrd for two expeditions to Antarctica, as an Arctic icebreaker and patrol vessel by the U.S. Coast Guard, and by the Navy as a patrol vessel out of Greenland during World War II. Intended finally for use as a stationery restaurant in Philadelphia, she foundered and sank in the North Atlantic in 1963 while under tow. The schooner Effie E. Morrissey was under command of Arctic explorer Robert Bartlett (1875–1946) from 1925 until 1945. During World War II it did survey work for the U.S. Navy in the Canadian Arctic.

11. Fort Chimo—probably from an Inuit word meaning "let's shake hands" and later renamed Kuujjuaq, meaning "Great River"—is on the western side of Koksoak River which flows into Ungava Bay east of Hudson Bay in northern Quebec. It was developed as an Army Air Force base early in World War II, is still used for air access to that part of the Canadian Arctic, and had a population of 2,375 as of 2011.

12. The SS *Norluna* was unloading into barges on 25 October 1942 and ran aground when its anchor dragged in the swift current. The rising tide contributed to her demise, and she was ultimately declared a constructive total loss.

13. Robert Merrill. A large archive of materials relating to the Merchants and Miner's Transportation Co., 1852–1952, is located at the Maryland Historical Society.

14. The SS *Thomas Hartley* was operated by the Merchants and Miners Transportation Co.

15. Designated Convoy JW-53 before its departure on 15 February 1943 from Loch Ewe, Scotland, what would become known as the "forgotten convoy" was accompanied to Russia by one cruiser, and 20 other warships including 11 destroyers. Morison, Vol. I, 368–369.

16. Compared to the 441-foot Liberty, Le Cato's last ship—SS *Norluna*—had been a 250-foot "Laker" built for transiting the locks of the St. Lawrence Seaway after construction in the area.

17. Convoy JW-53 was scouted by German aircraft on 23 and 24 February, and then attacked by JU-88 or JU-89 bombers from high altitude on 25 and 26 February 1943.

18. The number of merchant ships in Convoy JW-53 is usually put at 22, of which six (or eight) were American. One history indicates there were six American ships, while Le Cato recalled there were six. Morison, vol. 1, 368–369.

19. Poor visibility, and improved defensive firepower, aided the convoy, and prevented low-level attack. No serious damage nor casualties were reported.

20. The Convoy made it to the Kola Inlet near Murmansk on 27 February 1943.

21. The *Ocean Freedom* was sunk by aircraft bombs in Murmansk on 13 March 1943. The Ocean-type cargo ships, some commenced in early 1941 and all delivered in 1942, were built for the British in American shipyards. While having a somewhat different outward profile, the design later evolved into the Liberty type—such as SS *Thomas Hartley*—which would be built in such unprecedented numbers during World War II.

22. Convoy RA-53 with 30 merchant ships (11 American) departed Murmansk on 1 March 1943 with a large escort that included three cruisers and 11 destroyers. At least two of the merchant ships were lost to enemy action en route, and one to heavy seas.

23. The other American ship was the Sun Oil Co. tanker *Beacon Hill*.

24. Renamed Senerodvinsk in 1957, Molotovsk had a population of but 21,000 in 1939, and 32,900 in 1948. But, as a key submarine and ship construction and repair center during the Cold War period, its population swelled to a peak of nearly 250,000 by 1992, before then entering a period of some decline.

25. The one they did not make was said Convoy RA-53. See note 9 above.

26. Scotland's third longest river, the Clyde runs through Glasgow and out beyond Greenock. Oban, on the west coast of Scotland north of the Clyde, was used as a key base for convoy and naval activity during the Battle of the Atlantic.

27. As part of Operation Overlord, the initial landings at Normandy took place on 6 June 1944, which was D-Day. They took place on five beaches, code-named Juno, Gold, Omaha, Utah and Sword. At Omaha, the American sector, some 314,504 men, 41,000 vehicles and some 116,000 tons of supplies—largely carried in merchant ships—were moved ashore by 19 June, D-Day plus 13. Bunker, *Liberty Ships*, 168. For more regarding logistical support for the Omaha Beachhead see Morison, vol. 11, 166.

28. The DUKW—not acronym but a GMC code designation for a model designed in 1942 (D), utility (U), front-wheel drive (K), with two powered rear axles (W)—was a 31-foot long, six-wheel-drive amphibious truck. More than 21,000 were built.

29. These breakwaters—code-named "Gooseberry"—included 27 American merchant ships of various types, many of World War I-vintage but also at least a half dozen new Liberty ships that had been damaged or otherwise deemed unfit for service. Moore, 549.

30. There were two "Mulberry" artificial harbors, one of which was located in support of the Omaha Beach head. Consisting largely of pre-fab concrete sections, they were towed into place and were operational by D-Day plus three.

## Chapter 11

1. Interview conducted 13 May 1982 aboard SS *Jeremiah O'Brien*, National Liberty ship Memorial, San Francisco, CA. Established as a nautical school by the Pennsylvania Assembly in 1889, and known formally as the Pennsylvania State Nautical School and later Pennsylvania Maritime Academy, the Pennsylvania Schoolship remained in operation until 1947, by which time some 2,000 students had been graduated and prepared for careers at sea and related fields. Training was received on a series of ships, such as the *Annapolis* (1920–40) and *Keystone State* (1942–46).

2. Built in Tampa, FL, in 1940, MS *Sea Witch* was the first of a new class of standardized American merchant cargo ships, the C-2. As such, she had a length of 459 feet 2½ inches.

3. Prior to entry of the U.S. in the war, an arrangement was entered into with the British wherein military equipment would be "loaned" in exchange for lease of property for military installations.

4. Manila was bombed by the Japanese on Monday, 8 December (local time) some eight hours after the attack on Pearl Harbor. Evacuation of American forces from Manila, which was declared an "open city" to spare further destruction (to no avail), was ordered for 24 December 1941, the day *Sea Witch* got underway. The Japanese Army entered the city on 2 January 1942.

5. Period jargon for Balikpapan, located on the east coast of Borneo, Indonesia.

6. These were P-40 fighters.

7. Now known as Cilacap, in southwest central Java, Indonesia (then Netherlands East Indies).

8. Initially launched as the collier USS *Jupiter* (AC-3) in 1912, the ship was converted in 1920 to USS *Langley* (CV-1), the first U.S. Navy aircraft carrier. She was converted again to a seaplane tender in 1937 and given new designation (AV-3). Moving from anchorage in Cavite after the Japanese attack on Manila, *Langley* departed on 8 December 1941 for the Dutch East Indies and arrived in Darwin, Australia, on 1 January 1942, thence to Fremantle to transport aircraft—P-40 fighters, as *Sea Witch*—to Tjilatjap. Leaving in convoy on 22 February with *Sea Witch* and others, she was ordered to separate from convoy on 27 February and was attacked later that day by nine Aichi "Val" dive bombers. Seriously damaged some 75 miles from Tjilatjap, *Langley* was fired upon by escorts and sunk to prevent her capture by the Japanese.

9. The unsuccessful attempt by *Langley* to deliver 32 assembled P-40s, and the successful delivery by *Sea Witch* of 27 crated P-40s to Tjilatjap, is chronicled in Morison,

*History of United States Naval Operations in World War II, Vol. 2, The Rising Sun in the Pacific, 1931–1942*, pp. 359–363.

10. One period description of the approach and arrival to Tjilatjap is as follows: "After threading a very hazardous pass one entered a long, narrow bay with more shoals than deeps. Ships had to moor in line in the middle of the harbor, interfering with traffic and furnishing neat targets for enemy aircraft." Morison, *The Rising Sun in the Pacific*, 298.

11. The light cruiser USS *Marblehead* (CL-12), which had been home ported in Cavite, The Philippines, was heavily damaged by Japanese aircraft in the Battle of Makassar Strait on 4 February 1942. It retired to Tjilatjap for repairs and departed 13 February. So *Sea Witch* would also have departed shortly before that date.

12. Launched at Bath Iron Works in 1917, USS *Isabel* (PY-12) was a 231-foot armed yacht that had once been flagship of Yangtze River operations in China. At Cavite Navy Yard when the Japanese attacked The Philippines, it soon provided anti-submarine convoy escort, later made her way to Australia (Fremantle) and remained in service until 1946.

13. The Brooklyn-class light cruiser USS *Phoenix* was launched in 1935 and commissioned at Philadelphia Navy Yard in 1938. She was at Pearl Harbor in December 1941 during the Japanese attack but not damaged. She escorted convoys in Australian waters and as far as Java in early 1942. In service throughout the war, *Phoenix* was transferred to the Argentinian navy in 1951, renamed *ARA General Belgrano* in 1956, and sunk by the British nuclear submarine HMS *Conqueror* during the Falkland Islands War on 2 May 1982.

14. The letter was published as part of an article in *Trenton Times*, 12 June 1942, written after MacMichael's sister, Elisabeth MacMichael Evans, recognized him in a photograph in an earlier article. She brought that to the paper's attention, and it was published as a follow up with the title "Spots Brother in Times Photo of Navy Operations in Pacific." The article in which this letter appeared was brought to the author's attention by MacMichael's son, Capt. John L. MacMichael, Sr.

15. The story of MacMichael's entrance into the U.S. Navy Reserve—presumably in a brief swearing-in ceremony aboard MS *Sea Witch* while in Manila in December 1941—was told to the author by MacMichael's son, Capt. John L. MacMichael, Sr.

16. Many of the details of MacMichael's wartime and postwar service are contained in his personal resume, which was sent to the author by his son, Capt. John L. MacMichael, Sr.

## Chapter 12

1. Interview conducted and recorded in Bethany Beach, DE, in 1981.

2. Built at Hog Island, NJ, in 1920, this was one of about 110 cargo ships commonly known as the Hog Islander type. Operated by the Cuba Distilling Co., Inc., SS *Catahoula* was one of three ships in its fleet at that time; all three would be lost—two by submarine attack (SS *Catahoula* and SS *Carabulle*), the third (SS *Cassimir*) in collision, by the end of 1942. On this, last, voyage SS *Catahoula* was under the command of Capt. G. B. Johannesen.

3. It's not clear who this seaman was, though two Fireman-watertenders—Alfred K. Neilsen and Antonio Rey—were lost in the sinking of the SS *Catahoula*. Moore, 490.

4. The SS *Catahoula* was attacked by *U-154* (Kolle) which was subsequently sunk with no survivors by USS *Inch* (DE-146) and USS *Frost* (DE-144) on 3 July 1944.

5. Probably Joseph Tralie, AB.

6. Both Emil Christensen, AB, and Joseph Tralie, AB, were listed as lost.

7. The only seaman listed as lost from the steward's department was Norris W. Litch, Cook.

8. This was probably Julius Lynch, Bosun, also listed as lost.

9. Garrett M. Brownrigg, First Assistant Engineer.

10. It's not clear who this was since a pumpman is not on the official list of those who were lost. However, he might have been one of the two FWTs listed as lost (see note 3, above).

11. USS *Sturtevant* was a Clemson-class four-stack destroyer launched in 1920 by

New York Shipbuilding Corp. Assigned to duty in Caribbean Sea Frontier in 1942, under command of Lt. C. L. Weigle, she sank with loss of 13 sailors after running into a minefield soon after leaving Key West, FL, on 26 April 1942. Morison, vol. 1, 136.

12. The North Channel is the strait between north-eastern Ireland and south-western Scotland, connecting the Irish Sea with the Atlantic Ocean.

13. The SS *Jacksonville*, a T-2 tanker operated by Deconhil Shipping Co. and under command of Capt. Edgar Winter (lost), was hit by torpedo from *U-482* (Graf von Matuschka) at 0830 GCT on 30 August 1944. For additional description see Moore, 139.

14. The SS *Jacksonville*'s total complement was 78: 49 merchant crew and 29 Armed Guard. Only two survived, one from each group.

## Chapter 13

1. Interview conducted and recorded in Brooklyn, NY, on 21 June 1981.

2. The SS *John Witherspoon* was a new, 441-foot Liberty ship completed at Bethlehem Fairfield Shipyard in Baltimore, MD, in April 1942. She was "laying under a blanket of snow" there when McCusker went aboard. Operated by Seas Shipping Co., New York, the *John Witherspoon* was under the command of Captain Clark.

3. Convoy PQ-17 departed Reykjavik (Hvalfjordur fjord), Iceland for Archangel, Russia on 27 June 1942, and included 21 American merchant ships (of a total of 33). Commonly referred to as the "July 4th" convoy, the first major attacks on it, by German submarine, high altitude and torpedo-bomber aircraft, began on 2 July, with little effect. Bad visibility on the next day also prevented a successful attack by German aircraft. On 4 July the situation changed dramatically, beginning early that morning with the torpedoing by aircraft and loss of the Liberty ship *Christopher Newport*. As a result of reports of German capital ships (including the Battleship *Tirpitz*) setting out from ports in Norway, the British Admiralty ordered the escorting vessels to withdraw from the convoy, hoping to divert the German surface fleet; the convoy in turn was ordered to scatter. Thus resulted, in the words of historian Samuel Eliot Morison, in the "grimmest convoy battle of the war." As a result of the Admiralty order, and subsequent lack of convoy organization and protection, far more ships were lost in this convoy than might otherwise have occurred, including the SS *John Witherspoon* and two-thirds of the American merchantmen. Morison, *History of United States Naval Operations in World War II, Vol 1, The Battle of the Atlantic, 1939–1943* (Boston: Little, Brown and Co., 1947), 179–192; Dan Van Der Vat, *The Atlantic Campaign: World War II's Great Struggle at Sea* (New York: Harper and Row, 1988), 282–88.

4. Under command of Capt. William L. Graves, the Liberty ship *William Hooper* took on a load of general war cargo in Philadelphia before joining Convoy PQ-17. The ship received a fatal blow from a torpedo that hit the engine room on the starboard side. As a result, three seamen on watch in that area were killed. Moore, 308.

5. The orders from British Admiralty in London were not well received, apparently, by escorting cruiser force either. Rear Admiral L.H.K. "Turtle" Hamilton in HMS *London*, in command of that force, sent this message out after those orders were received: "I know you will be as distressed as I am at having to leave that fine collection of ships to find their own way to harbor." Morison, vol. 1, 185, n26.

6. At 1450 GCT SS *John Witherspoon* was hit by a torpedo on the starboard side between #4 and #5 cargo holds. This was followed by another torpedo hit on the same side underneath the bridge. After the ship was abandoned two more torpedoes struck on the port side amidship, breaking *John Witherspoon* in two, causing her to sink soon after. Moore, 158.

7. This was the *U-25*, which ultimately surrendered at Trondheim, Norway, in May 1945.

8. Ensign Rudolph S. Kroetz.

9. Otis F. Tydings, O.S.

10. The Morgan Line began in Texas in 1837 and initially operated steamships largely between Galveston, TX, and New

Orleans, and then Houston. It was sold in the late 1870s or early 1880s to the Southern Pacific Railroad, but continued to operate under its original name. Its fleet was sold to the U.S. Maritime Commission in 1941.

11. This is reference to a 4-engine German aircraft (Focke-Wulf FW 200) used for long-range reconnaissance and bombing against maritime targets. *El Capitan* was more likely damaged by German Junkers JU-88 dive-bombers. Morison, vol. 1, 190.

12. According to one account, 19 survivors in lifeboat #4 of the SS *John Witherspoon*—16 merchant seaman and three Armed Guard crew—were picked up and eventually put ashore in Archangel by the SS *Hoosier*. Moore, 158. However, that source makes no mention of *El Capitan*, and SS *Hoosier*, presumably in that same mini-convoy was also bombed and abandoned. Morison, 190. So it seems likely McCusker and others from boat #4 were brought into Archangel by one of the designated convoy rescue vessels after transferring from *El Capitan*.

13. The heavy cruiser USS *Tuscaloosa* was used by President Roosevelt at various points in the period just prior to U.S. entry in World War II for high level meetings to discuss such things as the Lend-Lease program of support for Great Britain. It was on hand for the Atlantic Conference in Argentia, Newfoundland, in August 1941, and became part of the task force supporting North Russia convoys in September 1941. Under command of Capt. Norman C. "Shorty" Gillette it was part of the Convoy PQ-17 task force.

14. On 2 October 1942 *Queen Mary* was in collision off the Irish coast with the light cruiser HMS *Curacoa*, which sank with the loss of 239.

15. Entering service with Cunard Line in 1936, the 1,019-foot (LOA) SS *Queen Mary* soon set records for the fastest Atlantic crossings—in excess of 30 knots—by a passenger ship. She was converted for carrying troops during World War II and, because of her speed, ran unescorted. She set a record in December 1942 when 16,082 U.S. troops were carried in one crossing between New York and Great Britain. Known as the "Grey Ghost" during the war, *Queen Mary* continued in commercial service until retired in 1967. She was saved from the breakers after being bought by the city of Long Beach, CA, and established there permanently as a combination hotel, restaurant and museum.

## Chapter 14

1. Interview with Chief Engineer Harry Morgan conducted 13 May 1982 on board the restored Liberty ship SS *Jeremiah O'Brien* (National Liberty ship Memorial) at San Francisco, CA.

2. The 437-foot, 8,151 gross ton SS *Julia Luckenbach* was launched in Quincy, MA, in 1917, and then converted to a troopship and transferred to the U.S. Navy late in World War I. She was decommissioned in September 1919 and returned to commercial use.

3. But the *Julia Luckenbach* was not fast enough—or could not see well enough—to avoid collision with another ship, the tanker SS *British Resolution*, near Cape Agulhas, South Africa, on 23 September 1943. The damage was severe and the ship sank with the loss of its Chief Mate. Moore, 406.

4. Named for an American Civil War general officer, the SS *William S. Rosecrans* was one of more than 2,700 Liberty ships—a new standard type cargo ship (EC2-S-C1) of 4,555 net tonnage, 10,850 deadweight tonnage, and 7,176 gross tonnage—constructed with phenomenal speed using prefab methods during World War II.

5. The city of Beaverton lies not far from and west of the Willamette River in Oregon. Portland straddles the Willamette.

6. Trincomalee, Ceylon, now SLN Dockyard, Sri-Lanka.

7. The island of Malta—a British colony at the time of World War II—is strategically located between Sicily and Africa in the Mediterranean. Requiring a steady supply of ship-borne goods and war materiel, it was besieged and bombed by Axis forces throughout the war.

8. In his seminal work on the Atlantic battle, Admiral Morison noted the "biggest concentration of submarines" encountered

in the area north and south of Recife occurring in the "July Blitz" of 1943. While Morgan's figure of 12 ships lost in one convoy seems inflated, the record does show that some 18 merchant ships were sunk in the Brazilian area between 1 May and the end of July 1943, when Morgan's convoy—presumably one of the northbound TF-designated convoys—was attacked. Morison, vol. 10, *The Atlantic Battle Won*, 215–222.

9. Morgan might be confusing this ship with another. According to various sources, the Liberty ship SS *Jedediah S. Smith* was never torpedoed, nor seriously damaged in other war-related incidents. The ultimate fate of this ship was to be scrapped in Oakland, CA, in 1964. L.A. Sawyer and W.H. Mitchell, *The Liberty Ships: The History of the "Emergency" Type Cargo Ships Constructed in the United States During World War II* (Newton Abbot: David & Charles, 1973), p. 68.

10. British Guiana became Guyana after independence in 1966. While the importance of walnuts to the war effort is not entirely clear—perhaps for a form of lubrication oil—that of bauxite is clear: it is essential for the production of aluminum.

11. The Liberty ship SS *Charles D. Poston* was built at California Shipbuilding Corp., Los Angeles, in June 1943. After postwar service, and time spent in a reserve fleet, she was scrapped at Panama City in 1971.

12. The Liberty ship SS *Luis Arguello* was built at California Shipbuilding Corp. in December 1942, and scrapped at Kure, Japan, in October 1960.

13. Port Moresby is the capital and largest city of Papua, New Guinea.

14. The SS *Simmons Victory* was built at Oregon Shipbuilding Corp., Portland, in May 1945. Later, in 1964, and after being withdrawn from reserve, it was converted by Willamette Iron & Steel Co., Portland, OR, to a mobile base technical ship for research on communications and electromagnetic radiation. Renamed *Liberty* (AG-168), later reclassified as AGTR 168, and then again as AGTR 5. Under Navy control, with a crew largely comprised of merchant seamen, it was considered an Electronic Intelligence (ELINT) Ship, and as such, on 8 June 1967, "was mistakenly attacked by Israeli aircraft and torpedo boats 15 miles off Sinai, western Mediterranean, during the Israel/Arab War." The ship was eventually returned to the United States and sold for scrapping in Boston in 1970. Sawyer and Mitchell, *Victory Ships and Tankers*, 64–65.

15. An explosion occurred at the Concord Naval Weapons Station, Port Chicago, north of San Francisco on 17 July 1944 at about 10:19 p.m. (PMT) aboard the Liberty ship *E. A. Bryan* (Master: J.L.M. Henrikson), which was loading 1,000-lb., incendiary, and fragmentation cluster bombs at the time. The ship and its entire Merchant Marine and Armed Guard crew, as well as the ship and its crews across the dock—the Victory Ship SS *Quinault Victory* (Master: Robert John Sullivan)—which was preparing to load, were obliterated. Some 70 merchant seamen, 40 Armed Guard personnel, and more than 200 naval personnel and civilians in the vicinity of the explosion were also killed. Robert L. Allen, *The Port Chicago Mutiny*. (Berkeley, CA: Heyday Books, 2006).

16. Completed at the Permanent Metals Corp., Yard No. 1 near Richmond, CA, in August 1943, this ship changed owners and names a number of times in postwar years, finally, as SS *Agios Ioannis*, running aground and breaking in two sections near Osaka, Japan, in 1963. The stern section was towed to Yokosuka, where it was scrapped. Sawyer and Mitchell, *The Liberty Ships*, 125.

## Chapter 15

1. Interview conducted and recorded in Astoria, NY, on 17 June 1982.

2. The 402-foot, 5,984 GT SS *Sawokla* was built in Tampa, FL, in 1920 for American Export Lines.

3. The German auxiliary cruiser *Michel* (Schiff 28) was initially constructed in 1938–39 as the freighter *Bielsko* for a Polish shipping company. Subsequently requisitioned by the Kriegsmarine, she was converted to the hospital ship *Bonn* before being converted again and commissioned as *Schiff 28 (Michel)* on 7 September 1942. During her first raiding voyage, from March 1942

until March 1943, she sank 15 ships, at least five of which were American. At the end of her second raiding voyage, during which an additional three ships were sunk, she was in turn sunk on 17 November 1943, by the American submarine USS *Tarpon* while en route—and just 50 miles from—Japan.

4. The SS *Sawokla* was then under command of Capt. Carl Wink.

5. Chief Officer Elmar Saar was believed to have been suffering from conjunctivitis.

6. Roland described his "going-over-the-side" kit as generally containing: "flashlight, knife, candy, gum, and other personal possessions."

7. Ruiz presumably survived. Sixteen merchant seamen—including Captain Carl Wink—and four Naval Armed Guard personnel were lost as a result of the attack on SS *Sawokla*.

8. Korvettenkapitan Helmuth von Ruckteschell survived the war, but was imprisoned in Hamburg where he died in 1948.

9. Prior to arriving in Japan for refit at the end of its first raiding voyage, *Michel* put all prisoners ashore in Singapore on 19 February 1943, to begin internment as prisoners of war under the Japanese.

10. The 7,040-ton British freighter *Empire March* was fired upon and sunk in the southern Atlantic on 2 January 1943.

11. The 4,816 ton Greek freighter *Eugenie Livanos* was fired upon, torpedoed and sunk by *Michel* in the southwest Indian Ocean on 8 December 1942. Nineteen survivors were taken prisoner.

12. Tanjung (Tandjoeng) Priok is the port for Jakarta, Indonesia, known as Batavia under Dutch colonial rule.

13. Two bridges were actually built by the Japanese in early 1942—using forced labor—in vicinity of Tamarkan, Siam (Thailand). The bridges—one wooden, the other steel—spanned the Mae Keong River, renamed Kwai Yai in 1960. Thousands of allied P.O.W.s—and a far greater number of civilians—died while working on the railway and bridge.

14. The film "The Bridge on the River Kwai" was released in 1957, and subsequently won seven Academy Awards including best picture. Directed by David Lean and starring Alec Guinness, William Holden, and Jack Hawkins, it was largely a work of fiction.

15. The Kempei Tai (lit: "Military Police Corps"), generally known as Japan's secret police, was formed in 1881 and lasted until 1945 when the war ended.

16. A novena is a Roman Catholic period of prayer.

## Chapter 16

1. Phone interview conducted and recorded 9 December 1985. The SS *Mary Luckenbach* was in the outside (starboard) column of convoy when hit by plane-launched torpedoes. It exploded with great force, disintegrated, and all 41 merchant seamen and 16 Armed Guard crew members were lost.

2. According to one account, shrapnel from the explosion hit a ship—probably the SS *Nathaniel Greene*—to the left which caused serious injuries to seven seamen on deck, and requiring their transfer to an escort vessel for medical attention. Moore, 186; Morison, vol. 1, 361–363.

3. The SS *Wacosta*, already damaged by force of explosion to *Mary Luckenbach* and losing headway, was hit by an aerial torpedo which landed on #2 hatch, holing the ship and causing it to begin sinking by the bow. Moore, 288.

4. Capt. Victor E. Tyson later became Assistant Superintendent of the U.S. Merchant Marine Academy in Kings Point, NY, from which he had graduated in 1943, the year following his experience in PQ-18.

5. There are contradictions in the historical record regarding the date of attack on and loss of the SS *Mary Luckenback*. Shearer's detailed eye-witness description of the ship's explosion as result of aerial torpedo attack places that on 13 September 1942, the day his own ship was sunk. Other accounts either support or contradict that, dating the loss of *Mary Luckenback* on 13 September or the following day. See, for example, Moore, 288; Morison, I, 262–263.

6. Jens Jensen.

7. The antiaircraft cruiser USS *Scylla* was flagship for Rear Admiral Burnett in Convoy PQ-18, and provided escort along with some 16 destroyers, two submarines,

and a number of smaller rescue vessels and other craft. Morison, vol. 1, 360.

8. Scapa Flow is a body of water in the Orkney Islands, Scotland. As an exceptional anchorage area, it was the location for the United Kingdom's primary naval base during both World Wars I and II. It was discontinued for that purpose in 1956.

9. *Queen Mary* was in collision off the coast of Ireland on 2 October 1942 with light cruiser HMS *Curacoa*, which sank with the loss of 239 members of her crew.

10. There were no casualties or serious injuries reported in loss of SS *Wacosta*. From phone interview, Capt. William J. Shearer, 9 December 1985.

## Chapter 17

1. Interview conducted and recorded 14 May 1982 in San Francisco, CA.

2. This is the port near Lihue, the largest city on Kauai, the fourth largest of the islands in the Hawaiian group.

3. This was the Liberty ship *Hall J. Kelley*, launched at Oregon Shipbuilding Company in Portland, OR, in March 1943.

## Chapter 18

1. Interview conducted and recorded 17 June 1981 in New York, NY. While attempting to contact Smolen and members of his family years later, and with last known address and phone number no longer current, the author went to the U.S. Merchant Marine Academy Alumni Foundation, hoping for some assistance. While there was no Robert B. Smolen listed as having graduated during the war period, I was informed that there was a person with same last name listed, but with different given name, which, for privacy reasons, they could not reveal. They did say, however, that there was no member of Smolen's family listed for contact purposes. Research elsewhere uncovered a Barnet R. Smolen at last known address in my records for him. Presumably, the person I knew and interviewed as Robert R. Smolen had, for his own purposes, dropped the use of Barnet as his given name in favor of Robert, no doubt what had been his middle name. Nonetheless, this revelation has still not lead the author as yet to a surviving member of Smolen's family.

2. In the sinking of the SS *Fairfield City* on 5 July 1942, eight members of her merchant crew were lost: Laurits P. Antonsin, AB; Domingo R. Fernandes, Steward; Cadenza Fernandez, Messman; Gordon P. Grey, Jr. Officer; Wambola Holm, Second Mate; Fredrick B. Nilsson, Bosun; Ralph S. Pratt; Chief Mate; James M. Scantlebury, Oiler.

3. According to report filed by Lt. (JG) Morton E. Wolfson, in command of ship's Navy Armed Guard, two planes were hit and set on fire by the *Daniel Morgan*'s guns. One plane was seen crashing into the sea "about 3 miles to the west of the ship."

4. Three merchant seamen were lost when one of three lifeboats capsized: Jacob Blazer, Messman; William L. Sirles, Fireman-Watertender; Richard C. Stowell, Chief Mate. One member of the Navy Armed Guard (name not available) was reported lost as a result of bomb blast.

5. This was the German submarine *U-88* (Bohmann) which was subsequently sunk on 14 September 1942 south of Spitzbergen by HMS *Onslow* (G-17). There were no survivors. Moore, 69.

6. The actual cargo included: steel, food, explosives, tanks, and cars. Moore, 69.

7. Survivors of Daniel Morgan were picked up by the Russian tanker *Donbass* at 0200 GCT on 6 July 1942.

8. Convoy PQ-18 departed Scotland for Russia on 2 September 1942. See Chapters 2, 16.

9. The naval attache in north Russia at this time was S.B. Frankel, generally referred to with rank of Captain. Morison, vol. 1, 172, 373.

## Chapter 19

1. Interview conducted and recorded in 1979, New York, NY.

2. The Seaman's Church Institute, commonly called the "Doghouse" by seamen,

was located variously on State St., and also at The Battery in New York City for many years. It provided rooms, library, chapel and other services to seamen, and received notices of available jobs on merchant ships.

3. Referred to as a Laker type, the 251 × 44 × 24-foot, 2,398 ton *Lake Osweya* was built at Saginaw, MI, in 1918. As a Laker she was sized to move through the locks of the St. Lawrence Seaway.

4. The *Lake Osweya*, under the command of Capt. Karl E. Prinz, was torpedoed by the German submarine *U-96* at 0253 GCT on 19 February 1942. All 30 crewmembers aboard were lost.

5. The new designation for northbound convoys was JW. Convoy JW-51A departed on 15 December and arrived "unruffled"—as one account has put it—10 days later on Christmas Day, 1942.

6. Merchant seaman were routinely assigned to assist Naval Armed Guard personnel at gun stations.

7. These lights, the result of collision between gasses from the sun and the Earth's magnetic field, are known as *Aurora Borealis* in northern latitudes, and as *Aurora Australis* in the southern hemisphere.

8. Designed in 1939 and initially produced in 1940, the Oerlikon 22 mm antiaircraft cannon were introduced by the U.S. Navy and placed on merchant ships beginning in 1942, to replace the M2 Browning machinegun and provide more firepower. It used a 60-round drum magazine (replaced later by belt-feed) placed on top of the gun. Guns were typically in single, double or quad configuration. *Naval Weapons of World War Two*. (Annapolis, Naval Institute Press, 1985).

9. Erie Basin is a port area in Brooklyn, NY, whose development began in 1864 and would eventually comprise some 135 acres of largely filled-in land for ship docking and warehouse space.

## Chapter 20

1. Interview conducted and recorded 11 March 1982 in New York, NY.

2. Built in Baltimore in February 1942, the Liberty ship SS *Roger B. Taney* was operated by Waterman Steamship Corp. and was under the command of Capt. Thomas J. Potter.

3. The three seamen killed were: Arthur L. Hand, F/W; Alfred T. Schulte, 3rd Engineer; and Hugh E. Williams, Oiler.

4. The SS *Roger B. Taney* was torpedoed by *U-160* (Lassen) at 22-00 south/7-45 west in the south Atlantic. The *U-160* was sunk on 14 July 1943 south of the Azores by aircraft from USS *Santee* (CVE-29); there were no survivors.

5. While some 11 American and neutral merchant ships were listed as lost in the Southeast Atlantic in March (Morison, I, 414), a figure is not available for February.

6. The Arquipelago de Trindade é Martim Vaz is a group of five islands totaling about 10.4 square kilometers—with Trindade being the largest at 10.1 square kilometers—approximately 1,200 kilometers due east of Vitoria, Brazil. It houses a base and small group of Brazilian naval personnel.

7. The #2 Lifeboat, under command of the Chief Mate and numbering 15 merchant seamen and 13 Armed Guard crew, was picked up after 22 days by the British SS *Penrith Castle* on 1 March 1943 and landed at Bahia on 5 March.

8. A goalie with the Chicago Blackhawks before the war, Sam LoPresti was born in Eveleth, MN, on January 30, 1917, and died on December 11, 1984 at the age of 67.

9. Twenty-one ships were reported sunk by submarine attack in the Brazilian designated area in the months of November and December 1942. Morison, vol. 1, *The Battle of the Atlantic*, 414.

10. The 26 survivors in lifeboat #4 were picked up on 22 March 1943 by the Brazilian passenger ship SS *Bage* about five miles offshore between Rio de Janeiro and Santos.

11. Uruguayan Air Force Flight 571 crashed with 45 persons on board while on a flight from Montevideo Uruguay to Santiago, Chile, on 13 October 1972. With members of a Uruguayan rugby team, family members, friends and associates, and five crewmembers aboard, the plane went down in the Andes at an altitude of 11,800 feet, with little food and water on board,

and no source of heat. Fourteen were killed outright, another five by the next morning, and another eight subsequently in an avalanche. Rescue did not come until 22 December—some 70 days later—at which time there were 16 survivors. As a group, it was decided that for survival's sake they would engage in anthropophagy—cannibalism—of persons who had already died of wounds, exposure and malnutrition.

# Bibliography

Banigan, John J., and Phil Richards. *How to Abandon Ship*. New York: Cornell Maritime Press, 1942.
Bunker, John Gorley. *Liberty Ships: The Ugly Ducklings of World War II*. Annapolis, MD: Naval Institute Press, 1972.
\_\_\_\_\_. *Heroes in Dungarees: The Story of the American Merchant Marine in World War II*. Annapolis, MD: Naval Institute Press, 1995.
Campbell, Ian, and Donald Macintyre. *The Kola Run: A Record of Arctic Convoys, 1941–1945*. London: Frederick Muller, Ltd.
Carse, Robert. *There Go the Ships*. New York: William Morrow, 1942.
\_\_\_\_\_. *Lifeline: The Ships and Men of Our Merchant Marine at War*. New York: William Morrow and Co., 1943.
Cornell, Felix M., and Allan C. Hoffman, eds. *American Merchant Seaman's Manual*. New York: Cornell Maritime Press, 1940.
Howe, Leslie. *The Merchant Service To-Day*. London: Oxford University Press, 1941.
Hoyt, Edwin P. *U-Boats Offshore: When Hitler Struck America*. Briarcliff Manor, NY: Stein and Day, 1978.
Karig, Walter, Cmdr., et al. *Battle Report: The Atlantic War*. New York: Farrar & Rinehart, 1946.
Lane, Frederic C., et al. *Ships for Victory: A History of Shipbuilding Under the U.S. Maritime Commission in World War II*. Baltimore: The Johns Hopkins Press, 1951.
Lent, Henry B., *Ahoy, Shipmate!: Steve Ellis Joins the Merchant Marine*. New York: Macmillan, 1945.
McEvoy, Joan, esq. *Request for a Determination that the World War II Service of the American Merchant Marine be Considered Active Military Service for Purposes of All Laws Administered by the Veterans Administration*. Washington, DC: Proskauer Rose Goetz and Mendelsohn, 1980.
Moore, Arthur R., Capt. *A Careless Word...A Needless Sinking: A History of the Tremendous Losses in Ships and Men Suffered by the U.S. Merchant Marine During World War II*. Kings Point, NY: American Merchant Marine Museum, 1983.
Morison, Samuel Eliot. *History of United States Naval Operations, Vol. I: The Battle of the Atlantic, September 1939–May 1943*. Boston: Little, Brown, 1947.
\_\_\_\_\_. *History of United States Naval Operations, Vol. III: The Rising Sun in the Pacific, 1931–April 1942*. Boston: Little, Brown, 1948.
\_\_\_\_\_. *History of United States Naval Operations, Vol. IX: Sicily-Salerno-Anzio, January 1943–June 1944*. Boston: Little, Brown, 1954.
\_\_\_\_\_. *History of United States Naval Operations, Vol. X: The Atlantic Battle Won, May 1943–May 1945*. Boston: Little, Brown, 1956.

———. *History of United States Naval Operations in World War II, Vol. XI: The Invasion of France and Germany, 1944–1945.* Boston: Little, Brown, 1953.
———. *History of United States Naval Operations in World War II, Vol. XIV: Victory in the Pacific 1945.* Boston: Little, Brown, 1960.
Palmer, M. B. *We Fight with Merchant Ships.* New York: Bobbs Merrill, 1943.
Rayner, D. A. *Escort: The Battle of the Atlantic.* London: William Kimber, 1955.
Reynolds, Quentin. *Convoy.* New York: Random House, 1942.
Sawyer, L. A., and W. H. Mitchell. *The Liberty Ships: The History of the "Emergency" Type Cargo Ships Constructed in the United States During World War II.* Newton Abbot: David & Charles, 1973.
———. *Victory Ships and Tankers: The History of the "Victory" Type Cargo Ships and of the Tankers Built in the United States of America During World War II.* Cambridge, MD: Cornell Maritime Press, 1974.
Standard Oil Company of New Jersey. *Ships of the Esso Fleet in World War II.* Second printing, 1946.
Turpin, Edward A., and William A. MacEwen. *Merchant Marine Officers' Handbook.* New York: Cornell Maritime Press, 1944.
Van der Vat, Dan. *The Atlantic Campaign: World War II's Great Struggle at Sea.* New York: Harper & Row, 1988.
War Shipping Administrator. *The United States Merchant Marine at War: Report of the War Shipping Administrator to the President.* Washington, DC: USGPO, 1946.

# Index

Ship names appear in *italics*. Page numbers in ***bold italics*** indicate photographs.

Abraham Lincoln Brigade 7
Acapulco, Mexico 43
*African Dawn* 145
Alaska Transportation Co. 141
Alcoa Aluminum Corp. 63
*Alcoa Cutter* 62, 63
Aleutian Islands, Alaska 9
Alexandria, Egypt 116
Algiers, Algeria 57
*Alive!* (book) 168
Ambrose Light 26
American Export Line 60
*American Leader* 36, ***38***, 41–42
American Mail Line 139
American President Lines (APL) 37, 119, 141
angel (vision of) 168
Archangel, Russia 20–22, 65, 67–68, 77–79, 103–104, 107–108, 111–112, 143–144, 153
Arctica (hotel) 76
Argentia, Newfoundland 27
*Arizpa* 63
Armed Guard *see* U.S. Naval Armed Guard
Army Air Corps *see* U.S. Army Air Corps
Aruba, Dutch West Indies 25, 27, 31, 139–140
*Asahi Shimbun* (newspaper) 131
Asbury Park, New Jersey 11, 26
*At Dawn I Die* (film) 111
Auckland, New Zealand 115–116
*Augustine Heard* 58–***59***
*Augustus S. Merriman* 113

Australia 27, 36, 39, 41, 85, 89–90, 115, 116
auto-alarm 91
*Azerbaidjan* 102–103, 110

*Badger State* 98
bagpipes 113
Bahia, Brazil 116
Bailey, William J. "Bill" 7–10, ***8***, ***9***
Bali 131
Balipap (Balikpapan), Indonesia 85
*Balladier* 72–74
Baltimore, Maryland 1, 3, 32, 35, 46, 50, 58, 70, 80, 102, 119, 146, 161
barrage balloons 50–54, 81
Basra, Iraq 47–48
bauxite 62–63, 76, 114, 117
*Beacon* (tanker) 25
Beacon Hill 185n23
*Bear* 74
Bear Island, Barents Sea 18, 144
Beaverton, Oregon 115–116
Beck's Beer 128
Belchite, Spain 7
Belfast, Ireland 151–152
*Bellingham* 68
Beresford Hotel, Glasgow 138
*Bering* 78
*Berkshire* 70
*The Best Friend* (NRHS) 83
Bethell, Howard 2, 4, 11–23, ***12***, ***23***
"Betsy" Bomber (Japanese) 132
Biloxi, Mississippi 82
Bishop (U.S.M.M. Academy cadet) 100
Bizerte, Tunisia 57

"Black Friday" 89
"Black Gang" 40, 41
Black Horse Ale 147
blackout, procedures 14, 15, 25, 37, 41, 44, 71, 88, 148
USS *Boise* 36–37
Bombay, India 48
USS *Borie* 180c4n3
Borneo 132
Boston, MA 3, 11, 13–14, 22, 25, 26, 31, 41, 69, 80, 81, 120, 138, 145
Boxell's School of Navigation 31
Bradley, Daniel J. 25–31, **26**
Bradley, Marie **26**
Brazil 50, 116, 139–140, 161, 164, 166
*Brazil* (ship) 102
Brazilian Navy 166
Brisbane, Australia 40, 115
Bristol Channel (England/Wales) 80
British Guiana 63, 117
Brooklyn, NY 61, 114, 115, 117, 161
Brooklyn Navy Yard 115
Buckner Bay, Okinawa 58–59
Burma-Siam Railroad ("Railroad of Death") 128–129, 134
Byrd, Adm. Richard 74

C-1 (ship type) 11, 36, 39, 99
C-2 84, 145
Calcutta, India 116, 120, 121, 126
Callous, Captain 76
Canadian (troops) 84–85
cannibalism 168–169
Cape Cod Canal 17
Cape Frio (Brazil) 166
Cape Hatteras, North Carolina 41, 61, 91, 140
Cape Horn 161
Cape May, New Jersey 46
Cape of Good Hope 15
Cape San Antonio (Cuba) 92
Cape Town, South Africa 11, 13, 46–48, 120, 161, 164
Cape Verde Islands 49
*El Capitan* 107–108
Cardiff, Wales 82
Caribbean 17, 23, 25, 26, 46–47, 63, 91, 93, 102, 139
*Carpathia* 11
*Carrabulle* 91
Carson, Rachel 167
Cartagena, Colombia 28
*Catahoula* 91–**96**, 98
Caven's Point, New Jersey 150
Cavite, P.I. 37–38

Ceylon 87, 89
Chanaral, Chile 115
*Charles D. Poston* 117–118
Charleston, South Carolina 82, 83
Charleston (SC) Army Depot 82
*Chatham* 70–71
*Cherokee* 60
*Cherry Valley* 27
Chester, Pennsylvania 26, 98
Chicago Blackhawks 165
Chicago, Illinois 113
Childs, Capt. Richard 17
Chile 63, 115, 168
Christensen, Emil 93–94
Christmas 127–128, 151–160, 161
chrome ore 77
Churchill, Prime Minister Winston 153
Cisco Brothers, Ernie 42
*City of Omaha* 78
The Clyde (Scotland) 80–81
Coast Guard *see* U.S. Coast Guard
*Collis P. Huntington* **109**, 113
Colombo (Ceylon) 87, 120, 121, 126
Columbia, North Carolina 142
*Columbian* 48
"Condor" (German aircraft) 108
*Conoyes* 135
Constable Hook, NY 139
Convoy, HX-designated 63
Convoy JW-51A 151–152
Convoy JW-53 ("Forgotten Convoy") 75–80
Convoy PQ-17 18, 63–67, 102–108, 109, 113, 142–**144**, 151
Convoy PQ-18 18–20, 135–138, **137**
Convoy SC-95 71–74
Corpus Christi, Texas 114
corvette (escort vessel) 149, 155
"Couvoisier" 106
*Cristobal* 27
*Crosby Noyes* **77**, 81–82
cryolite (ore) 74
Cuba 91–92
Cuba Distilling Company 91
Cumberland, Maryland 135, 138
Curaçao (Dutch Caribbean) 31

*Dakotan* 43–46
*Daniel Getson* 43
*Daniel P. Morgan* 142
Darwin, Australia 90
Deep Water Point, New Jersey 91
degaussing (cables) 27
Delaware Bay 82
Delaware River 91

# Index

Denmark 74
Diamond Shoals 91–92
Dickey, Rexford 32–35, **33**
*Dixie Arrow* 151
Doby School 9
"Doghouse" *see* Seamen's Church Institute
*Donbass* 143
"donut" raft 73, 125
*Dorothy Cahill* 91
DUKW (landing craft) 81
Durban, South Africa 11, 13
Dutch Guiana 62–63
Dvina River (Russia) 77–79

Eastern and Gulf Sailors Union 36
USS *Edgecomb* 90
*Edward L. Shea* 151
Eighth Army, British 46
Emanuel, Marshall E. 65
*Empire March* 126
*Empress of Australia* 98–99
English Channel 149
Ensenada, Puerto Rico 91–93
Erie Basin, Brooklyn, NY 160
Espiritu Santos 28
*Esso Harrisburg* **28**
*Esso Manhattan* 26
*Esso Pittsburgh* 27
*Eugenia Levonis* 127
*Excellency (Sawokla)* 120

*Fairfield City* 142
Finland 21, 76–77, 91, 153
Florida 41, 47, 91, 92, 147
Florida Straits 91–92
fog buoy 82, 99
Ford Shipping Co. 147
"Forgotten Convoy" *see* Convoy JW-53
Fort Chimo (Hudson's Bay) 75
Ft. Trumball (U.S.M.S. training station) 71
*Francis Scott Key* 78
*Francis Vigo* 146
Frankel, Cmdr. S.B. 67
Franklin, Capt. Sir John, expedition 74
Fremantle, Australia 85–87, 89, 116
Friendly Islands 28
Fullerton, California 114

gas, poison 82
*Gateway City* 151–154
George, Lloyd Livingston 121–122
*George Henry* 27–28
*George Powell* 10

*George W. Woodward* 160
*George Walton* 80, 82
Gibraltar 51
Glasgow, Scotland 17–18, 138, 145
*The Good Fight* (film) 10
Gorski, Stanley E. 36–42
Gowanus Canal, Brooklyn, NY 117
Grand Banks 99, 147
Great White Fleet 18
Greenland 74
Greenock, Scotland 27, 107–108, 112, 138
Greenwich Village (New York City) 120
"Grey Ghost" *see* Queen Mary
Guanica, Puerto Rico 93
Guantanamo Bay, Cuba 25
"guarantee engineer" 13–14
Gulf Pacific Line 114

"H Force" 128
Halifax, Nova Scotia 17, 35, 63, 71, 102, 142, 151
*Hall J. Kelley* 141
Hamilton, Scotland 145
Havana, Cuba 25
Hawaii 24, 36, 117–118
Hayden (second mate) 30
*Henry M. Stephens* 141
*Hercules* (steam tug) 119
Hiroshima, Japan 10
Hispaniola 91
Hobart, Tasmania 115–116
Hog Islander 78
Holt, Jack A. 43–49, **45**
Hong Kong 84
*Honolulan* 46–**47**, 48–49
hopper (dredge) 75
hot shell (gun position) 29
Hudson Bomber 48
Hull, England 80
hypnosis (use in medicine) 130–131

Iceland 18, 63, 71–74, 102, 103, 142, 147–148
*Idaho* 11–14
I.J.A. (Imperial Japanese Army) 133
"Ink Spots" (musical group) 50
International Club (Archangel) 109
Intourist Hotel 16, 67, 79, 109, 144
Irish Sea 81
*Isaac Coles* 23–24
USS *Isabel* 88

Jacksonville 101
*James Lick* 119
*James Longstreet* 61

# Index

*James R. Randall* 61
Japan, invasion of 118–119
Jarvis, Paul J. 50–59, **51**
Java (Dutch East Indies) 87
*Jean* 160
*Jedediah S. Smith* 116
Jensen, Captain Jens 138
*Jeremiah O'Brien* 90, 119
Johanson, Eric H. 60–61
*John Bell* 54–56
*John Paul Jones* **9**, 10
*John Sergeant* 57
*John W. Brown* 1–**2**, **121**
*John Witherspoon* 102–105, 109
Johnstone (Scotland) 69
Jones, David "Casey" 97
*Joseph Hewes* 32
*Josiah Royce* 141
*Julia Luckenbach* 114, **117**
"July 4th Convoy" *see* Convoy PQ-17
*Junyo Maru* 42

Kamikaze (aircraft) 58–59
Kaneohe Bay (Hawaii) 44
kapok 123
Kauai (Hawaii) 140
Kempei Tai (Japanese secret police) 131
*Kentucky* 17–20, **19**
*Kettle Creek* 98, 101
Key West, Florida 92
Kings Point, New York 142
Koksoac River (Hudson's Bay) 75
Kola River, Russia 80

*Lake Gaither* 7
*Lake Osweya* 147–**150**
*Lake Treba* 147
"Laker" (ship type) 72, 91
*Lane Victory* 90
USS *Langley* 87
Lansdowne, Pennsylvania 84
*Laredo Victory* 10
La Romana, Dominican Republic 93
USS *La Salle* 90
Lawrence, Ruel N. 62–69
Le Cato, John M. 70–83, **71**
lend lease 84, 139
Lewis, Capt. Ernest 80
USS *Lexington* 85
Leyte Gulf, Philippines 118
*Liberty see Simmons Victory*
Liberty ships 8–10, 18, 58, 61, 78, **109**, 115, 141, 164
*Lihue* 14–**16**, 17
Lind (second mate) 104

Liverpool, England 145
Lloyd-Brasilero Line 166
Loch Ewe, Scotland 18, 101, 151, 158–159
Londonderry, Ireland 101
Lopresti, Sam 165
*Lord Ashton* 103
HMS *Lotus* 66–67
Lourenço Marques 11
LSMR 189 (rocket ship) 69
LST (landing craft) 81–82
Luckenbach, ships 47, 114–115, **117**, 135–137
*Luis Arguello* 118
Lykes Brothers Steamship Co. 78

MacArthur, Gen. Douglas 43
MacMichael, Capt. Edward A. 84–90, **86**
Malta 116
Manila, P.I. 36–40, 84–85
Manila Bay 36–40
USS *Marblehead* 87
March, Edward C. 91–101, **92**
*Marcidoc* 91
Marin County, California 139
Marine Hospital, New York 166
Marine Workers Historical Association (MWHA) 10, 59, 113
Mariner's Medal 98
Marshall, Harry "hetri" 78–79
*Mary Luckenbach* 135–137
Matthews County, Virginia 76, 80
McCarthyism 4
McCormick Steamship Co. 60
McCusker, John S. "Jack" 102–113, **104**
McKenzie River, British Guiana 116–117
Melbourne, Australia 85–87
Merchant Marine Academy *see* U.S. Merchant Marine Academy
Merchants and Miners Transportation Co. 70, 75, 83
Merrill, Capt. Robert 75
MERSIGS 98
Miami, FL 31
*Michel* (German raider) 42, 120, 129
Milne Bay, New Guinea 27
Mobile, Alabama 61, 62–63, 65, 69
USCGC *Mojave* 36
Molotovsk, Russia 77–79, 81, 143
Mona Pass (Passage) 92–93
Montana 113
Montgomery, Bill 53–55
Morgan, Harry E. 114–119, **115**
Moro Bay, New Guinea 118
*Morrissey* 74
*Morro Castle* 11

# Index

Moscow, Russia 21
"Mulberries" (harbors and piers) 81
Murmansk Run 8, 63
Murmansk, Russia 18, 63, 67, 76–77, 79–80, 111, 151–158, 160

Nagasaki, Japan 10
Nags Head 91–92
Naha, Okinawa 10, 58
Nakagusuku Wan (Buckner Bay) 58–59
*Nantucket* 91
National Liberty Ship Memorial (*Jeremiah O'Brien*) 90, 119
National Maritime Union (NMU) 36, 108
Naval Air Station, Kaneohe Bay, Hawaii 44
*Navarino* 102
Nawiliwili, Kauai, Hawaii 139–141
New Caledonia 40
New Jersey (coast) 115
New Orleans, Louisiana 107, 115, 118
New York 2, 7, 11, 14, 15, 17, 19, 23, 24, 26, 27–28, 31, 32, 35, 36, 46, 49, 51, 56–57, 59, 60, 61, 63, 71, 75, 80, 81, 83–84, 100–101, 102, 107, 109, 113, 117, 120, 121, 124, 126, 134, 139, 142, 145, 146, 147, 148, 151, 159, 160, 161
*New York Times Magazine* 42
New Zealand 28, 115–116
Newburyport, Massachusetts 14
Newell, Blackie 111
Newport News Shipbuilding and Drydock Co. 70
*Norfolk* (tanker) 27
*Norluna* 70–**73**, 74–75
Normandy (invasion) 80–81, 146
North Cape (Scandinavia) 76, 79, 102–103, **144**
North Carolina Shipbuilding Co. 109
North Channel (Great Britain) 101
North Dakota 113
North River (New York) 15
*Northern Sword* 153–154
Novaya Zemlya 105

Oban, Scotland 80
O'Brien, Davey 29
*Ocean Freedom* (British) 76, 80
Oerlikon (anti-aircraft cannon) 66
Okinawa 58–59, 90
USS *Oklahoma* 44
*The Oklahoma Kid* (film) 145
Olympic Steamship Co. 141
*Only Yesterday* (book) 53
*Oriente* 27

P-51 (aircraft) 100
Pacific Coast Marine Firemen, Oilers, Watertenders and Wipers Association 7
Palermo, Sicily 24
Pan American Clipper 31
SS *Pan Atlantic* 63, **64**, 69
Panama 115
Panama Canal 27, 40, 44–46, 115, 118, 139–140, 161
Paramount Theater (New York) 7
paravane 26
*Pat Doheny* 69
Patton, Gen. George 130
PBY (aircraft) 96, 98
Pearl Harbor, Hawaii 7, 11, 25, 37, 43, 50, 60, 62, 70, 84–85, 91, 102, 114, 120, 139–140, 142, 147–148, 161
Pederson, Capt. Haakon A. 39
pemmican (lifeboat ration) 164
Penang Bay (Malaysia) 89
USS *Pennsylvania* 58
Pennsylvania Nautical School 84
Pennsylvania School ship 84
Perkins, Captain 160
Persian Gulf 109, 126
Peterson (seaman) 136
Philadelphia, PA 50, 63, 84, 91, 114
Philippines 36, 115
USS *Phoenix* 88
"Pilot" (short wave radio) 140
Piru, California 114
Pittsburgh, Pennsylvania 113
Point Lobos 114
Point "Zed" 26
Polaris (submarine type) 83
Pomona College (California) 114
"pom-pom" gun 66
Port Chicago, California 118–119
Port Churchill, Hudson's Bay 74
Port Elizabeth 13
Port Moresby, New Guinea 89, 118
Port o' Spain, Trinidad 62–63, 116–117
Port Said, Egypt 116
Portland, Oregon 115
*President Grant* 37
*President Harding* 84
*President Jackson* 24
*President Jefferson* 139
HMS *Prince of Wales* 13
Project Liberty Ship 1–2, 134, 146

Quartermaster 24, 36, 70, 85, 98, 139
Queen Mary 69, 113, 138, 145
Queen Wilhemina (Dutch destroyer) 30

Racine, Wisconsin  36, 41–42
Radio Tokyo  134
Rand-McNally (Atlas)  87
Recife, Brazil  116
Red Cross, American  24, 69
Red Hook Basin (Brooklyn, NY)  114
Reeves, Ted  111
HMS *Repulse*  13
Reykjavik, Iceland  18, 102, 142, 148
*Richard Henderson*  50–58
Richfield Oil Co.  114
Rio de Janeiro, Brazil  139, 166
River Kwai Bridge  128–130
*Roger B. Taney*  161–162, **163**
Roland, Dennis A.  120–134, **121**
Roosevelt, Pres. Franklin D.  7, 18, 139, 153
Rotterdam  82
Ruckteschell, Korvettenkapitan Helmuth von  126
Ruiz (wounded seaman)  125
*R.W. Gallagher*  151

*Sacajawea*  141
Sailors Union of the Pacific (S.U.P)  108
St. Louis, Missouri  82
St. Nicholas Day  127
Saldana Bay, South Africa  161
Salvation Army  97–98
*Samuel Putnam*  78
San Francisco, California  9, 10, 90, 115, 117, 119, 141
San Juan, Puerto Rico  97
San Pedro, California  36; Bay 139
San Pedro de Macoris  93
Sandova, John  180c4n6
Sangerville, Maine  32
*Santa Louisa*  120–123
Santa Marta, Colombia  30–31
Santos, Brazil  139, 140, 166
São Paulo, Brazil  140
USS *Saratoga*  85
Savannah, Georgia  147
NS *Savannah*  90
*Sawokla*  120–**129**
Scapa Flow (Scotland)  138
scurvy  78
USS *Scylla*  138
*The Sea Around Us* (book)  167
*Sea Witch*  84–89
Seafarers International Union (S.I.U.)  32, 35
Seamen's Church Institute  147, 177n2, 192–193n2
Seattle, Washington  102, 113, 139
Shearer, William J.  135–138, **136**

Sheepshead Bay Training Station  99
Sicily, invasion of  23–24
Sievers, Henrik E.  139–142, **140**
Silk, Capt. Lawrence J.  56
*Simmons Victory*  118
Singapore  128
Sixth Fleet  118
Smolen, Robert B.  142–146
Smyrna, Delaware  83
HMSAS *Southern Maid*  56
Southern Pacific Morgan Line  107
"Spam"  57, 80, 112
Spitzbergen  18, 66
Squadron Seven (PT-boat)  27
Standard Oil Company of California  139, 141
Staten Island, New York  27
"Steam Schooner"  119
*Steel Navigator*  131
"Stuka" (JU-87), aircraft  153, 155–157
USS *Sturtevant*  96
Suez Canal  116, 161
Sumatra  42
Sun Ship (yard)  98
Sundoxford (diesel)  27, 147
Surabaya, Java  85, 89
Sydney, Australia  40
Sydney, Nova Scotia  147

T-2 (tanker)  3, 27, 98–101
T-3 (tanker)  26–27
Tampa, Florida  186n2, 190n2
Tanjung Priok, D.E.I.  128
Tarawa  90
*Thomas Hartley*  75–80
Thursday Island, Australia  40, 90
Thurso, Scotland  138
Tiencken, John H.  147–160, **148**
Tjilatjap, D.E.I.  87
Tocopilla, Chile  63
Tokyo, Japan  134
Tokyo Rose  87
HMS *Tradewind*  42
Trincomalee, Ceylon (Sri-Lanka)  116
Trinidad  15, 17, 62–63, 116–117
Trinidade e Martim Vaz (island group, Brazil)  164
Trujillo, Rafael (dictator)  93
USS *Tuscaloosa*  108, 112, 160
*Typhoon* (tanker)  25–27
Typhoon Louise  59
Tyson, Victor E.  135

Union Station (Washington, D.C.)  70
United Seamen's Service (U.S.S.) Club  31

U.S. Army Air Corps  132
U.S. Coast Guard  14, 27, 36, 39, 41, 42, 75, 102
U.S. Coast Guard Cutter, Campbell Class  72
United States Lines  17, 84
U.S. Marine Corps  4, 46, 139
U.S. Maritime Service Training Station, Ft. Trumball, New York  71
U.S. Merchant Marine Academy  100, 142, 145
U.S. Naval Academy  70
U.S. Naval Armed Guard  18, 64, 69, 103, 152–153, 156–157, 164–165
U.S. Naval Reserve  15, 89, 139
U.S. Navy  15, 18, 26, 27–28, 29, 30, 41, 42, 45, 67, 69, 74, 83, 87, 91–92, 93, 97, 118, 125, 132, 153, 160, 166
Utah Beach (Normandy invasion)  81

Valparaíso, Chile  115
Very pistol, signals  164
Vezina Trophy  165
USNS *Victoria*  83
USS *Victoria*  28
Victory Ship  118
Virgin Islands  63
Vitória, Brazil  161, 164
*Von Tirpitz* (battleship)  64

*Wacosta*  135, *137*–138
*Wade Hampton*  32, *34*
walnuts  116
War Shipping Administration (W.S.A.)  57, 75, 89
SS *Washington*  84, *86*
USS *Washington*  160
Washington, D.C.  43, 70, 90
Waterman Steamship Co.  63, 68, 161
*West Nilus*  145
*West Notus*  60–*61*
Westport, Connecticut  121
White Sea (Russia)  20, 77–78, 108, 112, 143
*William Few*  50
*William Glackens*  69
*William Hooper*  102
*William S. Rosecrans*  115
Wilmington, Delaware  154
Wilner, Stanley  120, 123–124, 126, 130
*Winchester Castle*  49
WINS  98
"Wolf pack"  116
*W.S. Miller*  139, *141*

*Yale Victory*  141

"Zed," Point  24
Zubrod, Donald E.  161–169, *163*

www.ingramcontent.com/pod-product-compliance
Ingram Content Group UK Ltd.
Pitfield, Milton Keynes, MK11 3LW, UK
UKHW042002140426
5217IPUK00015B/943